Lesson Plans for the First 30 Days

Getting Started With HighScope

Lesson Plans for the First 30 Days

Getting Started With HighScope

Second Edition

Beth Marshall

*with Shannon Lockhart
and Moya Fewson*

HIGHSCOPE PRESS®

Ypsilanti, Michigan

Published by
HighScope® Press

A division of the
HighScope Educational Research Foundation
600 North River Street
Ypsilanti, Michigan 48198-2898
734.485.2000, FAX 734.485.0704

Orders: 800.40.PRESS; Fax: 800.442.4FAX; www.highscope.org
E-mail: *press@highscope.org*

Copyright © 2012 by HighScope Educational Research Foundation. All rights reserved. Except as permitted under the Copyright Act of 1976, no part of this book may be reproduced or distributed in any form or by any means, electronic or mechanical, including photocopy, recording, or any information storage-and-retrieval system, without either the prior written permission from the publisher, or authorization through payment of the appropriate per-copy fee to the Copyright Clearance Center, Inc., 222 Rosewood Drive, Danvers, MA 01923, 978.750.8400, fax 978.646.8600, or on the web at www.copyright.com. The name "HighScope" and its corporate logos are registered trademarks and service marks of the HighScope Foundation.

Editor: Jennifer Burd
Cover design, text design, production: Judy Seling, Seling Design, LLC
Photography: Gregory Fox

Library of Congress Cataloging-in-Publication Data
Marshall, Beth, 1959-
 Lesson plans for the first 30 days : getting started with highscope / by Beth Marshall with Shannon Lockhart and Moya Fewson. — 2nd ed.
   p. cm.
 ISBN 978-1-57379-323-0 (soft cover : alk. paper) 1. Education, Preschool—Curricula—United States. 2. Classroom management—United States. I. Lockhart, Shannon. II. Fewson, Moya. III. Title.
 LB1140.4.M375 2012
 372.21—dc23
                                    2012028387

Printed in the United States of America
10 9 8 7 6 5 4 3 2 1

Lesson Plans for the First 30 Days

Table of Contents

Introduction: An Overview of the HighScope Curriculum 1

The HighScope Preschool "Wheel of Learning" 2
    Active Participatory Learning 2
    Adult-Child Interaction 3
    The Daily Routine 6
    The Learning Environment 12
    Curriculum Content and Key Developmental Indicators 14
    Assessment 14
Teamwork 15
    Team Planning 15
Family Involvement 15
How to Use This Book 16
    Weekly Overviews 16
    The Lesson Plans 16
Getting Started: Things to Do Before Week 1 18
    Room Arrangement 18
    Daily Routine 18
    Letter Links 18

Chapter 1: The First Week 22

Chapter 2: The Second Week 41

Chapter 3: The Third Week 63

Chapter 4: The Fourth Week 85

Chapter 5: The Fifth Week 108

Chapter 6: The Sixth Week 131

Chapter 7: Sample Growing Readers Activities 157

Appendix A: Reproducible Planning Sheets 177

Appendix B: Music CD Selections for Lesson Activities 183

Acknowledgments

It is sometimes said that implementing HighScope is a journey. Many have been fortunate enough to have had training to help them along the way. Others have worked with a mentor teacher who showed them the ins and outs. Still others are self-taught, having read curriculum books and watched video footage. However, a few folks are simply plunked down on the path and asked to do their best in getting started — immediately! *Lesson Plans for the First 30 Days* was written with the latter group in mind. The book is meant to be a guide or support to teachers as they take their first steps toward implementing HighScope. These plans are made of up activities that have been favorites of both children and teachers at the HighScope Demonstration Preschool in Ypsilanti, Michigan. It is my hope that you find them helpful as you begin to implement the HighScope Curriculum in your setting.

I am indebted to the people who were instrumental in helping me take my first baby steps with HighScope: Mary Hohmann, Becki Perrett, and Sam Hannibal. I am grateful for the support and contributions of the staff in HighScope's Early Childhood Department, who have continually worked to make the path smoother, shorter, and easier. Ann Epstein, Mary Hohmann, Suzanne Gainsley, Kay Rush, and Polly Neill all gave valuable feedback and shaped the ideas shared here. I would like to acknowledge Patricia Murphy, Eilis McKay, Margaret Fullerton, Pam Lafferty, Rachael Underwood, René King, Phakama Mzileni, and Fioni Murray, who helped widen that path to include a world perspective and who will always hold a special place in my heart. I would also like to thank Clay Shouse for his encouragement in the development of this book. I am grateful to Jennifer Burd, whose support and enthusiasm made the editing process a breeze. I also thank HighScope staff members Carol Markley and Karen Sawyers for sharing their expertise. From the field, Kathie Preistley, Amy Goerl, and Jan Berry reviewed the plans and offered valuable insights. A big thanks to my fellow authors, Shannon Lockhart and Moya Fewson, whose contributions enriched these plans immensely. I'd also like to thank the next generation of HighScope teachers who helped me understand what it's like to be a new teacher with today's demands. Late night conversations with Sara Krugielki and Emily Marshall were particularly valuable. Appreciation also goes to the Mary and Robert Pew Public Education Fund, which provided partial funding for the development of this material. Finally, I'd like to thank all the workshop participants who have offered insights about their journey to HighScope.

— Beth Marshall

Introduction
An Overview of the HighScope Curriculum

Welcome to ***Lesson Plans for the First 30 Days: Getting Started With HighScope.*** This series of sample lesson plans is designed to help you begin to use the HighScope Curriculum. Whether you are a teacher, administrator, or a supervisor or trainer of teachers, this book will help you and your teaching team get up and running with active participatory learning the HighScope way! Once you work through this book, you will be able to develop your own daily plans using our proven approach.

◆

The HighScope Curriculum may be distinguished from other curricula by its emphasis on these components: **active participatory learning, adult-child interaction,** and the **plan-do-review process.** You will learn a bit more about these components as you read on, but let's start at the beginning.

◆

The HighScope Curriculum began as a result of the landmark research study known as the HighScope Perry Preschool Study. Through continuing study and use, the curriculum has evolved to what it is today.

We know through evidence from the HighScope Perry Preschool Study and several other studies that high-quality preschool programs make a difference in children's lives. Research shows that children who participate in such programs achieve greater success as students and adults. They go further in school, earn more money, commit fewer crimes, and ultimately contribute in a positive way to society.

◆

Research has validated HighScope as a high-quality, effective curriculum. But what do we mean by that statement? Aren't most curricula research validated? The answer is *no.* They might be *research based,* meaning that the developers of the program have studied the work of significant early childhood theorists (such as Piaget, Vygotsky, and Bronfenbrenner) and used the research of others as a starting point for developing their own curriculum. However, they may not have taken the next step of studying whether the program they have developed actually works — that is, to *validate* the curriculum using research. Unlike other curricula you may have heard of, the HighScope Curriculum has been validated through direct research on its effectiveness.

HighScope integrates all aspects of young children's development. It uses research-based and validated strategies to enhance growth in academics as well as social-emotional, physical, and creative development. It provides a comprehensive and complete system of child instruction, staff development, and child and program assessment. By learning to use this system effectively, you can make a significant difference in children's lives. This book of sample daily lesson plans will help you take the first steps toward understanding how HighScope can work in your classroom.

HighScope also offers workshops, conferences, and customized training in addition to books, DVDs, curriculum and assessment tools, and other resources. For more information, visit the HighScope Web site at *www.highscope.org*.

The HighScope Preschool "Wheel of Learning"

Now let's start learning more about the HighScope Curriculum. The diagram below, called the HighScope Preschool "Wheel of Learning," illustrates the curriculum principles that guide practitioners in their daily work with children.

Active Participatory Learning

The HighScope educational approach is based on the belief that young children build or "construct" their knowledge of the world. That means learning is not simply a process of adults giving information to children. Rather, children are *active learners* — discovering things through direct experience with people, objects, events, and ideas. They learn best from pursuing their own interests while being actively supported and challenged by adults. In the classroom, HighScope teachers are as active and involved as the children. They give thoughtful attention to the materials they provide, the

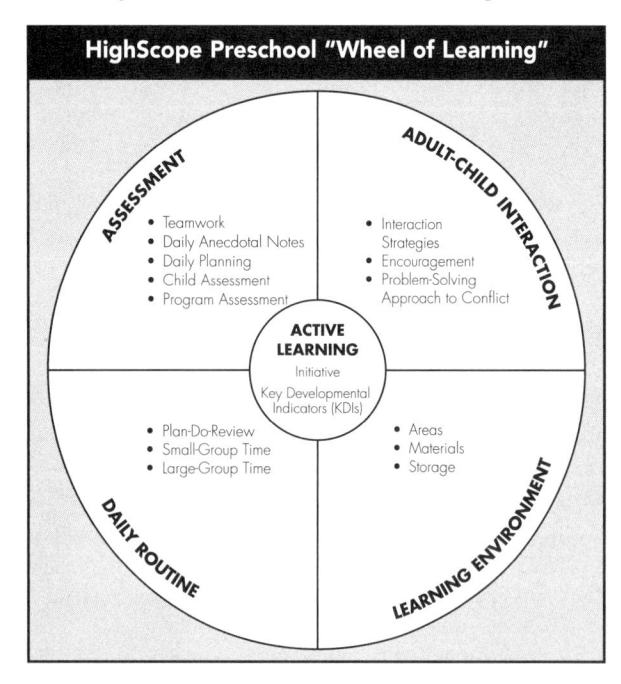

Active learning takes place when children make discoveries through their experiences with people, objects, events, and ideas.

activities they plan, and the ways they talk with children to both support and challenge what children are experiencing and thinking. HighScope calls this approach **active participatory learning** — a process in which teachers and children are partners in the learning process. Active learning is at the center of the wheel of learning to highlight its importance in every other aspect of the curriculum.

HighScope Preschool "Wheel of Learning"

ASSESSMENT
- Teamwork
- Daily Anecdotal Notes
- Daily Planning
- Child Assessment
- Program Assessment

ADULT-CHILD INTERACTION
- Interaction Strategies
- Encouragement
- Problem-Solving Approach to Conflict

ACTIVE LEARNING
Initiative
Key Developmental Indicators (KDIs)

DAILY ROUTINE
- Plan-Do-Review
- Small-Group Time
- Large-Group Time

LEARNING ENVIRONMENT
- Areas
- Materials
- Storage

Active learning has five ingredients, all of which must be present:

Materials: Abundant supplies of interesting materials are readily available to children. Materials are appealing to all the senses and are open ended — that is, they lend themselves to being used in a variety of ways and help expand children's experiences and stimulate their thinking.

Manipulation: Children handle, examine, combine, and transform materials and ideas. They make discoveries through direct hands-on and "minds-on" contact with these resources.

Choice: Children choose materials and play partners, change and build on their play ideas, and plan activities according to their interests and needs.

Child language and thought: Children describe what they are doing and understanding. They communicate verbally and nonverbally as they think about their actions and modify their thinking to take new learning into account.

Adult scaffolding: "Scaffolding" means adults both support children's current level of thinking and challenge it. Adults encourage children's efforts and help them extend or build on their work by talking with them about what they are doing, by joining in their play, and by helping them learn to solve problems that arise.

Adult-Child Interaction

In the HighScope Curriculum, **shared control** is central to how adults and children interact. The curriculum has many specific strategies for accomplishing this goal. Children are in control of child-sized decisions such as where to play, how to play, and what and who to play with. Adults are in charge of adult-sized decisions, including establishing the daily routine, arranging and equipping the classroom, and keeping children physically and psychologically safe. HighScope classrooms have neither a directive nor an "anything-goes" atmosphere. Instead, HighScope promotes a supportive climate in which adults and children are partners throughout the day.

Research indicates that the way adults interact with children plays a very important role in children's learning and development. Studies of the relationship between teachers' interaction styles and positive outcomes for children support the importance of a child-oriented interaction style. These studies demonstrate that in classrooms where teachers are responsive, guiding, and nurturing, children take more initiative and are more likely to be actively involved and persistent in their work. (Clarke-Stewart; Fagot; and Schweinhart, Weikart, and Larner as cited in HighScope Educational Research Foundation, 1996.) A directive approach is inconsistent with developmentally appropriate practices and our understanding of the importance of active learning, intrinsic motivation, and the engagement of young children.

Interaction Strategies That Encourage Active Learning

As you go through the 30 days of lesson plans in this book, you'll be slowly introduced to these interaction strategies. Although the strategies are given in particular daily routine segments, they can be used throughout the daily routine.

Offer children comfort and contact:

- *Look for children in need of comfort and contact.* Children who are expressing anxiety or discomfort, watching others play, moving quickly from one thing to another, or frequently asking for an adult may need your support.

- *Offer reassuring physical contact.* Children sometimes need a hand to hold, a lap to curl up in, reassuring arms around them, or just an adult's calm presence nearby.

- *Offer simple acknowledgements.* Occasionally all that is needed is acknowledgement of children's efforts — a simple nod, a smile, or a comment that shows you notice their efforts.

Participate in children's play:

- *Look for natural play openings.* It is easier and less disruptive to join children's exploratory play (for example, squeezing dough, pouring water, finger painting), pretend play (for example, being a party guest, putting the baby figure to bed in the dollhouse, pretending to drive cars down a block road), or games (for example, simple card games children make up), rather than their constructive play (for example, building a block road, painting a picture, making a duplo tower).

- *Join children's play at their physical level.* Kneel, sit, and even lie down on the floor so that the children are not "looking up" at you and you are not "looking down" on them.

- *Play in parallel with children.* This strategy can be an effective way to show children you accept what they are doing. Simply play near the children, using the same materials in the same way or in a similar way as the children are using them.

- *Play as a partner with children.* This works well with children involved in pretend play or games.

Lesson Plans for the First 30 Days

A child is able to use his own words to explain that the sponge balls are food for the journey because the adult referred one child to another instead of answering the question herself.

- *Refer one player to another.* This enables children to use their own abilities for the benefit of others, recognize one another's strengths, regard one another as a valuable resource, and play cooperatively.

- *Suggest new ideas within ongoing play situations.* Adults may also wish to challenge young children's thinking to expand their play and understanding. Strategies include

  - Offering suggestions within the children's play themes
  - Addressing the roles rather than the children themselves (for example, the mommy or the puppy dog children are pretending to be)
  - Respecting the children's reaction to your idea

Converse with children:

- *Be available for conversation throughout the day.* Children are more likely to talk with adults when they feel that adults enjoy these conversations. Be prepared for any subject — the past, things from the classroom, things that happen at home, speculations about the future, imaginings. Responding to children's chosen topics with interested comments and honest questions is more supportive than changing the subject or trying to get your own point across.

- *Join children at their level for conversation.* Since it is difficult to maintain a conversation when there is a major difference in the participants' head or eye levels, it is important to sit, kneel, or crouch down so you are at the children's level. This lets children know they have your full attention for conversation.

- *Respond to children's conversational leads.* When adults are silent yet attentive and listen patiently and with interest to ongoing conversations, children will likely address them directly or make the first move toward involving them in conversation.

- *Converse as a partner with children.* Pass control of the conversation back to children at every opportunity. Strategies include

  - Sticking to the topics children raise
  - Making comments that allow the conversation to continue without pressuring children for a response
  - Waiting for children to respond before taking another turn
  - Keeping comments fairly brief

- *Ask questions responsively and sparingly.* When adults ask questions, they take control of the conversation. Research shows that this actually limits conversational sharing from children. Here are some additional strategies:

  - Relate questions directly to what children are doing. Questions that discourage conversation tend to be questions about facts the adult already knows. (What color is that? How many do you have? Which stack is higher?) When questions are asked out of genuine interest and they relate directly to what children are doing, they may stimulate discussion.

  - Ask questions about children's thought process. The best kinds of questions are those that encourage children to talk about what they are thinking. (How can you tell? What do you think made that happen? How did you get the ball to…? What do you think would happen if…? What will you try next?)

Encourage rather than praise:

Research shows that there are many drawbacks to using praise and rewards as ways to motivate young children.

Praise may lead to dependence on adults because it encourages children to rely on authority figures to solve problems for them and to evaluate what is right or wrong. Praise can discourage children's efforts, have a negative effect on self-image, and can make children feel insecure and defensive.

Encouragement is an alternative to praise. It shows children that we notice their accomplishments and that we respect their efforts. Encouragement allows children to feel they can make mistakes and learn from them without being judged. Here are some strategies that support encouragement:

- *Participate in children's play:*
    - Get involved in children's play.
    - Observe what children are doing and saying.
    - Be responsive to children's actions and interests.
- *Encourage children to describe their efforts and products:*
    - Encourage reflective thinking.
    - Ask open-ended questions.
    - Repeat what children say: listen carefully.
- *Acknowledge children's work or ideas by making specific comments:*
    - Notice the details in the work and comment on them without making a judgment.

Encourage children's problem solving:
- *Look for children involved in problem situations.*
- *Allow children to deal with problems* and conflicting viewpoints if they can.
- *Interact with, rather than manage, children.* Adults who *manage* (pass out instructions, warnings,

By interacting with children rather than managing them, and by remaining nonjudgmental, adults help children learn to be problem solvers.

Lesson Plans for the First 30 Days

solutions) rather than *interact* prevent children from confronting and working with child-sized problems.

- *Assist matter-of-factly with unresolved conflicts.* When intervention is necessary, adults should be patient, respectful, and nonjudgmental. Remember, the goal is not just to solve the problem — you as an adult can do this easily. The goal is to have the children engage in a problem-solving approach so they can learn the skills necessary to be problem solvers themselves!

- Use the Six Steps to Conflict Resolution, described on page 107.

The Daily Routine

The HighScope daily routine is designed to provide the consistency and predictability that children and adults need while providing enough flexibility that children feel neither rushed nor bored as they carry out their activities. The parts of the day include time for children to plan, to carry out their plans, to recall and reflect on their actions, and to engage in small- and large-group activities. The schedule is the same every day, with each component taking a specified amount of time. This regularity gives children a sense of control and helps them to act independently.

You may schedule the parts of the daily routine in any order, depending on the hours and structure of your program, with the exception that planning time, work time, cleanup time, and recall time *always* occur in that order. In half-day programs, each part typically happens once. In full-day programs, one or more parts may be repeated, and you may also include a rest or nap period.

The Daily Routine Chart

The daily routine chart helps children understand what they will be doing during the day. The chart lists the time periods of the day in sequence. Next to the name of each time period is a photograph, picture, symbol, or drawing that illustrates that segment of the routine (for example, next to "Outside Time" there might be a drawing of the swing set).

At right and below are two examples of how a daily routine poster can be made using symbols to illustrate the segments of the daily routine.

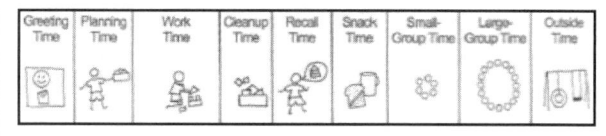

(You might try inventing your own creative variations!) The word "time" is consistently used with each segment, as it helps children recognize that separate time periods make up their daily routine.

TIP: Use a large clip or clothespin to indicate which part of the daily routine you are in. As you progress through the day, children can move the clip to the next part of the routine.

The children "read" the vertical chart from top to bottom and the horizontal chart from left to right. The size of each section in the horizontal chart represents how long each part of the routine takes. This helps children understand that some segments of the routine last longer than others.

Components of the HighScope Daily Routine

Here's a summary of each segment of the HighScope daily routine.

Greeting Time (15–20 Minutes). Greeting time provides a smooth transition from home to school. Teachers greet children, connect with parents, and read books in a cozy setting. Typically, one adult is available to greet children and parents and the other adult sits in a comfortable area ready to read books to the children

Adults use a combination of words and symbols on the message board to share important information about the day with children.

Lesson Plans for the First 30 Days

Sample Daily Routines

Half-Day Program

▷ Greeting time
▷ Planning, work, cleanup, and recall time
▷ Snack
▷ Large-group time
▷ Small-group time
▷ Outside time
▷ Departure

Double Half-Day Sessions

Morning arrival group:
▷ Greeting time
▷ Planning, work, cleanup, and recall time
▷ Small-group time
▷ Large-group time
▷ Outdoor time
▷ Lunch
▷ Departure

Afternoon arrival group:
▷ Lunch
▷ Greeting time
▷ Large-group time
▷ Planning, work, cleanup, and recall time
▷ Small-group time
▷ Snack
▷ Outdoor time
▷ Departure

Full-Day Program

Children arrive and depart at the same time:
▷ Breakfast
▷ Greeting time
▷ Large-group time
▷ Planning, work, cleanup, and recall time
▷ Small-group time
▷ Outside time
▷ Lunch
▷ Books and rest
▷ Snack
▷ Outside time
▷ Departure

Staggered arrivals and departures through the day:
▷ Free play
▷ Breakfast
▷ Greeting time
▷ Planning, work, cleanup, and recall time
▷ Small-group time
▷ Large-group time
▷ Outside time
▷ Lunch
▷ Books, nap
▷ Snack
▷ Small-group time
▷ Planning, work, and cleanup, and recall time with parents

as they arrive. Adults rotate this role so that, over time, each has opportunities to both greet and read to children. You might consider inviting parents to participate with you and the children for this part of your day.

The last five minutes of greeting time are used to read the **message board** with the children. The message board gives children and adults a chance to share important information for the day. An adult writes the messages ahead of time using pictures and words so children of all literacy levels can "read" them together. Adults share announcements and let children know about upcoming special events, new materials, visitors, and so on. The message board can also be used as a starting point for group problem solving. Two or three messages each day are plenty.

The Plan-Do-Review Process. The longest segment of the HighScope daily routine, generally over an hour in length, is devoted to a *planning time, work time,* and *recall time* sequence called *plan-do-review.* At planning time, children meet in small groups with an adult. Each child then decides what to do during work time — what area to play in, what materials to use, and who else will be involved — and shares this plan with

TIP: A wipe-off board, whiteboard, or chalkboard makes a great message board.

> **TIP:** Planning time, work time, cleanup time, and recall time always occur in that order.

the adult. Work time is when children carry out their plans, alone and/or with others, and then clean up. At recall time, they meet with the same adult and small group of children with whom they planned to share and discuss what they did and learned during work time.

The plan-do-review process in a HighScope program differs from choice time, center time, or free play commonly seen in other programs in that HighScope adults do not direct children's plans or work-time activities. They do not tell children what materials to use, what activities to complete, or where to play; they do not close certain areas of the classroom.

Planning Time (10–15 Minutes). Planning time begins the "plan-do-review" process. When young children plan, they begin with an intention or idea. Depending on their age and ability to communicate, they might express their plan in actions (picking up a block), gestures (pointing to the block area), or words ("I want to make a tall, tall building — like where my mommy works"). Planning is different from simply making a choice because it involves children in developing specific ideas about what they want to do, how they will do it, and who they will do it with. In other words, planning involves more purpose and intentionality than choosing. It is also important to remember that young children can change their plans. In fact, children often do this as they get interested in what someone else is doing or notice interesting materials they previously overlooked. Therefore, in a HighScope program, children are not required to stick to their initial plans, nor are they criticized for not completing them. Instead, adults follow up with children at work time and help them express a new plan.

Planning Time How-To's:
- Divide children into two groups, each with its own adult. The membership of each group remains consistent.
- Invite children to share what they want to do during work time (typically what they will do first).
- Support the planning process by encouraging children to plan in ways that are consistent with their development. The adults
    - Use interesting activities or props to capture children's interest and facilitate the sharing of their plans

> **TIP:** As you use this book, notice how the planning strategies progress from being simple and concrete to being more complex and abstract.

- Keep in mind that children's planning skills will move from the simple and concrete to the more complex and abstract as they become familiar with the planning process
- Help developing planners extend their plans, asking not only "Where will you go?" but also "What will you do in that area?" "What materials will you use?" and "How will you get your plan started?"
- Let children know they are free to begin work time once they have made a plan.

Work Time (45–60 Minutes). Work time — the "do" part of plan-do-review — is when children carry out their plans. During this time, children can work with any of the materials in any of the classroom interest areas. In other words, children decide where they will play, what they will play, and who they will play with. Children use materials creatively at work time, repeating and building upon activities that interest them; there are no preset activities. Children may move materials from one area of the classroom to another. Adults also do not limit the number of children who can work in each area — if too many children are in one area at a time, the adults use this as a problem-solving opportunity.

During work time, adults focus on the children. They interact with children in calm and respectful tones. Adults observe and listen to children during this part of

Teachers support children's planning process by offering interesting planning props or activities and asking questions to help children extend their plans.

Lesson Plans for the First 30 Days

At work time, children carry out their plans, working creatively and repeating and building upon activities that interest them.

Work Time How-To's:

- Make sure interest areas and play materials are easily accessible and contain a wide range of materials.
- Find out what children are doing: observe their plan status, social interactions, specific types of play, and learning through play.
- Choose children to interact and play with.
- Use the interaction strategies described in your lesson plans.
- Record your observations of children — what they do and say.
- Bring work time to an end by giving a transition warning.

> **The Find-Use-Return Cycle**
>
> During plan-do-review, children engage in the *find-use-return cycle* as they find the materials they wish to play with, use the materials, then return the materials at cleanup time. Adults arrange and label the learning environment so children have easy access to materials. This helps establish the find-use-return cycle, which also engages children with the developmental experience of classification while empowering them to select and care for materials. For more on arranging and labeling the classroom environment to promote active learning see pages 12–14.

the day, conversing in a give-and-take manner. They avoid asking children many questions with predetermined, correct answers. Adults participate as partners in children's play, assuming roles suggested by the children and following the children's cues about the content and direction of play. Adults encourage children to

> **TIP:** As you use the lesson plans in this book, notice how the work-time plans focus on adult-child interaction strategies you can try out.

explore and use materials in their own way and support children when the children choose to repeat an activity. Adults encourage children's efforts and ideas and put children in control of evaluating their own work and efforts. Adults in a HighScope classroom involve children in resolving conflicts.

Cleanup Time (About 10 Minutes). Cleanup time helps children further understand the "find-use-return" principle. Children and adults work together to return materials and equipment to their storage spaces and, when appropriate, put away or find display space for children's personal creations. It's important to remember to keep a light and playful attitude during cleanup time. Accept children's level of involvement and skill while supporting their learning.

As you go through the lesson plans in this book, notice how the strategies for cleanup time offer fun and engaging ways for children to put away their materials.

Recall Time (10–15 Minutes). Recall time brings closure to the plan-do-review process. In their small groups, children are encouraged to reflect on, talk about, and/or show what they have done at work time. Younger preschoolers often recall the last thing they did, since it is freshest in their minds. Older preschoolers are more able to recall the sequence of what they

Lesson Plans for the First 30 Days

At recall time, children reflect on what they did during work time. Strategies used for planning time also often make effective recall strategies.

did at work time, or they may even recall their original plans. Recall should always immediately follow the work time-cleanup time sequence. Adults use a variety of strategies to encourage children to share and recall their experiences. They avoid strategies that result in rote recalling (such as the questions "Where did you go?" and "What did you do?"). Rather, they assist children in reflecting on their actions, feelings, and plans. Adults encourage children to recall in ways that are consistent with their developmental levels.

Recall Time How-To's:
- Meet back in the same group children planned in (each group has its own adult).
- Listen and support children as they share what they did at work time. You can support the recall process by encouraging children to recall in ways that are consistent with their development (see "Planning Time How-To's" on p. 8).

Small-Group Time (15–20 Minutes). During small-group time, the same group of children meets each day with the same adult, starting out in the same place. Small-group time is adult initiated; the adult plans the small-group activity and provides the materials for each

> **TIP:** The same children meet together with the same adult for planning time, recall time, small-group time and, often, for meals. These stable groups help adults get to know each child and help the children feel comfortable with each other.

child. Small-group time is not, however, adult directed — active participatory learning continues throughout the daily routine! Children contribute their own ideas, use the materials in ways that they find interesting, and participate at their own developmental level. Small-group time gives children the opportunity to build on their own interests; have experiences in a variety of curriculum content areas; and explore new, unexplored, or underused materials they might not use during work time — all with adult support in an intimate setting.

Adults use many strategies to support and extend children's small-group activities. They observe what children do, move from child to child, comment on what children are doing and saying, and imitate and add to children's actions and ideas while using the materials themselves.

While small-group time is adult-planned, this part of the daily routine offers children an opportunity to explore materials in unique ways in an intimate and supportive setting.

Small-Group-Time How-To's:
- Meet consistently with the same small group that children planned and recalled in (one adult per group). *Note:* Depending on the nature of your

small-group activity, you may need to move to another location (for example, the floor, the water table, and so forth).

- After a brief introduction, give each child his or her own set of materials. Small baskets, paper lunch bags, large yogurt containers, and shoeboxes make great containers for individual sets of small-group-time materials (for example, scissors, glue stick, and paper scraps in each basket for an art activity). Also have extra materials in the center of the table for the group to use as needed (for example, more paper scraps, yarn, and feathers).
- Once children have their materials, carefully observe how they respond to the materials; listen to their comments.
- Try using the materials yourself, imitating the children's actions.
- Be ready for children to use materials in ways you don't expect. This is fine!
- Move from child to child to provide individual support.
- Give children a three-minute warning before ending the activity.
- Encourage children to help you clean up the materials.
- Remind children where they can find the materials if they want to use them again at work time.

TIP: You may find the block area works well for large-group time, or you may have to move equipment aside to make a big enough space — the children can help you with this!

Large-Group Time (10–15 Minutes). Large-group time is a segment of the daily routine that adds to the sense of community in the classroom. It is a time when everyone comes together to participate in a shared experience, such as a music and movement activity. As with every other part of the HighScope day, it involves the five ingredients of active participatory learning. Note that large-group times require a space that can accommodate vigorous activities involving the whole class.

As with small-group time, large-group time is planned and initiated by the adults but children have many choices. For example, children decide how to move their bodies to music, or they make suggestions for motions to a favorite song or rhyme. It is also a time of day when children can take turns being leaders. For example, if the group is singing "Old MacDonald Had a Farm," children can suggest the next animal to sing about and what noise that animal might make.

Large-Group-Time How-To's:
- Begin large-group time by gathering together in your large-group space. There is no need to sit and wait for all the children to "be ready" before starting. As children finish their previous activity, they will be eager to join in this part of the day.
- Introduce the activity but readily share control with children by planning ahead of time for children to make choices and incorporate their ideas in the activity.
- Encourage children to move in their own ways and to try out each other's ideas for singing and moving. Do not ask children to follow directions during large-group time — for example, children are not expected to sing to a recording or to move in a predetermined way.
- Participate in large-group time along with all the other adults and children.
- Give children a warning when the activity is coming to an end. ("We'll sing about one more animal.")
- Have a plan ready for transitioning to the next part of the daily routine.

Outside Time (30–40 Minutes). During outside time, children can enjoy physical, noisy, and vigorous play. Rather than standing to the side and passively watching, HighScope adults join children in their outdoor play, supervising for safety but also becoming engaged with children, scaffolding their learning and discoveries. Being outside also lets children and adults connect to their neighborhood community and use all their senses to appreciate nature.

TIP: Supplement your outdoor environment with loose materials that you can take in and out every day. Add items like balls, boards, old sheets, tires, shovels, rakes, water hoses, chalk, and so on. You can also take out materials from your art, house, sand and water, and music areas.

Children have an abundance of choices about what they can do outside. The outdoors is a place where young children can run, jump, throw, kick, swing, climb, dig, and ride, playing alone or with others. Their pre-

Lesson Plans for the First 30 Days

Large-group time offers an opportunity for all adults and children to come together for a shared experience, such as a movement and music activity, game, or group project.

tend play takes on new dimensions as they move over a larger area and incorporate trees, rocks, leaves, and play equipment.

Mealtimes (15–20 Minutes). In most part-day programs, children and adults share a snack, while full-day programs include both meal- and snacktimes. It's preferable for children to eat with the same adult and children who gather together for planning, recall, and small-group times.

The emphasis during mealtimes is on social interaction. It is important for adults to sit down and eat with children, not just as a natural social situation but also as an opportunity to share relaxed conversation with children and support children's ideas. Mealtimes are also occasions when children enjoy practicing self-help skills such as pouring their own juice, serving themselves food, wiping up spills, and so forth. (*Note:* In some of the lesson plans included in this book you will find conversation starters to use during mealtimes under "Other Ideas.")

Transitions. Adults in HighScope programs plan ways for children to make transitions and give children reasonable choices as they move from one activity to the next. For example, if there's a short waiting time, children can decide how to move or they can join in singing songs. Adults always let children know transitions are coming by giving the children a warning.

The Learning Environment

Planning the Indoor Learning Environment

Environments that foster active learning require thoughtful planning. Unlike some other types of programs in which the adults plan and set out specific materials for children to use each day, in HighScope programs, it's the *children* who decide what they need for their work-time plans. Careful attention to the room arrangement, types of materials provided, and storage of those materials help children follow through on their ideas and build on their learning experiences.

Guidelines for Arranging the Play Space

- Divide the space into well-defined interest areas for distinctive types of play:

- Start with the basic interest areas: the house area, the art area, the block area, and the toy area.
- Add to the areas as you observe the children's interests.
- Each interest area should be carefully placed in the learning environment to suit the types of play carried out in the space.
    - The block area should provide enough space for the children to build.
    - Because children often use materials from the house area and block area together in play, the house area and block area are ideally located next to one another. (For example, children might bring pretend food from the house area to the boat they've built in the block area, use small blocks as ingredients in a soup pot, and so forth.)
    - The art area should be placed close to a water source or on tile floor to accommodate activities and make cleanup easier.
- Choose names for the areas that the children can understand (for example, "toy area" instead of "manipulatives").
- Establish visual boundaries between the interest areas that are low enough so the adults and children can see what is happening in all areas. Some additional considerations:
    - Well-defined spaces help children make purposeful decisions when planning because they know what is available and where to find it.
    - Well-defined areas make it easier for children and adults to put things away.

Well-planned classroom areas allow children to carry out their work-time plans and build on their interests.

Guidelines for Choosing Materials
- Choose materials that reflect the children's interests:
    - Observe children and identify what materials they are using.
    - Select additional materials to support their learning and play.
    - Introduce new materials at small-group time and observe how children use the materials.
- Choose materials that are developmentally appropriate.
- Provide open-ended materials that can be used in a variety of ways:
    - When selecting materials, don't think of equipment and materials as having a specific purpose or function — rather, think of them as being used in *many* ways!
    - Choose materials that children of different ages and abilities can use in different ways.
- Choose materials that support the following different types of play:
    - Exploratory play (string, glue, play dough, water)
    - Constructive play (blocks, tubes, boxes, fabric pieces)
    - Dramatic play (dress-up clothes, suitcases, pots and pans, dolls)
    - Games (cards, paper, counters, dice, and other materials children can use to make up their own simple games)
- Choose materials that reflect the experiences and cultures of the children.
- In addition to natural materials, add real, everyday items to the classroom (for example, old cell phones, purses, tools). This enables children to imitate the important adults in their lives. Consider items made of wood, paper, metal, liquid, and so forth.
- Make sure materials are safe, clean, and well-maintained.

Guidelines for Storing Materials
- Store materials so children can reach them.
    - Store materials on low, open shelves so they are always accessible to children.
- Use see-through containers to store materials in plain view.
    - Use boxes or baskets with no lids, tubs, or other sturdy containers.

Lesson Plans for the First 30 Days

- Make sure materials are always stored in the same place.
  - Store materials so children can find what they need without adult assistance.
  - Store the same types of materials together (for example, crayons, pencils, and chalk on the same shelf; glue, tape, and staplers on the same shelf)
- Label the shelves and containers so children can easily find and put away materials. The container and the shelf where the container goes should be labeled with identical labels.
- Use labels children can easily "read." Some suggestions:
  - Use one of the actual items attached to the container.
  - Use a tracing of the item; for example, for blocks, pots, or cooking tools.
  - Use a photograph or drawing as a label (both on the container and on the space where it belongs on the shelf). Use photocopies or catalogue pictures to make labels for hard-to-draw materials.

HighScope classrooms also use **letter links** for children's nametags and to label areas of the classroom used for children's belongings. For more on this name-learning system, see pp. 18–19 in "Getting Started: Things to Do Before Week 1."

Curriculum Content and Key Developmental Indicators

The HighScope Preschool Curriculum includes 58 Key developmental indicators (KDIs) in eight different content areas. The KDIs are statements of active behaviors that reflect the concepts and skills that children naturally use as they interact with materials, people, ideas, and events. The role of adults is to support children in their activities and help develop these learning behaviors.

The HighScope KDIs are organized around these eight content areas: Approaches to Learning; Social and Emotional Development; Physical Development and Health; Language, Literacy, and Communication; Mathematics; Creative Arts; Science and Technology; and Social Studies. You can find a complete listing of the content areas and the KDIs that comprise them on pp. 20–21.

At the beginning of each day's lesson plan, you will see a section titled "Curriculum Content – Key Developmental Indicators," which will show you which KDIs are reflected in that day's activities. The KDIs for individual parts of the daily routine are listed next to the headings for those parts of the day. Please use the complete list of KDIs on pp. 20–21 to identify specific areas of learning that you see your children engaged in. Compare this list to your state standards or learning objectives of your program.

Assessment

Observation and Anecdotes

In HighScope classrooms, adults take daily notes on their observations about children. These notes are called *anecdotes* and focus on what children do and say. Anecdotes enable adults to see the children and the classroom objectively. They also help to answer these important questions:

- What are the children's interests?
- What are children learning?
- What areas of learning are we currently supporting?
- Are any of the areas of learning overlooked or not supported?
- What materials or experiences might be added?

How to Record Anecdotes

Adults may select two or three children and take anecdotes on what they do and say throughout the entire day, or they might record whatever anecdotes they see happening in a specific area of the room or part of the daily routine.

- Start by noting down the date, the segment of the daily routine during which the observation took place, where the observation took place, and who was involved.

For example,

May 16, at work time, in the block area, Shannon…

- Write down what the child did and said, and record the child's language in quotes. For example:

  May 16, at work time, in the block area, Shannon put the blocks end-to-end, making a big circle. She said, "I made a big swimming pool for horses." She put the horse figures inside and moved them around like they were swimming.

- When recording an anecdote, try to be as factual, specific, and brief as possible.

TIP: Have anecdote-taking material handy. Try using sticky notes, small pads of paper, an apron with pockets, a device for using OnlineCOR Mobile, or whatever works best for you!

For more on observation and anecdote-taking, see page 84.

Assessing Children's Learning

HighScope has developed and validated assessment instruments to measure children's development and growth. HighScope's **COR Advantage** assesses children's overall development. It is available in both print and online versions. This assessment system is based on teacher's anecdotal notes made during normal classroom activities. It enables adults to look at the whole child, and it respects and accommodates cultural differences. COR Advantage is used to observe children in their natural program setting and rate their development.

Teamwork

HighScope sees each adult working with the children as a member of the team. Teamwork is a process of active learning that requires a supportive climate of mutual respect. Team members support each other and can enhance each other's strengths. They also share the same expectations, which are based on a shared philosophy and mutually agreed-upon goals. Decisions are made by consensus, and clear communication is respected and practiced. Members of the team know what to expect from one another. All team members work together to achieve team goals. Everyone — adults, parents, and children — benefit from this kind of teamwork.

Team Planning

Adults experienced in the HighScope Curriculum use their observations about children to develop daily lesson plans that scaffold children's discoveries and learning. (For an explanation of scaffolding, see p. 3) Each day, teaching team members discuss their anecdotes, describing what they saw children doing and learning that day, and together they develop lesson plans for the next day.

This book is designed to supplement this planning process while adult team members are learning more about the HighScope Curriculum. Although the book can be used on a daily basis, adults might also page through it to find ideas and strategies suitable to the needs and interests of individual children they are working with. So don't be afraid to play around with the ideas you'll find in this book, use activities out of order, or substitute materials or toys that you know your children are interested in!

See the next section for more about how you can get the most out of this book as you implement the HighScope approach in your daily routine.

Family Involvement

Family involvement is a key aspect of the HighScope Curriculum. A HighScope program provides a variety of opportunities for parents to become involved and to support their own children's development at home. Adults in a HighScope program work to create a partnership with families by doing the following:

- Encouraging family members to participate in classroom activities with children, as they are able

- Exchanging information with family members and other staff about the curriculum and its relationship to children's development

- Interacting informally with family members and other staff to share information about the day's activities and children's experiences

- Exchanging information with other staff and family members about how to promote and extend children's learning and social development at home

Encouraging family members to participate in classroom activities also helps families to support their child's development at home.

How to Use This Book

Each of the next six chapters of this book represents one week, with **five days of lesson plans** included for each week. This section describes what you will find in each of these chapters, along with tips for getting the most out of the lesson plans. (*Note:* Chapter 7 contains the sample Growing Readers Curriculum activities used in Weeks 3 and 5, Appendix A contains reproducible observation and planning forms, and Appendix B contains a chart showing how the music CD included with this book can be used with lesson plan activities.)

Weekly Overviews

Each week starts with an **overview** complete with goals, prompts for things you'll need to do or prepare, specific strategies or ideas for the week, and a helpful calendar with reminders. The overview helps give you a sense of where you are headed for the week.

The Lesson Plans

Next, you'll find five days of lesson plans. Keep in mind that the plans are sequential, building on one another throughout the book. They start out simply, beginning with ideas for introducing the HighScope daily routine to your children in Week 1. As you progress through the plans they become increasingly more complex, reflecting both the children's development and your understanding of the HighScope Curriculum.

Each day's plan includes the following:

Curriculum Content (KDIs)

At the top of the lesson plan you will see a list of the learning areas highlighted for the day (Key developmental indicators [KDIs]).

Next to each daily routine component in the lesson plan, you will see the KDIs you are likely to observe children expressing for the activity given. (Note that the KDIs listed represent behaviors that may or may not be seen, depending on children's actions.) Remember to be on the lookout for other KDIs that may be occurring!

Greeting Time and Message Board

The plans provide prompts for greeting-time activities and offer ideas for drawing and writing messages about the day's events on your message board.

Planning Time

The lesson plans offer planning ideas for two planning groups. Be sure to read the plans for your group (for example, if you are the adult working with Group 2, always read the activity and strategy for Group 2). Note that each group uses each of the planning strategies, but on different days.

Work Time

Adult-child interaction strategies that promote active learning — including s and examples — are provided in these sections. Remember, you can use these ideas any time you work with children!

Cleanup Time

These sections offer strategies for helping to keep your cleanup times fun and engaging while promoting active learning and important developmental experiences. See Appendix B for selections from the music CD included with this book that you can use at cleanup time.

Recall Time

As with planning time, the lesson plans in this book offer recall ideas for two groups. Be sure to read the plans for your group (Group 1 or Group 2). Note that each group uses each of the recall strategies, but on different days.

Lesson Plans for the First 30 Days

- **Outside time** — materials to take outside and interaction strategies to try.
- **Meal conversations** — ideas for conversation starters during snacks or mealtimes.
- **Home-school connections** — ideas for communicating with children's family members. You may wish to communicate these ideas in a note home if children arrive on a bus, or you might share them on a parent board and verbally if family members drop off or pick up their child.

Observation and Follow-Up Ideas

At the end of each lesson plan, you'll be reminded to record your observations of children. You'll also be given some ideas for following up on the day's activities and/or prompted to develop your own follow-up ideas. You will find reproducible sheets for recording your observations and follow-up ideas on pages 178 and 179.

Working With Your Team. Together with your teaching team, discuss and record your observations (anecdotes) of what you saw individual children do and say. You might find the following questions helpful:

- What did you learn about the child's understanding?
- What did you learn about the child's interests?
- What did you learn about the child's developmental levels?
- What ideas do you have to support the child's interests and learning in the future?
- What did you learn about using HighScope?

Working through this process will also help you develop the next day's plan and follow-up ideas that support your children's unique interests and developmental needs.

Finally, **be sure to read through the next day's plans** with the other members of your teaching team. Talk about how you'll handle that day's activities and transitions. Using your observations about children, discuss whether you will modify the plans in any way, then gather and prepare the materials you'll need.

Small-Group Time

Each lesson plan provides a small-group activity for each of the two groups. These activities include a description of materials needed for each child and instructions for what to do at the beginning, middle, and end of the activities, including prompts for supporting children as they work.

Also note that six of the small-group times are sample activities from the Growing Readers Early Literacy Curriculum (used in Weeks 3 and 5). Growing Readers is a set of detailed plans for 90 teacher-led small-group activities. The activities are designed around the four key areas of early literacy learning:

- Comprehension
- Phonological awareness
- Alphabetic principle
- Concepts about print

You will find a complete description of these activities along with materials needed on pages 157–175.

Large-Group Time

Each lesson plan offers a unique large-group-time activity. If you need any materials they'll be listed, followed by the steps to carry out the activity. See Appendix B for selections from the music CD included with this book that you can use at large-group time.

Other Ideas

These sections give you additional ideas and strategies for building active learning into your daily routine. You'll find ideas for

> **TIP:** Preparing your materials the night before helps reduce the stress and time crunch before the children arrive the next day. When you are prepared ahead of time, you can be ready to greet and support the children when they arrive.

Lesson Plans for the First 30 Days

Weekly Summaries

At the end of each chapter, you'll find a review of the week titled **"Building on What You Already Know."** These handy summaries highlight the past week's content. In each you'll see a summary of the activities that you led, the developmental experiences and curriculum content areas in which you provided support to children, and the adult-child interaction strategies that you practiced.

◈

Now that you know how to get the most out of the material presented in the lesson plans, you are ready to prepare your classroom for active learning! See the next section for some important preparation steps.

Getting Started: Things to Do Before Week 1

Before you begin using the lesson plans, there are a few things you will need to do set the stage for active learning. The list below will help you organize the learning environment, the daily routine, and children's letter links.

Room Arrangement

- **Arrange your classroom into four to seven main interest areas** (for example, a block area, art area, house area, toy area, and book area are common interest areas for preschool children).

With a well-arranged classroom, children have abundant opportunities to use materials in ways that interest them and are appropriate to their developmental levels.

- **Make signs** for each of the interest areas that include a simple symbol and written name that children can easily understand. (You can also purchase area signs from HighScope. See the HighScope Web site at *www.highscope.org* to access the online store for more information.)

Daily Routine

- **Assign the children to one of two consistent groups,** one of which will meet with Adult 1, and the other, with Adult 2. The members of these groups will be together for planning time, recall time, small-group time, and, ideally, snack- or mealtime (if you eat in your classroom instead of a lunchroom).

- **Prepare a daily routine chart** using the simple drawings on page 6 as a model, or using photographs taken during the first days of school.

- **Create a set of cards showing each classroom area** using words and simple drawings on the cards. The children will use this card set for planning and recall time. See the sample below.

- **Take photos of the areas of the room** to use for planning and recall time.

- **Make a daily routine book** and make enough photocopies of it for each child to take home on the first day. This daily routine book can simply be what you use for your daily routine chart, put in booklet format.

Letter Links

Letter links is an important part of the HighScope classroom. It is a name-learning system that pairs a child's printed name with a letter-linked picture of an object that starts with the same letter and sound; for example, *F*lora and ❄, *S*am and ✂, *A*aron and ✈. Using nametags and letter links as labels in a variety of ways throughout the classroom and having children write their names to "sign in" each day engages children in a meaningful way with both phonological awareness and the alphabetic principle.

Prepare letter-link choices for children corresponding with the letter sounds of their first name. Children will select their letter link symbol at greeting time on Day 1. After that, you will create cards with each child's name and letter link symbol (see the Week 1 overview, "Materials to Add to the Classroom," on p. 22). Letter links are used in many of the lesson plans in this book.

(The material in this section was adapted from *Growing Readers Early Literacy Curriculum Teacher Guide,* by Mary Hohmann, p. 10)

HighScope Preschool Curriculum Content
Key Developmental Indicators

A. Approaches to Learning
1. Initiative: Children demonstrate initiative as they explore their world.
2. Planning: Children make plans and follow through on their intentions.
3. Engagement: Children focus on activities that interest them.
4. Problem solving: Children solve problems encountered in play.
5. Use of resources: Children gather information and formulate ideas about their world.
6. Reflection: Children reflect on their experiences.

B. Social and Emotional Development
7. Self-identity: Children have a positive self-identity.
8. Sense of competence: Children feel they are competent.
9. Emotions: Children recognize, label, and regulate their feelings.
10. Empathy: Children demonstrate empathy toward others.
11. Community: Children participate in the community of the classroom.
12. Building relationships: Children build relationships with other children and adults.
13. Cooperative play: Children engage in cooperative play.
14. Moral development: Children develop an internal sense of right and wrong.
15. Conflict resolution: Children resolve social conflicts.

C. Physical Development and Health
16. Gross-motor skills: Children demonstrate strength, flexibility, balance, and timing in using their large muscles.
17. Fine-motor skills: Children demonstrate dexterity and hand-eye coordination in using their small muscles.
18. Body awareness: Children know about their bodies and how to navigate them in space.
19. Personal care: Children carry out personal care routines on their own.
20. Healthy behavior: Children engage in healthy practices.

D. Language, Literacy, and Communication[1]
21. Comprehension: Children understand language.
22. Speaking: Children express themselves using language.
23. Vocabulary: Children understand and use a variety of words and phrases.
24. Phonological awareness: Children identify distinct sounds in spoken language.
25. Alphabetic knowledge: Children identify letter names and their sounds.
26. Reading: Children read for pleasure and information.
27. Concepts about print: Children demonstrate knowledge about environmental print.
28. Book knowledge: Children demonstrate knowledge about books.
29. Writing: Children write for many different purposes.
30. English language learning: (If applicable) Children use English and their home language(s) (including sign language).

---

[1] Language, Literacy, and Communication KDIs 21–29 may be used for the child's home language(s) as well as English. KDI 30 refers specifically to English language learning.

E. Mathematics

31. Number words and symbols: Children recognize and use number words and symbols.

32. Counting: Children count things.

33. Part-whole relationships: Children combine and separate quantities of objects.

34. Shapes: Children identify, name, and describe shapes.

35. Spatial awareness: Children recognize spatial relationships among people and objects.

36. Measuring: Children measure to describe, compare, and order things.

37. Unit: Children understand and use the concept of unit.

38. Patterns: Children identify, describe, copy, complete, and create patterns.

39. Data analysis: Children use information about quantity to draw conclusions, make decisions, and solve problems.

F. Creative Arts

40. Art: Children express and represent what they observe, think, imagine, and feel through two- and three-dimensional art.

41. Music: Children express and represent what they observe, think, imagine, and feel through music.

42. Movement: Children express and represent what they observe, think, imagine, and feel through movement.

43. Pretend play: Children express and represent what they observe, think, imagine, and feel through pretend play.

44. Appreciating the arts: Children appreciate the creative arts.

G. Science and Technology

45. Observing: Children observe the materials and processes in their environment.

46. Classifying: Children classify materials, actions, people, and events.

47. Experimenting: Children experiment to test their ideas.

48. Predicting: Children predict what they expect will happen.

49. Drawing conclusions: Children draw conclusions based on their experiences and observations.

50. Communicating ideas: Children communicate their ideas about the characteristics of things and how they work.

51. Natural and physical world: Children gather knowledge about the natural and physical world.

52. Tools and technology: Children explore and use tools and technology.

H. Social Studies

53. Diversity: Children understand that people have diverse characteristics, interests, and abilities.

54. Community roles: Children recognize that people have different roles and functions in the community.

55. Decision making: Children participate in making classroom decisions.

56. Geography: Children recognize and interpret features and locations in their environment.

57. History: Children understand past, present, and future.

58. Ecology: Children understand the importance of taking care of their environment.

Chapter 1
The First Week

Getting Ready: Week 1 Overview

Goals for the First Week
- Get to know your children (if you are starting with a new group of children).
- Help children become familiar with the HighScope daily routine.
- Help children become familiar with the classroom arrangement (area and materials).
- Help children become familiar with their name and letter link symbol.

Things to Keep in Mind This Week
- Be sure to read each activity plan ahead of time so you will know what materials you need to prepare.

Daily Routine
- As you move from one part of the routine to the next, move a marker (for example, a clothespin or a giant clip) from one part of the daily routine chart to the next.
- To help children become familiar with the routine, be sure to always say the name of each part when it starts; for example, "It's planning time," or "Now, it's small group time."
- To help children become more familiar with the room and materials, each *small-group time* for this week will be spent exploring a particular area. Always meet with your group in your regular place first, then move to the area you will be exploring that day.
- On Friday, add this to the message board: Two simply drawn images of the school with a red circle and diagonal slash over them — the universal "no" symbol). Write *2 no-school days* and help the children interpret the drawings. Remind them that they will stay home for two days and then come back to school.

TIP: This week's small-group times have children exploring an interest area to learn what materials are found there. Use this strategy any time you've added or modified an interest area. For example, when we added a woodworking area to our classroom, each teacher took a small-group time to explore it with the children in her group.

Sign-In Sheets
Make simple sign-in sheets (to be introduced on Day 3) by doing the following:
1. Write out each child's name and letter link symbol followed by a long line:

   Sue ☼ _____

   Helen ♥ _____

2. Make one sheet for each small group and place it on a clipboard.

3. Each day, during the book reading time, children can write their names in whatever way they can. Some children might start out by writing squiggles, some might make some letters. Be sure to date each page and keep them to show children's progress over the course of the program.

Materials to Add to the Classroom
- After children have chosen their letter link symbol (see Day 1, "Greeting Time"), create cards with each child's name and letter link symbol. Make two sets — one to send home with children, and the other, to use in the classroom. These can easily be made using index cards. Simply print the child's name and draw the child's letter link symbol after it.

Lesson Plans for the First 30 Days

- Create a classroom song book. The song book is a binder or notebook that contains a selection of songs that are sung in the classroom. Each page of the song book includes just the song's title and a simple drawing to represent the title. The song book is used at large-group time as a way to give children the opportunity to select songs. It provides a visual reminder of the children's favorite songs. Here are some suggestions for making a song book:
    - Use a ring binder to hold the pages, or "song cards," so children can easily turn them.
    - Place each page in a plastic sheet protector, laminate it, or cover it with contact paper.
    - Keep the pictures simple. For example, a single star could represent the song "Twinkle, Twinkle Little Star," and a barn could represent the song "Old MacDonald Had a Farm."
    - Put a title on the front of the binder that reads "Song Book" and has a photo or simple drawing of your large-group time.
    - Place new song cards in the song book as you introduce the songs to the children.
    - Place the binder either in your book area or the area where you meet for large-group time. Keep the song book available for children to use at work time.

Note: These items will be used for large-group time on Day 5.

Other
- Have ready the photocopied daily routine booklets for each child. (See "Getting Started: Things to Do Before You Start Week 1" on pp. 18–19.)
- Create a photo page for each child to take home on Friday. See "Home-School Connections" on page 39 for more explanation.
- After children have chosen their letter link symbol, put their name and letter link symbol on their cubby and/or coat hook.
- After children have chosen their letter link symbol (see Day 1, "Greeting Time"), prepare a name chart for each small group and hang it by that group's table (use the children's and your names with letter links).

After Children Leave for the Day
- Record your observations of children and jot down any ideas you want to follow up on.
- Read tomorrow's lesson plans to see what preparations you will need to make before the children arrive.

Some Reminders for This Week					
Monday (Day 1)	**Tuesday** (Day 2)	**Wednesday** (Day 3)	**Thursday** (Day 4)	**Friday** (Day 5)
Children's daily routine books to take home	Children's letter link symbols to take home	Start sign-in sheets Cards with teachers' names and letter link symbols	Family note home: Donate containers and lids for activity next week	Song card for "The Wheels on the Bus" Family note home: Send home photo sheet

DAY 1

Curriculum Content — Key Developmental Indicators (KDIs)*

- 2. Planning
- 6. Reflection
- 7. Self-identity
- 9. Emotions
- 11. Community
- 12. Building relationships
- 13. Cooperative play
- 16. Gross-motor skills
- 22. Speaking
- 24. Phonological awareness
- 25. Alphabetic knowledge
- 26. Reading
- 40. Art
- 42. Movement
- 43. Pretend play

*See the KDIs listed under individual activities.

Greeting Time   *KDIs 12, 24, 25, 26*

Adult 1: As children come in to the classroom, ask each child to choose a letter link symbol from several choices that you have put out on the table for them to see. Join Adult 2 when all children have chosen their symbol.

Adult 2: Have about 10 books spread out on the floor. Read books with children who are not choosing their letter link symbol. (*Note:* This should last no more than 15 minutes.)

Message Board
Use a clothespin or clip with the daily routine chart, which is taped to the message board. Show the children the daily routine chart. Place the clip on "Greeting Time" and explain the purpose of the chart.

Draw an image of two tables. Say something like the following: "In our classroom we have two groups. One group will meet at the _____ table with (Teacher 1's name) and the other group will meet at the _____ table with (Teacher 2's name)." Teacher 1 stands up and says the names of the children in his/her group and goes with the children to that group's table. Teacher 2 stands up and says the names of the children in his/her group and goes with the children to that group's table.

Planning Time   *Group 1 — KDI 2/Group 2 — KDI 2*

Move the clip or marker on the daily routine chart to the next part of the routine and tell children it's planning time.

Group 1: Train
Ask everyone to hold hands as the group pretends to be a train. As the train moves around to each area, you can talk to children about the materials and name of the area. If a child plans to work in that area, he or she "gets off" the train. Then the train goes on to the next area.

Group 2: Snake
Ask everyone to hold on to a long jump rope or piece of yarn as the group pretends to be a snake. As the snake goes from area to area, you can talk to children about the materials and name of the area. If a child plans to work in that area, he or she can stay and play with those materials. The snake then "slithers" to the next area.

Work Time   *KDIs 9, 12, 13, 40, 43*

Move the clip or marker on the daily routine chart to the next part of the routine and tell children it's work time.

Both adults: Look for children in need of comfort and contact and offer them gentle reassurance (a hand to hold, a lap to sit in, or just your calm presence nearby). **Offer simple acknowledgments** such as a smile, a nod, or a comment such as "I see, you've got the doll." **Acknowledge children's feelings** by simply stating them nonjudgementally. ("You're feeling sad. You miss your Dad." "You're excited, you see lots of toys to play with.")

Day 1

Did You Know...?

It's not enough to simply read books with children — *how* we read them can help children connect with the stories, which is an important part of literacy comprehension.

Select and study storybooks. Children need to look at and read all kinds of books, but to develop story comprehension, they depend on you to do the following:

- Provide stories with plots — that is, stories that have a beginning, middle, and end and in which characters confront and solve a particular problem.
- Choose books with characters, events, or ideas that children can connect in some way to their own experience.

Converse during story reading. Children's talk about stories, once regarded as disruptive, is both a desirable and necessary form of story engagement. Do the following to promote sharing:

- Read one-to-one or in small groups to increase opportunities for adult-child dialogue.
- Use comments and open-ended questions to elicit child talk about a story as you read and look at pictures with children.
- Take a leisurely approach to story reading. Give children time to think and put their ideas into words. The less rushed children feel, the more likely they are to make their own contributions.

Create opportunities for thinking about the story. What you talk about with children during story reading determines what kind of thinking they will engage in. To help children form a coherent idea of stories and how they work, read the same book together with children many times. This shouldn't be a problem because children typically want to read favorite stories over and over again. What you can do, however, is to use a slightly different conversational focus each time, depending on where children are in their understanding of the story. These strategies can help you vary your readings and prompt thought-provoking conversations from one reading to the next:

- Encourage children to look at pictures and comment on story characters, objects and/or actions. ("I wonder what you see on this page?" or "What do you see the fox doing in this picture?")
- As children look at the pictures (which should be a critical part of the story), you might say something like, "I wonder what's going on here" or "What's happening now?"

— Adapted from "Interactive Reading: How 'Story Talk' Builds Comprehension," by Mary Hohmann, in *Let's Talk Literacy*, pp. 36–38.

Cleanup Time
KDI 11

Give a verbal warning 10 minutes and then 5 minutes before the end of work time. Move the marker to the next part of the routine and signal that cleanup is starting by shaking some jingle bells or playing some instrumental music. Work with the children in cleaning up and helping them through this transition. For example, you might say, "I'll help you put these toys away — they'll be right here if you'd like to play with them tomorrow."

Recall Time
Group 1 — KDI 6/Group 2 — KDI 6

Move the clip or marker on the daily routine chart to the next part of the routine and tell children it's recall time.

Group 1: Train
Ask everyone to hold hands as the group pretends to be a train. As the train moves around to each area, talk to children about what they may have done in that area. If children seem to want to play with the materials in that area, remind them that this is recall time and that they might want to make a plan to play with those things tomorrow at work time. Then the train goes on to the next area.

Group 2: Snake
Ask everyone to hold on to a long jump rope or piece of yarn as the group pretends to be a snake. As the snake moves from area to area, talk with the children about what they did in each area. If children seem to want to play with the materials in that area, remind them that this is recall time and that they might want to make a plan to play with those things tomorrow at work time. The snake then slithers to the next area.

Day 1

Small-Group Time
Group 1 — KDI 40/Group 2 — KDI 40

Move the clip or marker on the daily routine chart to the next part of the routine and tell children it's small-group time.

Group 1: Exploring the Art Area
Gather in your usual meeting place. Put a few crayons, scissors, and pieces of paper on the table. Ask the children where they think they might find these materials in the classroom. (Children might point or say "over there," indicating the art area.) Affirm that these materials all do belong in the art area, and say something like "Today we're going to jump like bunnies over to the art area for our small-group time." Once there, reassure children that they can use any of the materials they find there. During this time, **watch what children do** with the materials and **imitate their actions.** After 10 minutes, give a 3-minute warning. After 3 minutes, help the children clean up the materials, reminding children that they might want to make a plan to use these things at work time.

Group 2: Exploring the Toy Area
Gather in your usual meeting place. Put a few Legos, animal figures, and pegs on the table. Ask the children where they think they might find these materials in the classroom. (Children might point or say "over there," indicating the toy area.) Affirm that these materials all do belong in the toy area, and say something like "Today we're going to fly like birds over to the toy area for our small-group time." Once there, reassure children that they can use any of the materials they find there. During this time, **watch what children do** with the materials and **imitate their actions.** After 10 minutes, give a 3-minute warning. After 3 minutes, help the children clean up the materials, reminding children that they might want to make a plan to use these things at work time.

Large-Group Time
KDIs 16, 42

Move the clip or marker on the daily routine chart to the next part of the routine and tell children it's large-group time.

Singing and Moving Together
Step 1: Begin singing as soon as some children arrive at large-group time. To the tune of "Rock Around the Clock," sing the following words:

We're going to shake, shake, shake, shake, shake, shake, shake, shake, shake until we STOP (everyone freezes).

We're going to shake, shake, shake, shake until we STOP (everyone freezes).

We're going to shake, shake, shake until we STOP (everyone freezes).

Step 2: Continue singing, using ideas from children on how to move together.

Step 3: Ask children to choose one final way to move and then sing and move in that way as they proceed to the next part of your daily routine.

Other Ideas
Outside Time — KDIs 12, 16/Meal Conversations — KDIs 7, 22

Outside Time
Explore the outdoor space with the children. While watching for safety, also **be sure to play with children** and talk to them about what they are doing.

Meal Conversations
As you eat with the children, converse about who is in their family. You might start with a photograph, a statement about your own family, or ask an open-ended question. ("I'm curious about who lives with you.") Add contributions from your own experiences. For example, when asked about her family, if a child responds by mentioning her brother Jeremiah, you might say, "I have a brother, too." This will help you get to know the children.

Home-School Connections
Give each child a copy of the daily routine book you photocopied for children to take home (See "Getting Started: Things to do Before Week 1" on pp. 18–19). Encourage the children to share it with their family. Send a short note home to parents in which the teachers introduce themselves.

Day 1

Observations

Record what you saw individual children say and do today. You can use the reproducible sheet on page 178 to make your notes.

Follow-Up Ideas

- Prepare letter link symbols so each child can take a copy of his or hers home tomorrow.
- Write down your own follow-up ideas, using the reproducible sheet on page 179.

DAY 2

Curriculum Content — Key Developmental Indicators (KDIs)*

2. Planning
6. Reflection
7. Self-identity
9. Emotions
11. Community
12. Building relationships
13. Cooperative play
16. Gross-motor skills
22. Speaking
24. Phonological awareness
25. Alphabetic knowledge
26. Reading
40. Art
41. Music
43. Pretend play

*See the KDIs listed under individual activities.

Greeting Time *KDIs 12, 24, 25, 26*

Adult 2: As children come in to the classroom, ask them to find their name and letter link on their cubbies so they'll know where to put their belongings. Join Adult 2 when all children have put their things away.

Adult 1: Have about 10 books spread out on the floor. Read books with children. (*Note:* This should last no more than 15 minutes.)

Message Board
Use a clothespin or clip with the daily routine chart, which is taped to the message board. Show the children the daily routine chart. Place the clip on "Greeting Time."

Draw an image of two tables on the message board. Remind the children that they will be going to their group's table. **Adult 1:** One at a time, hold up each child's name and letter link symbol and ask the child whose name/symbol it is to go to your table. Repeat until all your children are at your table. **Adult 2:** Repeat the process with the children in your group.

Planning Time *Group 1 — KDI 2/Group 2 — KDI 2*

Move the clip or marker on the daily routine chart to the next part of the routine and tell children it's planning time.

Group 1: Snake
Ask everyone to hold on to a long jump rope or piece of yarn as the group pretends to be a snake. As the snake goes from area to area, you can talk to children about the materials and name of the area. If a child plans to work in that area, he or she can stay and play with those materials. The snake then "slithers" to the next area.

Group 2: Train
Ask everyone to hold hands as the group pretends to be a train. As the train moves around to each area, you can talk to children about the materials and name of the area. If a child plans to work in that area, he or she "gets off" the train. Then the train goes on to the next area.

Work Time *KDIs 9, 12, 13, 40, 43*

Move the clip or marker on the daily routine chart to the next part of the routine and tell children it's work time.

Both Adults: Continue to **look for children in need of comfort and contact** and offer them gentle reassurance (a hand to hold, a lap to sit in, or just your calm presence nearby). **Offer simple acknowledgments** such as a smile, a nod, or a comment such as "I see, you've got the doll." **Acknowledge children's feelings** by simply stating them nonjudgementally. ("You're feeling sad. You miss your Dad." "You're excited, you see lots of toys to play with.")

Day 2

Cleanup Time — KDI 11

Give a verbal warning 10 minutes and then 5 minutes before the end of work time. Move the clip or marker to the next part of the routine and signal that cleanup is starting by shaking some jingle bells or playing some instrumental music. Work with the children in cleaning up and helping them through this transition. For example, you might say, "I'll help you put these toys away — they'll be right here if you'd like to play with them tomorrow."

Recall Time — *Group 1 — KDI 6/Group 2 — KDI 6*

Move the clip or marker on the daily routine chart to the next part of the routine and tell children it's recall time.

Group 1: Snake
Ask everyone to hold on to a long jump rope or piece of yarn as the group pretends to be a snake. As the snake moves from area to area, talk with the children about what they did in each area. If children seem to want to play with the materials in that area, remind them that this is recall time and that they might want to make a plan to play with those things tomorrow at work time. The snake then slithers to the next area.

Group 2: Train
Ask everyone to hold hands as the group pretends to be a train. As the train moves around to each area, talk to children about what they may have done in that area. If children seem to want to play with the materials in that area, remind them that this is recall time and that they might want to make a plan to play with those things tomorrow at work time. Then the train goes on to the next area.

Small-Group Time — *Group 1 — KDI 40/Group 2 — KDI 40*

Move the clip or marker on the daily routine chart to the next part of the routine and tell children it's small-group time.

Group 1: Exploring the Toy Area
Gather in your usual meeting place. Place a few Legos, animal figures, and pegs on the table. Ask the children where they think they might find these materials in the classroom. (Children might point or say "over there," indicating the toy area.) Affirm that these materials all do belong in the toy area, and say something like "Today we're going to fly like birds over to the toy area for our small-group time." Once there, reassure children that they can use any of the materials they find there. During this time, **watch what children do** with the materials and **imitate their actions.** After 10 minutes, give a 3-minute warning. After 3 minutes, help the children clean up the materials, reminding children that they might want to make a plan to use these things at work time.

Group 2: Exploring the Art Area
Gather in your usual meeting place. Put a few crayons, scissors, and pieces of paper on the table. Ask the children where they think they might find these materials in the classroom. (Children might point or say "over there," indicating the art area.) Affirm that these materials all do belong in the art area, and say something like "Today we're going to jump like bunnies over to the art area for our small-group time. Once there, reassure children that they can use any of the materials they find there. During this time, **watch what children do** with the materials and **imitate their actions.** After 10 minutes, give a 3-minute warning. After 3 minutes, help the children clean up the materials, reminding children that they might want to make a plan to use these things at work time.

Day 2

Large-Group Time
KDIs 16, 41

Move the clip or marker on the daily routine chart to the next part of the routine and tell children it's large-group time.

Singing Songs

Step 1: As children gather, begin by singing the "Rock Around the Clock" song from yesterday. Sing a few verses, and when most children have joined the large group, sing

> We're going to sit right down, sit right down, sit right down for large-group time...

Step 2: Sing several familiar songs with the children (such as "Itsy Bitsy Spider," and "Twinkle, Twinkle, Little Star"). When singing, be sure to

- Slow the tempo so all the children can join in and sing.
- Pause at the end of one line before going on to the next.
- Keep any hand movements or motions very simple and limit them to about 4–5 per song.

Step 3: Ask children to jump to the next part of the daily routine.

Other Ideas
Outside Time — KDIs 12, 16/Meal Conversations — KDIs 7, 22

Outside Time
Continue to explore the outdoor space with the children. While watching for safety, also **be sure to play with children** and talk to them about what they are doing.

Meal Conversations
To find out more about individual children, talk with them about what they like to do at home.

Ask open-ended questions and then pause, listening to children's responses. This strategy enables children to share their thoughts with you.

Home-School Connections
Give each child a copy of their name and letter link symbol to take home. Encourage them to share it with their family.

Observations

Record what you saw individual children say and do today. You can use the reproducible sheet on page 178 to make your notes.

Follow-Up Ideas

- Prepare sign-in sheets for tomorrow.
- Write down your own follow-up ideas, using the reproducible sheet on page 179.

DAY 3

Curriculum Content — Key Developmental Indicators (KDIs)*

- 2. Planning
- 6. Reflection
- 9. Emotions
- 11. Community
- 12. Building relationships
- 13. Cooperative play
- 16. Gross-motor skills
- 22. Speaking
- 24. Phonological awareness
- 25. Alphabetic knowledge
- 26. Reading
- 29. Writing
- 35. Spatial awareness
- 40. Art
- 41. Music
- 43. Pretend play

*See the KDIs listed under individual activities.

Greeting Time
KDIs 12, 24, 25, 26, 29

Adult 1: Greet children as they enter the classroom and assist them as needed as they put their belongings away.

Adult 2: Have about 10 books spread out on the floor. Read books with children. (*Note:* This should last no more than 15 minutes.)

Message Board
Draw an image of two clipboards on the message board or put up actual clipboards. Introduce the sign-in sheets to the children, and tell them the sign-in sheets will be in the book area.

Write teachers' names and their letter link symbols on the message board. Introduce the teacher's written names and letter link symbols to the children.

Planning Time
Group 1 — KDI 2/Group 2 — KDI 2

Ask a child to move the clip or marker on the daily routine chart to the next part of the routine. State that it's planning time.

Group 1: Point With a Magic Wand
Pull a child's name and letter link symbol out of a bag. That child can use the magic wand to point to something she would like to work with. Ask the child what she will be doing with that item. After sharing, that child can get started on her plan. Repeat for all the children in your group.

Group 2: Area Cards and Objects From Areas
Before planning time, gather one representative object from each area (for example, a pan to represent the house area, a block to represent the block area, a paintbrush to represent the art area). At planning time, lay the area cards out on the table and ask children to match the objects to the correct area card. Then ask each child to point to the area where he or she would like to work and ask the child to share his or her plan. After responding, the child is free to go and begin his or her plan.

Work Time
KDIs 9, 12, 13, 40, 43

Ask a child to move the clip or marker on the daily routine chart to the next part of the routine. State that it's work time.

Join the play at the children's level (on the floor, sitting, kneeling, squatting, and so forth). **Play in parallel** with children; that is, use the materials yourself, copying what the children are doing. Continue to **acknowledge children's feelings.** ("You're anxious to go to the water table." "You seem frustrated that your blocks keep falling down. I wonder what ideas you have about building them again?") **Adult 2:** Specifically watch what children in your group are using. At the end of work time, collect one item per child to use at recall. Place these items in a basket.

31

Day 3

Cleanup Time
KDI 11

Give a verbal warning 10 minutes and then 5 minutes before the end of work time. Move the marker to the next part of the routine and signal that cleanup is starting by shaking some jingle bells or playing some instrumental music. Work with the children in cleaning up, pointing out that the labels help remind everyone where the materials belong in the classroom.

Recall Time
Group 1 — KDI 6/Group 2 — KDI 6

Ask a child to move the clip or marker on the daily routine chart to the next part of the routine. State that it's recall time.

Group 1: Bring Back Something You Played With
Ask each child, one at a time, to bring to recall time one thing he or she played with and show it to the group, sharing what he or she did with the material. After sharing, the first child can return the item as the next child goes and gets something. You can also identify the area where the child gets the item. ("I see Allie going to the block area. I wonder what she'll bring back.")

Group 2: Mystery Bag
Toward the end of work time, for each child in your group, gather an item that you saw the child play with. Place the item in your "mystery bag." At recall time, tell children that you saw them playing with different things today and that for recall time you'd like to see if they can guess who played with which item. As you pull each item from the bag, children can share who they saw playing with the item. You can also state which area the item came from. ("Yes, Jason was playing with the pan. He was playing in the *house area*.")

Small-Group Time
Group 1 — KDIs 25, 26/Group 2 — KDIs 35, 40

Ask a child to move the clip or marker on the daily routine chart to the next part of the routine. State that it's small-group time.

Group 1: Exploring the Book Area
Gather in your usual meeting place. Put a few books and other items from the book area on the table. Ask the children where they think they might find these materials in the classroom. (Children might point or say "over there," indicating the book area.) Affirm that these materials all do belong in the book area, and say something like "Today we're going to creep quietly like mice over to the book area for our small-group time. Once there, reassure children that they can use any of the materials they find there. During this time, **watch what children do** with the materials. You might find it easier to look at a variety of books that children have chosen rather than trying to read just one story to all the children. After 10 minutes, give a 3-minute warning. After 3 minutes, help the children clean up the materials, reminding children that they might want to make a plan to use these things at work time.

Group 2: Exploring the Block Area
Gather in your usual meeting place. Put a few different blocks on the table. Ask the children where they think they might find these materials in the classroom. (Children might point or say "over there," indicating the block area.) Affirm that these materials all do belong in the block area and show children the area card for the block area. Say something like "Today we're going to slide over to the block area for our small-group time." Once there, reassure children that they can use any of the materials they find there. During this time, **watch what children do** with the materials and **imitate their actions.** After 10 minutes, give a 3-minute warning. After 3 minutes, help the children clean up the materials, reminding children that they might want to make a plan to use these things at work time.

Day 3

Large-Group Time
KDIs 16, 41

Ask a child to move the clip or marker on the daily routine chart to the next part of the routine. State that it's large-group time.

Singing Songs
Step 1: As children gather, begin by singing the "Rock Around the Clock" song from Day 1. Sing a few verses and, when most children have joined the large group, sing the following words:

> We're going to sit right down, sit right down, sit right down for large-group time...

Step 2: Sing several familiar songs with the children (such as "Itsy Bitsy Spider" and "Twinkle, Twinkle, Little Star"). When singing, be sure to

- Slow the tempo so all the children can join in and sing.
- Pause at the end of one line before going on to the next.
- Keep any hand movements or motions very simple and limit them to about 4–5 per song.

Step 3: Ask children to creep to the next part of the daily routine.

Other Ideas
Outside Time — KDIs 9, 12/Meal Conversations — KDIs 12, 22

Outside Time
Continue to explore the outdoor space with the children. While watching for safety, join the play at the children's level (on the ground, running, kneeling, squatting and so forth). **Play in parallel** with children; use the materials yourself, imitating what the children are doing. Continue to **acknowledge children's feelings,** as in the following examples: "You're anxious to have a turn on that bike." "You are running so fast and I see a big smile on your face. It must mean you're feeling happy."

Meal Conversations
During the meal, play a guessing game to help children get to know the materials in the different areas. Name a material and see if someone can guess what area the material is from. ("What area are the cars in? If I wanted to use the crayons, where would I find them?") Continue by having children take turns naming materials and guessing the area.

Observations

Record what you saw individual children say and do today. You can use the reproducible sheet on page 178 to make your notes.

Follow-Up Ideas

- Continue to put song cards in plastic sleeves and add them to the classroom song book. As you sing new songs with the children, be sure to add a page with the new song to the book. (See p. 23 for suggestions for making the classroom song book.)
- Prepare a family note home about donating containers and lids for an activity next week (see Day 4).
- Write down your own follow-up ideas using the reproducible sheet on page 179.

DAY 4

Curriculum Content — Key Developmental Indicators (KDIs)*

- 2. Planning
- 6. Reflection
- 9. Emotions
- 11. Community
- 12. Building relationships
- 13. Cooperative play
- 16. Gross-motor skills
- 22. Speaking
- 24. Phonological awareness
- 25. Alphabetic knowledge
- 26. Reading
- 28. Book knowledge
- 29. Writing
- 40. Art
- 42. Movement
- 43. Pretend play

*See the KDIs listed under individual activities.

Greeting Time
KDIs 12, 24, 25, 26, 29

Adult 2: Greet the children. Remind them to write their name on the sign-in sheet over where the books are. After all children have arrived, assist any children who haven't signed in with locating their group's clipboard and finding the space for their name, if necessary.

Adult 1: Have about 10 books spread out on the floor. Read books with children. (*Note:* This should last no more than 15 minutes.)

Message Board
Draw an image of two clipboards on the message board or put up actual clipboards. Ask the children for their ideas about what this message means (it is a reminder to sign-in when they come to school).

Draw an image of children's cubbies or lockers along with a question mark (?). Point to the question mark and say to children "We use the question mark as a sign for mystery." Ask the children what is in the drawing. Ask them what belongs in their cubbies. (Use this message as a way of reminding children that their work goes in their cubbies and that they can take their work home with them.)

Planning Time
Group 1 — KDI 2/Group 2 — KDI 2

Ask a child to move the clip or marker on the daily routine chart to the next part of the routine. State that it's planning time.

Group 1: Look Through a Tube
Pull a child's name and letter link symbol out of a bag. That child can look through a tube (for example, a paper towel tube) to see what she would like to work with. Ask the child what she will be doing with those materials. After sharing, that child can get started on her plan. Repeat for all the children in your group.

Group 2: Point With a Magic Wand
Pull a child's name and letter link symbol out of a bag. That child can use the magic wand to point to something he would like to work with. Ask the child what he will be doing with those materials. After sharing, that child can get started on his plan. Repeat for all the children in your group.

Work Time
KDIs 9, 12, 13, 40, 43

Ask a child to move the clip or marker on the daily routine chart to the next part of the routine. State that it's work time.

Join the play at the children's level (on the floor, sitting, kneeling, squatting, etc). **Play in parallel** with children; that is, use the materials yourself, copying what the children are doing. **Make comments** about what you see children doing. ("Sandra, you've made your tower really tall and Mario has made his very long.")

Adult 1: Specifically watch what children in your group are using. At the end of work time, collect one item per child to use at recall. Place these items in a basket.

34

Day 4

Cleanup Time — KDI 11

Give a verbal warning 10 minutes and then 5 minutes before the end of work time. Move the marker to the next part of the routine and signal that cleanup is starting by shaking some jingle bells or playing some instrumental music. Work with the children in cleaning up, pointing out that the labels help remind everyone where the materials belong in the classroom.

Recall Time — *Group 1 — KDI 6/Group 2 — KDI 6*

Ask a child to move the clip or marker on the daily routine chart to the next part of the routine. State that it's recall time.

Group 1: Mystery Bag
Toward the end of work time, for each child in your group, gather an item that you saw the child play with. Place the item in your "mystery bag." At recall time, tell children that you saw them playing with different things today and that for recall time you'd like to see if they can guess who played with which item. As you pull each item from the bag, children can share who they saw playing with the item. You can also state which area the item came from. ("Yes, Jason was playing with the pan. He was playing in the *house area*.")

Group 2: Area Cards
Show the children the area cards. Together with the children, discuss who played in each area and what those children did.

Small-Group Time — *Group 1 — KDI 43/Group 2 — KDIs 26, 28*

Ask a child to move the clip or marker on the daily routine chart to the next part of the routine. State that it's small-group time.

Group 1: Exploring the House Area
Gather in your usual meeting place. Put a few cooking items and dress-up clothes on the table. Ask the children where they think they might find these materials in the classroom. (Children might point or say "over there," indicating the house area.) Affirm that these materials all do belong in the house area and show children the area card for the house area. Say something like "Today we're going to tiptoe over to the house area for our small-group time. Once there, reassure children that they can use any of the materials they find there. During this time, **watch what children do** with the materials and **imitate their actions.** After 10 minutes, give a 3-minute warning. After 3 minutes, help the children clean up the materials, reminding children that they might want to make a plan to use these things at work time.

Group 2: Exploring the Book Area
Gather in your usual meeting place. Put a few books and other items from the book area on the table. Ask the children where they think they might find these materials in the classroom. (Children might point or say "over there," indicating the book area.) Affirm that these materials all do belong in the book area, and say something like "Today we're going to creep quietly like mice over to the book area for our small-group time." Once there, reassure children that they can use any of the materials they find there. During this time, **watch what children do** with the materials. You might find it easier to look at a variety of books that children have chosen rather than trying to read just one story to all the children. After 10 minutes, give a 3-minute warning. After 3 minutes, help the children clean up the materials, reminding children that they might want to make a plan to use these things at work time.

Day 4

Large-Group Time
KDIs 16, 42

Ask a child to move the clip or marker on the daily routine chart to the next part of the routine. State that it's large-group time.

Moving Our Bodies

Bring out enough carpet squares for each child and adult.

Step 1: Start with our easy-to-join song — "We're going to shake, shake, shake" — like you've done before.

Step 2: Ask each child to get a carpet square and find a place to put it (this gives the children some boundaries for personal space). Tell children that they can stand on their carpet as they move their bodies. Show children how you can twist and untwist your arms. Ask them to try it. Ask them if there is anything else they could twist, then try their ideas together. Continue with other actions; for example, bending and straightening, curling and uncurling, or shaking or moving another part of their body up and then down. Throughout this time, **remember to ask children for their ideas and try them out.** Also remember that whatever ideas children share are acceptable.

Step 3: Ask children to shake their hands as they walk to the next part of the daily routine.

Other Ideas
Outside Time — KDIs 12, 16/Meal Conversations — KDIs 12, 22

Outside Time

While playing outside, **observe children and make comments** about what you see children doing (also see "Work Time" for this lesson plan). Here are some examples of comments: "Jennifer, you're running really fast"; "Grace, you've found the big trucks and now you're pushing them under the tree."

Meal Conversations

Use this mealtime to continue to talk with children about what they did at work time. After asking children an initial open-ended question, pause and listen carefully to their comments. You can add statements about what you saw children doing, drawing other children into the conversation. "Marcella, I saw you with some blocks, too. Were you working with Ethan?"

Home-School Connections

Ask families to donate recyclable containers. You will use these in small-group time next week and you can add them to the classroom materials. Include the following container types in your request:

- Lids that attach in various ways (twist or screw top, snap-on, squirt-top)
- Containers that are transparent (clear) as well as opaque; containers in different colors
- Containers that still have labels or writing on them as well as blank ones

Observations

Record what you saw individual children say and do today. You can use the reproducible sheet on page 178 to make your notes.

Follow-Up Ideas

- Add the carpet squares to the classroom materials. You may want to put them near where you hold large-group time or in the block area.
- Prepare the song card for "The Wheels on the Bus" and add it to the classroom song book for tomorrow's large-group time (see Day 5).
- Prepare a family note home summarizing the week; include a page with the child's name and letter link symbol and a request for photos of the child's family and friends (see Day 5).
- Write down your own follow-up ideas using the reproducible sheet on page 179.

DAY 5

Curriculum Content — Key Developmental Indicators (KDIs)*

- 2. Planning
- 6. Reflection
- 9. Emotions
- 11. Community
- 12. Building relationships
- 13. Cooperative play
- 24. Phonological awareness
- 25. Alphabetic knowledge
- 26. Reading
- 29. Writing
- 35. Spatial Awareness
- 40. Art
- 41. Music
- 42. Movement
- 43. Pretend play
- 57. History

*See the KDIs listed under individual activities.

Greeting Time
KDIs 12, 24, 25, 26, 29, 57

Adult 1: Greet the children. Remind them to sign-in over where the books are. After all children have arrived, assist children in finding their group's clipboard and finding the space for their name if necessary.

Adult 2: Have about 10 books spread out on the floor. Read books with children. (*Note:* This should last no more than 15 minutes.)

Message Board
Place a carpet square on the floor below the message board and draw an arrow on the message board pointing down. Help the children read the message reminding them about the carpet squares that they used at large-group time yesterday. Tell the children that they may want to use these carpet squares for work time. Ask children for ideas on how they might want to use them.

Draw two simple images of the school, with a red circle and diagonal slash over them — the universal "no" symbol. See page 22 for a sample of what this might look like. Write *2 no school days* and help the children interpret the drawings. Remind them that they will stay home for two days and then come back to school.

Planning Time
Group 1 — KDI 2/Group 2 — KDI 2

Ask a child to move the clip or marker on the daily routine chart to the next part of the routine. State that it's planning time.

Group 1: Area Cards and Objects From Areas
Before planning time, gather one representative object from each area (for example, a pan to represent the house area, a block to represent the block area, a paintbrush to represent the art area). At planning time, lay the area cards out on the table and ask children to match the objects to the correct area card. Then ask each child to point to the area where he or she would like to work and ask the child to share his or her plan. After responding, the child is free to go and begin his or her plan.

Group 2: Look Through a Tube
Pull a child's name and letter link symbol out of a bag. That child can look through a tube (for example, a paper towel tube) to see what he would like to work with. Ask the child what he will be doing with those materials. After sharing, that child can get started on his plan. Repeat for all the children in your group.

Day 5

Work Time
KDIs 9, 12, 13, 40, 43

Ask a child to move the clip or marker on the daily routine chart to the next part of the routine. State that it's work time.

Continue to **play in parallel** with children and **look for children who need extra support.** Especially look for children who may be having trouble becoming engaged in their play and give them support. For example, you might say, "I remember you planned to make dinner in the house area. Is that still your plan? Would you like to walk with me and see if there is something else you'd rather do?"

Cleanup Time
KDI 11

Give a verbal warning 10 minutes and then 5 minutes before the end of work time. Move the clip or marker to the next part of the daily routine chart and signal that cleanup is starting by shaking some jingle bells or playing some instrumental music. Work with the children in cleaning up, pointing out that the labels help remind everyone where the materials belong in the classroom.

Recall Time
Group 1 — KDI 6/Group 2 — KDI 6

Ask a child to move the clip or marker on the daily routine chart to the next part of the routine. State that it's recall time.

Group 1: Area Cards
Show the children the area cards. Together with the children, discuss who played in each area and what those children did.

Group 2: Bring Back Something You Played With
Ask each child, one at a time, to bring to recall time one thing he or she played with and show it to the group, sharing what he or she did with the material. After sharing, the first child can return the item as the next child goes and gets something. You can also identify the area where the child gets the item. ("I see Allie going to the block area. I wonder what she'll bring back.")

Small-Group Time
Group 1 — KDIs 35, 40/Group 2 — KDI 43

Ask a child to move the clip or marker on the daily routine chart to the next part of the routine. State that it's small-group time.

Group 1: Exploring the Block Area
Gather in your usual meeting place. Put a few different blocks on the table. Ask the children where they think they might find these materials in the classroom. (Children might point or say "over there," indicating the block area.) Affirm that these materials all do belong in the block area and show children the area card for the block area. Say something like "Today we're going to slide over to the block area for our small-group time." Once there, reassure children that they can use any of the materials they find there. During this time, **watch what children do** with the materials and **imitate their actions.** After 10 minutes, give a 3-minute warning. After 3 minutes, help the children clean up the materials, reminding children that they might want to make a plan to use these things at work time.

Group 2: Exploring the House Area
Gather in your usual meeting place. Put a few cooking items and dress-up clothes on the table. Ask the children where they think they might find these materials in the classroom. (Children might point or say "over there," indicating the house area.) Affirm that these materials all do belong in the house area and show children the area card for the house area. Say something like "Today we're going to tiptoe over to the house area for our small-group time." Once there, reassure children that they can use any of the materials they find there. During this time, **watch what children do** with the materials and **imitate their actions.** After 10 minutes, give a 3-minute warning. After 3 minutes, help the children clean up the materials, reminding children that they might want to make a plan to use these things at work time.

Day 5

Large-Group Time
KDIs 41, 42

Ask a child to move the clip or marker on the daily routine chart to the next part of the routine. State that it's large-group time.

Singing Songs
Bring out the classroom song book.

Step 1: Sing the "We're gonna shake, shake, shake" song. When all children have joined, sing one more verse and end by having everyone sit down on the floor.

Step 2: Show the children the new song card for "Wheels on the Bus." (See p. 23 for an explanation of how to make a classroom song book.) Sing additional verses using the children's ideas.

Step 3: Add the song card to the classroom song book. Then show children a sticky note with a child's name and letter link symbol written on it. Let the children know that this child can look through the book and choose a song to sing and place the sticky note on that song. When that child has chosen a song, sing that song (along with other verses if appropriate). Let the class know that other children will have a turn to choose a song on other days.

Step 4: Ask children to wiggle as they move to the next part of the daily routine.

Other Ideas
Meal Conversations — KDIs 12, 24, 25

Meal Conversations
Describe several children's letter link symbol and see if they can guess whose it is (for example, "This child's symbol is an animal." Children guess. "The animal has sharp teeth." Children guess. "The animal starts with a /b/.") Continue giving clues until children guess whose symbol it is. After children catch on to the game, they may want to give the clues.

Home-School Connections
Send parents a short note that summarizes your week. Also send home a page with the child's first name and letter link symbol on the top center (for example, Henry ♥ 's Family). Invite the parent to work with their child over the weekend to select several photos of the child's family, friends, etc., and put them on this page. Explain that this page will be added to a notebook titled "Our Class" and that the photos will be returned at the end of the program year.

Observations

Record what you saw individual children say and do today. You can use the reproducible sheet on page 178 to make your notes.

Follow-Up Ideas

Write down your own follow-up ideas using the reproducible sheet on page 179.

Building on What You've Learned: Week 1 Summary

This week you did the following in your classroom:
- Established a consistent HighScope daily routine
- Helped children become familiar with the HighScope routine in concrete ways
- Used transitions as a way of moving from one part of the routine to the next
- Introduced the message board as a means of communicating important classroom information to all the children

The children were particularly were supported in the following areas:
- Forming relationships with the classroom adults
- Beginning to form relationships with other children
- Beginning to express their plans, choices, and intentions
- Beginning to talk with others about things that are important to them
- Beginning to develop phonemic awareness through the use of letter-linked symbols
- Beginning to write in various ways by using daily sign-in sheets

You developed your own adult-child interaction skills by using these HighScope interaction strategies:
- Offering children comfort and contact
- Looking for children in need of comfort and contact
- Offering reassuring physical contact
- Offering simple acknowledgments
- Acknowledging children's feelings
- Participating in children's play
- Joining play on children's level
- Playing in parallel with children
- Using comments and observations to start conversations

Learn More About...*Large-Group Time*

HighScope's large-group times are those parts of the daily routine when all children and adults participate in an activity together (traditionally referred to as "circle time"). Even at large-group time, adults plan to include the ingredients of active learning in children's activities. You'll notice the large-group plans in this book build in ways to give choices to children, allow children to share their ideas, and let adults and children share control by encouraging children to become leaders of activities. Following this simple format can help make your large-group times fun, engaging, and meaningful learning experiences for young children.

Opener:
- Draw children in with an easy-to-join activity.
- Start right away.

Activity:
- For each activity, provide a brief introduction.
- Join children on their level.
- If you are using props, give them to the children.
- Participate, observe, and listen.
- Ask for children's ideas; use their language.
- Let children lead; imitate their actions.

Transition:
- Give children a warning that the activity is coming to an end.
- Make putting materials away part of the transition.
- Make the final activity a transition to the next part of your daily routine.

Chapter 2
The Second Week

Getting Ready: Week 2 Overview

Goals for the Second Week
- Continue to form relationships with your children.
- Continue to help the children feel comfortable in the classroom, with the routine, and with you.
- Begin implementing HighScope small-group times.

Things to Keep in Mind This Week
Be sure to read each activity plan ahead of time so you will know what materials you need to prepare.

Daily Routine
- Continue to ask a child to move the daily routine marker to the next part of the routine. Children may volunteer or spontaneously move the marker without your bringing attention to it. This is fine! It means the children are starting to take ownership of the routine and are understanding what comes next.
- At greeting time, continue to have the clipboards available with a fresh sign-in sheet and books for browsing. You will do this for the rest of the year.
- This week you will start singing a transition song during greeting time to help signal the end of looking at books and the beginning of reading the message board. Do this as a part of every greeting time.
- This week at planning and recall times, you will use the cards you made in Week 1, with each child's name and letter link symbol on a card.
- Be sure to alternate adults when leading large-group time — Adult 1 can lead one day, then Adult 2 can lead the next day. When you aren't leading large-group time, you will still be an active participant in the activity. Your modeling will help the children understand more about what's expected of them and how to participate. You can also provide support to children who may need help participating and sharing their ideas with the large group.
- On Friday, add this to the message board: Two simply drawn images of the school with a red circle and diagonal slash over them — the universal "no" symbol. Write *2 no school days* and help the children interpret the drawings. Remind them that they will stay home for two days and then come back to school.

Materials to Add to the Classroom
- Locate the books *Good Night, Gorilla,* by Peggy Rathmann, and an edition of *Mother Goose* and have them as a book choice during the morning greeting time. *(Note:)* you will also be using these books for small-group time in Week 3.)
- Continue to add song cards to the classroom song book (see Days 8 and 10).
- Create an *Our Class* book: Use a three-ring binder and plastic sleeves. As children bring in their photo pages (see "Home-School Connections" in Day 5), help the children add them to the book. Be sure to also include a page for the teachers. Always have this book available as a greeting-time choice.

After Children Leave for the Day
- Record your observations of children and jot down any ideas you want to follow up on.
- Read tomorrow's lesson plans to see preparations you will need to make before the children arrive.

Some Reminders for This Week				
Monday (Day 6)	**Tuesday** (Day 7)	**Wednesday** (Day 8)	**Thursday** (Day 9)	**Friday** (Day 10)
Group 1: Name and letter link symbols on sticky notes for planning time	Group 2: Name and letter link symbols on sticky notes for planning time		Family note home: Encourage children to help with laundry	Family note home: Read books with children; borrow from the classroom lending library

DAY 6

Curriculum Content — Key Developmental Indicators (KDIs)*

1. Initiative
2. Planning
6. Reflection
9. Emotions
11. Community
12. Building relationships
13. Cooperative play

16. Gross-motor skills
23. Vocabulary
24. Phonological awareness
25. Alphabetic knowledge
26. Reading
29. Writing
34. Shapes

36. Measuring
40. Art
42. Movement
43. Pretend play
57. History

*See the KDIs listed under individual activities.

Greeting Time
KDIs 12, 24, 25, 26, 29

Adult 2: Greet children as they enter. Remind them where to put their things and to sign in on their group's clipboard. Join the other adult and children reading books when everyone has arrived.

Adult 1: Have about 10 books spread out on the floor, including the daily routine book. Read books with children. (*Note:* This should last no more than 15 minutes.)

To the tune of "Mary Had a Little Lamb," sing made-up words, such as the following:

> It's time to put the books away,
> the books away, the books away.
> It's time to put the books away
> and read the message board.

Message Board

Tape the message board clip to the message board and write the words *Daily Routine* on the board. Help children figure out where the clip came from and what we use it for. (We use this message to remind children about moving the clip for the daily routine.)

On the message board, draw two tables with a question mark (?) on each. Ask children if they remember which group they are in. Ask them to choose a way to move to their planning groups.

Planning Time
Group 1 — KDIs 2, 24/Group 2 — KDI 2

Group 1: Name and Letter Link Symbol on a Sticky Note

One at a time, show the sticky notes with children's name and letter link symbol written on them. For each, ask the children whose name is on the note. When the children respond, give the sticky note to that child and ask the child to put it on something he would like to play with at work time. When the child returns to the table, ask him what he will do with that item. After the child responds, he is free to begin his plan. Repeat for all the children in your group.

Group 2: Camera

Using an old camera (or even a small box made to look like a camera), children can take a pretend "picture" of something they would like to use in their plan for work time. Once they've shared their idea about what they'd like to do, they can get started on their plan.

Work Time
KDIs 1, 9, 12, 13, 40, 43

Work Time

Use this time to reconnect with children after the weekend. Try to make sure at least one of the adults spends *some* time with each child. Begin by looking for children who may need extra support getting started. Be sure to **physically get down on children's level and listen to what they say. Repeat and restate children's comments and acknowledge their feelings.**

Day 6

Cleanup Time
KDI 11

Give children a verbal warning 10 minutes and then 5 minutes before the end of work time. Signal that cleanup is starting by shaking some jingle bells or playing some instrumental music. Help the children clean up, keeping a light and playful attitude throughout this transition.

Recall Time
Group 1 — KDIs 6, 24, 26/Group 2 — KDIs 6, 36

Group 1: Name and Letter Link Symbol Cards

Pull a child's name and letter link symbol out of a bag. Tell the children that when you hold up their name and symbol they can tell you what they did at work time. After each child shares, everyone can use the child's name and letter link symbol to chant; for example, "Hannah Heart, Hannah Heart played with the _____." Or "Connie Coat, Connie Coat, Connie Coat played with the _____."

Group 2: Large and Small Bags

Have both a large and a small bag at your group's table. Addressing the children one at a time, tell them they can go to get something they used at work time and bring it back in one of the bags. Ask children if they think they'll need the big bag or the small bag to put their item in. While you are waiting for the recalling child to return, engage the other children in conversation about what they saw that child doing. You might say something like, "Did anyone see what Davie was doing today? What do you think he'll bring back?" Or you might say, "Did anyone work with Davie today? You did, Anna? What did you do together?" You can use this strategy for other recall times if there is any waiting involved. When a child comes back, he or she can show the object selected and share what he or she did (and you can send the next child to get a recall item).

Day 6

Small-Group Time
Group 1 — KDIs 23, 34/Group 2 — KDI 40

Group 1: Where's My Lid?

Materials:

- Clean and empty plastic containers and bottles of various shapes and sizes with matching lids/tops
- Two large baskets or bins — one to hold the containers and one to hold the lids

Beginning: Tell the children you have a bunch of containers that got separated from their lids — that they're all jumbled up. Show the children the two baskets (one with containers and one with lids) and ask them to help you figure out which top/lid goes on which container. Pick out a container and start searching through the lids, asking the children if they think the one you chose will fit. Some will guess based on appearance; others will want or need to try the lid to see if it will fit. Encourage the children to pick out one or more containers themselves and begin searching for a match.

Middle: As children try matching containers and lids, **listen to the children's comments and extend their observations and vocabulary.** For example, you might say, "I see your bottle has a small hole at the top. Which lid do you think will fit on that little round opening?" Or you might comment, "Your container is blue so you're looking for a top with the same color." Use words like *top, lid, round, square, big, little, open, closed, screw, twist, squeeze, narrow* and *wide*. If the containers have words on them, point out the letters and read the words together with the children.

End: Ask children to help you separate the containers and lids back into the two baskets/bins.

Group 2: Play dough and Cookie Cutters

Materials:
For each child, provide

- A hunk of play dough
- Three cookie cutters

Beginning: Give each child a hunk of play dough and tell the children that today everyone in the group is going to play with the play dough. Be sure to have a hunk for yourself.

Middle: Move around the table from child to child, observing what they are doing with the play dough. Try using your play dough in the same ways as the children. Halfway through the small-group time, place the cookie cutters in the middle of the table. Observe how children may add these into their work. Use the same interaction strategies you've been using at work time. For a list of these, see page 61 at the end of this week's plans.

End: After 10 minutes, give children a 3-minute warning and ask them to put all their cookie cutters back in the cookie cutter container and the play dough in the play dough tub.

Day 6

Large-Group Time
KDIs 16, 42

Scarves or Streamers

Materials: A basket (or tub or box) containing a scarf or streamer for each child and adult, plus a few extra

Step 1: Sing the "We're gonna shake, shake, shake" song from last week (see "Large-Group Time" in Day 1). When all children have joined the group, sing one more verse and end by having everyone sit down on the floor. Pass out scarves to the children and allow for some exploration time. Explain to the children that they will be keeping their scarves in their hands and finding ways to move with them. As children continue exploring, they will probably be more comfortable standing up.

Step 2: As children discover ways to move with the scarves, comment on what you see them doing, as in the following example.

Teacher: "Oh, I see that Liam is moving his scarf by holding one corner with one hand, one corner with the other hand and raising it up and down. Let's try it Liam's way."

Child (Ella): "I am doing it this way!" (Ella shows that she is holding the scarf with one hand and tapping it repeatedly on the floor.)

Teacher: "Now, let's try it Ella's way." (The teacher models what Ella has just shown.) "Let's try to remember Liam's way." (The group moves Liam's way.) "Now, let's do Ella's way." (The group tries it Ella's way again.)

Continue exploring the scarves, trying out different children's ideas.

Step 3: Tell the children that everyone will try one last way of moving their scarf — by floating them into the basket (demonstrate first). Then ask children if they can "float" themselves to the next part of your classroom's daily routine.

Other Ideas
Outside Time — KDIs 12, 16/Meal Conversations — KDIs 12, 57

Outside Time

Be sure to **play and interact** with the children outdoors. Look for children who may need extra support getting started with their outdoor play. Be sure to **get down on children's physical level, listen** to what they say, **repeat and restate children's comments, and acknowledge their feelings,** if appropriate. **Jot down observations** of what you see children doing.

Meal Conversations

Talk with the children about what they did over the weekend. Help them remember by saying something like "What did you do when you were at home for the two no-school days?" **Listen** to what children say, and **repeat and restate** their words to acknowledge their comments. ("You went to the laundromat and then saw your new baby cousin.")

Home-School Connections

Remind children and parents to bring in their photo page of their family (see "Home-School Connections" in Day 5 for the original request).

Observations

Record what you saw individual children say and do today. You can use the reproducible sheet on page 178 to make your notes.

Follow-Up Ideas

- Choose several classroom materials to take outdoors for outside time (balls, dolls, chalk, etc.).
- Add the container of scarves or streamers to the house area.
- Write down your own follow-up ideas, using the reproducible sheet on page 179.

DAY 7

Curriculum Content — Key Developmental Indicators (KDIs)*

1. Initiative
2. Planning
6. Reflection
9. Emotions
11. Community
12. Building relationships
13. Cooperative play

16. Gross-motor skills
23. Vocabulary
24. Phonological awareness
25. Alphabetic knowledge
26. Reading
29. Writing
34. Shapes

36. Measuring
40. Art
42. Movement
43. Pretend play
50. Communicating ideas

*See the KDIs listed under individual activities.

Greeting Time
KDIs 12, 24, 25, 26, 29

Adult 1: Greet children at the door. When everyone has arrived, join the children and Adult 2 reading books.

Adult 2: Have about 10 books spread out on the floor. Read books with children. (*Note:* This should last no more than 15 minutes.) To the tune of "Mary Had a Little Lamb," sing made-up words, such as the following:

> *It's time to put the books away,
> the books away, the books away.
> It's time to put the books away
> and read the message board.*

Message Board
Draw the materials you will be taking outside, then draw an arrow pointing to the outside time symbol and write the words "outside time." Ask children for their ideas on what this message says and help them read this message that today the class will be taking the _____ and the _____ outside to play with.

Tape a scarf to the message board, then draw the area sign for the house area. Help the children read this message that the scarves have been added to the house area.

Planning Time
Group 1 — KDI 2/Group 2 — KDIs 2, 24

Group 1: Camera
Using an old camera (or even a small box made to look like a camera), children can take a pretend "picture" of something they would like to use in their plan for work time. Once they've shared their idea about what they'd like to do, they can get started on their plan.

Group 2: Name and Letter Link Symbol on a Sticky Note
One at a time, show the sticky notes with children's name and letter link symbol written on them. For each, ask the children whose name is on the note. When the children respond, give the sticky note to that child and ask the child to put it on something she would like to play with at work time. When the child returns to the table, ask her what she will do with that item. After the child responds, she is free to begin her plan. Repeat for all the children in your group.

Work Time
KDIs 1, 9, 12, 13, 40, 43

Continue to **play in parallel** with children and **look for children who need extra support.** Especially look for children who may be having trouble becoming engaged in their play. To these children you might say something like the following:

> *"It looks like some children are building a boat. Should we go see if they need some more boat builders?"*

> *"Yesterday you found the tape and paper. Is that something you'd like to plan to use today?"*

> *"Would you like to walk with me and see if there is something else you'd rather do?"*

Cleanup Time   KDI 11

Give children a verbal warning 10 minutes and then 5 minutes before the end of work time. Signal that cleanup is starting by shaking some jingle bells or playing some instrumental music. Help the children clean up, keeping a light and playful attitude throughout this transition.

Recall Time   *Group 1 — KDIs 6, 36/Group 2 — KDIs 6, 24, 26*

Group 1: Large and Small Bags
Have both a large and a small bag at your group's table. Addressing the children one at a time, tell them they can go to get something they used at work time and bring it back in one of the bags. Ask children if they think they'll need the big bag or the small bag to put their item in. While you are waiting for the recalling child to return, engage the other children in conversation about what they saw that child doing. You might say something like, "Did anyone see what Davie was doing today? What do you think he'll bring back?" Or you might say, "Did anyone work with Davie today? You did, Anna? What did you do together?" You can use this strategy for other recall times if there is any waiting involved. When a child comes back, he or she can show the object selected and share what he or she did (and you can send the next child to get a recall item).

Group 2: Name and Letter Link Symbol Cards
Pull a child's name and letter link symbol out of a bag. Tell the children that when you hold up their name and symbol they can tell you what they did at work time. After each child shares, everyone can use the child's name and letter link symbol to chant; for example, "Hannah Heart, Hannah Heart played with the _____." Or " Connie Coat, Connie Coat, Connie Coat played with the _____."

Day 7

Small-Group Time

Group 1 — KDI 40/Group 2 — KDIs 23, 34

Group 1: Play dough and Cookie Cutters

Materials:

For each child, provide

- A hunk of play dough
- Three cookie cutters

Beginning: Give each child a hunk of play dough and tell the children that today everyone in the group is going to play with the play dough. Be sure to have a hunk for yourself.

Middle: Move around the table from child to child, observing what they are doing with the play dough. Try using your play dough in the same ways as the children. Halfway through the small-group time, place the cookie cutters in the middle of the table. Observe how children may add these into their work. Use the same interaction strategies you've been using at work time. For a list of these, see page 61 at the end of this week's plans.

End: After 10 minutes, give children a 3-minute warning and ask them to put all their cookie cutters back in the cookie cutter container and the play dough in the play dough tub.

Group 2: Where's My Lid?

Materials:

- Clean and empty plastic containers and bottles of various shapes and sizes with matching lids/tops
- Two large baskets or bins — one to hold the containers and one to hold the lids

Beginning: Tell the children you have a bunch of containers that got separated from their lids — that they're all jumbled up. Show the children the two baskets (one with containers and one with lids) and ask them to help you figure out which top/lid goes on which container. Pick out a container and start searching through the lids, asking the children if they think the one you chose will fit. Some will guess based on appearance; others will want or need to try the lid to see if it will fit. Encourage the children to pick out one or more containers themselves and begin searching for a match.

Middle: As children try matching containers and lids, **listen to the children's comments and extend their observations and vocabulary.** For example, you might say, "I see your bottle has a small hole at the top. Which lid do you think will fit on that little round opening?" Or you might comment, "Your container is blue so you're looking for a top with the same color." Use words like *top, lid, round, square, big, little, open, closed, screw, twist, squeeze, narrow,* and *wide*. If the containers have words on them, point out the letters and read the words together with the children.

End: Ask children to help you separate the containers and lids back into the two baskets/bins.

Day 7

Large-Group Time
KDIs 16, 42

Scarves or Streamers and Music With No Words

Materials:

- A scarf or streamer for each child and adult, plus a few extra
- A CD or cassette player
- Flowing or "floating" type of music with no words

Step 1: Sing the "We're gonna shake, shake, shake" song. When all children have joined the group, sing one more verse and end by having everyone sit down on the floor. Pass out scarves to the children and allow for some exploration time. Remind the children that they used these yesterday for large-group time. Ask children if they remember some of the ways they moved with the scarves. Use children's ideas.

Step 2: Tell children that today they have the chance to put on some music and decide how they might want to move to the music. Then invite children to stand up and put on the music. Watch and copy how children are moving to the music.

Step 3: As the music is finishing, ask the children to dance their scarves into the basket and then dance to the next part of the daily routine.

Other Ideas
Outside Time — KDIs 12, 16/Meal Conversations — KDIs 12, 50

Outside Time
In addition to the usual materials, take out other materials, such as balls, dolls, or chalk. Be sure to **play and interact with the children outdoors.**

Meal Conversations
During conversations with children, bring their attention to objects that are on the table, or are clearly visible from the table, that have similarities and differences. Invite children to describe the similarities and differences by using comments and observations; for example, you might say, "Koby, your fruit looks different from Margaret's now," inviting Koby to notice and comment on the comparison.

Observations

Record what you saw individual children say and do today. You can use the reproducible sheet on page 178 to make your notes.

Follow-Up Ideas

- Put the baskets with the containers and lids in the house area, next to a sand or water table, and/or bring them outside for the children to play with.

- Write down your own follow-up ideas, using the reproducible sheet on page 179.

DAY 8

Curriculum Content — Key Developmental Indicators (KDIs)*

1. Initiative
2. Planning
4. Problem solving
6. Reflection
11. Community
12. Building relationships
13. Cooperative play
16. Gross-motor skills
22. Speaking
24. Phonological awareness
25. Alphabetic knowledge
26. Reading
29. Writing
32. Counting
35. Spatial awareness
36. Measuring
40. Art
41. Music
42. Movement
43. Pretend play

*See the KDIs listed under individual activities.

Greeting Time
KDIs 12, 24, 25, 26, 29

Greeting Time
Adult 2: Greet children at the door. When everyone has arrived, join the children and Adult 1 reading books.

Adult 1: Have about 10 books spread out on the floor. Read books with children. (*Note:* This should last no more than 15 minutes.) To the tune of "Mary Had a Little Lamb," sing made-up words, such as

> *It's time to put the books away,*
> *the books away, the books away.*
> *It's time to put the books away*
> *and read the message board.*

Message Board
Tape a lid and container to the message board and draw the area sign for the place where you've added the lids and containers. Help the children read this message that the containers and lids have been added to the _____ area.

Draw your daily routine symbol for cleanup time and draw a simple robot. Help the children read this message that today for cleanup, everyone will pretend to be robots. You might ask children how robots move and what they sound like. Suggest that they move like robots to the next part of your daily routine.

Planning Time
Group 1 — KDI 2/Group 2 — KDI 2

Group 1: Simple Area Stories
Make up simple stories about the areas in the room; for example, "In this area there is paint, there are markers, there is a lot of paper…this area is called…? Yes, the art area. Who wants to work in the art area today?" **Help children extend their plan** by asking what they will do and what materials they will use. As each child shares his or her idea, that child is free to get started.

Group 2: Puppets
Materials: One puppet for the adult and one for children to take turns with

Give one child a puppet. Using a puppet yourself, ask the child to tell his plan to your puppet. When the child has shared his plan, he is free to get started. You can then pass the puppet to the next child and repeat the process until all the children have shared their plans.

> **TIP:** You'll find that many of the strategies you've used for planning time can be modified and used for recall time on other days!

Day 8

Work Time
KDIs 1, 12, 13, 40, 43

In addition to the other strategies you've been using, **look for natural openings in children's play and join children at their level.** Generally, it is more natural and less disruptive to join children who are exploring materials (for example, squeezing play dough but not necessarily making anything with it), children who are pretending, or children who are starting to play simple games.

Sometimes it can be disruptive to try to enter into play with children who are in the middle of making or building something. However, once the builders are finished, they may welcome additional play partners as they continue their plans. Be careful not to take over children's play; instead, let children maintain the direction and control.

Cleanup Time
KDIs 11, 42, 43

Give children a verbal warning 10 minutes and then 5 minutes before the end of work time. At the beginning of cleanup time, remind children that today everyone is going to clean up like robots. Invite children to share how they think a robot might move and sound. You can pretend to turn a switch on to get your cleanup robots started. You can make this really fun by talking in a robot voice and walking stiffly yourself.

Recall Time
Group 1 — KDIs 6, 22/Group 2 — KDIs 41, 42

Group 1: Magic Wand
Using a "magic wand" (such as a decorated tube or stick), children can point to what they played with and share what they did. Repeat for all the children in your group.

Group 2: Guessing Game
One at a time, ask children to show you what their hands did at work time. For each child whose turn it is, sing the following words to the tune of "All on a Monday Morning":

This is what (Jesse) did,
(Jesse) did, (Jesse) did,
This is what (Jesse) did, at work time.

You and the rest of the children can imitate the child's actions with your hands. Ask the children to guess what the child whose turn it is did. Repeat for the other children in your group.

Day 8

Small-Group Time
Group 1 — KDIs 4, 35/Group 2 — KDIs 32, 36

Group 1: Puzzles

Materials: For each child, provide a puzzle with the pieces placed in a bag that has the child's name and letter link symbol written on it; also create two to three extra sets.

Beginning: Give each child the base for his or her puzzle (it might be helpful to put the child's name on a small piece of masking tape on the back to help remember who has what puzzle to start with). Ask children what they think they need for this small-group activity. Wait for children to respond "Puzzles!" or "Pieces!" and give them their bags.

Middle: Move around the table from child to child, **making specific comments** on what you see children doing. ("You've got the feet pieces done." "You're trying to find where that piece goes.") Avoid putting the pieces in for children who may need help. Instead, point out similar colors, or shapes. ("This part of your piece is curved — is there a curved part on the puzzle?" "I see your piece is dark blue — are there any other dark blue parts on your puzzle?") If needed, **refer children to other children for help.** ("I think Theresa knows how to do this puzzle; let's ask her.") As children complete their puzzle, they can exchange it for one of the extra puzzles in the middle of the table if they like.

End: Give children a three-minute warning. As they finish up their last puzzle, they can either stack them in the center of the table or put them where they belong in the toy area before they move to the next part of the day.

> **TIP:** Small-Group Times and Anecdotes. As you are interacting with children during small-group time, remember that you can note down what children say and do. These make great anecdotal notes, which can provide useful information about children's development and interests.

Group 2: Using Funnels

Materials:
For each child, provide
- Funnels in various sizes
- Clear, dry plastic bottles (16 oz. soda, one-half pint water bottles, plastic ketchup or syrup bottles); plastic food containers (margarine, yogurt, etc.)
- Dry sand (or salt, cornmeal, or birdseed)
- Spoons or scoops
- Cafeteria trays to work on, if available

Beginning: Give each child a tray, a plastic container of sand, a funnel, a spoon, and several plastic bottles. Introduce the small-group activity by asking the children to help you fill up the bottles with the sand.

Middle: Watch children experiment with filling up the bottles. Expect some children to pour their sand directly from the container into the bottle, others to spoon the sand into the bottle, and others to use the funnel. **Support children** in whatever method they choose to fill their bottles by trying each child's method. **Talk to children** about the different amounts of sand each bottle holds. Suggest that some bottles may hold more sand than others. Watch to see whether children count the number of scoops of sand a bottle will hold. **Listen** to whether children use comparison words to describe the sizes or shapes of their containers or to describe and compare the weights of different containers. **Repeat and restate what children say, and use descriptive words** that focus on and extend the children's actions.

End: Ask children to pour their sand into the sand table to be used again at work time. Have children put their funnels and scoops in containers to be placed near the sand table.

Day 8

Large-Group Time
KDI 43

Singing Songs

Materials: Classroom song book

Step 1: Sing the "We're gonna shake, shake, shake" song from last week. When all children have joined the group, sing one more verse and end by having everyone sit down on the floor.

Step 2: Bring out the song book, and show a sticky note with a child's name and letter link symbol written on it. Let the children know that this child can look through the book and choose a song to sing and place the sticky note on that song. When the child has chosen a song, sing that song (along with other verses, if appropriate). Repeat for one more song, and let the class know that other children will have a turn to choose a song on other days.

Step 3: Add one more song card for "Old Mac-Donald Had a Farm." Start by singing about one animal, then ask children for their ideas about animals and the noises they make. Sing more verses, using the children's ideas. At the end, ask children to move like the last animal to the next part of the daily routine.

Other Ideas
Outside Time — KDI 12/Meal Conversations — KDIs 6, 12

Outside Time
Take some of the containers and lids outside. Suggest to children that they might use them to collect things found outside.

Meal Conversations
Together with the children, create a story that recalls some of the children's experiences throughout the daily routine. You might start by saying, "Let's tell a story together that starts like this: Once upon a time, there was a class of children. They came to school and they...." Be sure to let children contribute to the story. Children may find prompts about your daily routine helpful. ("After they looked through the tube and shared their plan, they went to work time. At work time they..." Or "After they cleaned up, they went to recall. At recall they...")

Observations

Record what you saw individual children say and do today. You can use the reproducible sheet on page 178 to make your notes.

Follow-Up Ideas

Write down your own follow-up ideas, using the reproducible sheet on page 179.

DAY 9

Curriculum Content — Key Developmental Indicators (KDIs)*

1. Initiative
2. Planning
6. Reflection
11. Community
12. Building relationships
13. Cooperative play
16. Gross-motor skills
22. Speaking

24. Phonological awareness
25. Alphabetic knowledge
26. Reading
29. Writing
32. Counting
36. Measuring
40. Art

41. Music
42. Movement
43. Pretend play
45. Observing
46. Classifying
51. Natural and physical world

*See the KDIs listed under individual activities.

Greeting Time
KDIs 12, 24, 25, 26, 29

Adult 1: Greet children at the door. When everyone has arrived, join the children and Adult 2 reading books.

Adult 2: Have about 10 books spread out on the floor. Read books with children. (*Note:* This should last no more than 15 minutes.) To the tune of "Mary had a Little Lamb," sing made-up words, such as

*It's time to put the books away,
the books away, the books away.
It's time to put the books away
and read the message board.*

Message Board
Draw an image of the *Our Class* book on the message board. Remind the children that this book is in the book area if they would like to look at it. (See p. 41 in the Week 2 overview for a description of how to make the *Our Class* book.)

Draw your daily routine symbol for cleanup time and draw a simple robot. Help the children read this message that, for cleanup time, everyone is going to clean up like robots again. You might ask children how robots move and what they sound like. Suggest to the children that they move like robots to the next part of the daily routine.

Planning Time
Group 1 — KDIs 2, 29, 40/Group 2 — KDIs 2, 22

Group 1: Write or Draw Plans
Ask children to write or draw what they would like to do today. Have the set of area cards laid out on the table. **Expect a range of responses** from the children, including scribbling and telling you their plans, drawing, and writing some words using the cards as a guide. Younger children may find it helpful to go get something they would like to use and draw around it. **Jot down notes** about what each child does with the materials.

Group 2: Simple Area Stories
Make up simple stories about the areas in the room; for example, "In this area there is paint, there are markers, there is a lot of paper…this area is called…? Yes, the art area. Who wants to work in the art area today?" **Help the children extend their plan** by asking what will they will do and what materials they will use. As each child shares his or her idea, that child is free to get started.

Work Time
KDIs 1, 12, 13, 40, 43

Continue to **look for natural openings in children's play so you can join children** in what they are doing. As you do this, remember to look for children who are exploring the materials, pretending, or starting to play simple games. Observe those children who are in the middle of making or building something and ask yourself these questions to guide your next steps:

- Are they progressing with their ideas on their own?
- Are they experiencing a problem with materials and need your support?
- Are they completing their plans and ready for an additional player to join them as they use what they've created?

Day 9

Cleanup Time
KDIs 11, 42, 43

Give children a verbal warning 10 minutes and then 5 minutes before the end of work time. At the beginning of cleanup time, remind children that today everyone is going to clean up like robots. Invite children to share how they think a robot might move and sound. You can pretend to turn a switch on to get your cleanup robots started. You can make this really fun by talking in a robot voice and walking stiffly yourself.

Recall Time
Group 1 — KDIs 41, 42/Group 2 — KDIs 2, 6

Group 1: Guessing Game
One at a time, ask children to show you what their hands did at work time. For each child whose turn it is, sing the following words to the tune of "All on a Monday Morning":

This is what (Jesse) did,
(Jesse) did, (Jesse) did,
This is what (Jesse) did, at work time.

You and the rest of the children can imitate the child's actions with your hands. Ask the children to guess what the child whose turn it is did. Repeat for the other children in your group.

Group 2: Hats
Have several hats at the table. One at a time, ask the children to choose their recall hat and point to or tell what they did at work time as they wear their hat.

Day 9

Small-Group Time
Group 1 — KDI 32, 36/Group 2 — KDIs 45, 46, 51

Group 1: Using Funnels

Materials

For each child, provide

- Funnels in various sizes
- Clear, dry plastic bottles (16 oz. soda, one-half pint water bottles, plastic ketchup or syrup bottles); plastic food containers (margarine, yogurt, etc.)
- Dry sand (or salt, cornmeal, or birdseed)
- Spoons or scoops
- Cafeteria trays to work on, if available

Beginning: Give each child a tray, a plastic container of sand, a funnel, a spoon, and several plastic bottles. Introduce the small-group activity by asking the children to help you fill up the bottles with the sand.

Middle: Watch children experiment with filling up the bottles. Expect some children to pour their sand directly from the container into the bottle, others to spoon the sand into the bottle, and others to use the funnel. **Support children** in whatever method they choose to fill their bottles by trying each child's method. **Talk to children** about the different amounts of sand each bottle holds. Suggest that some bottles may hold more sand than others. Watch to see whether children count the number of scoops of sand a bottle will hold. **Listen** to whether children use comparison words to describe the sizes or shapes of their containers or to describe and compare the weights of different containers. **Repeat and restate what children say, and use descriptive words** that focus on and extend the children's actions.

End: Ask children to pour their sand into the sand table to be used again at work time. Have children put their funnels and scoops in containers to be placed near the sand table.

Group 2: Looking at Pebbles

Materials:

- Container of small rocks or pebbles for each child
- Magnifying glasses
- A piece of chart paper
- A marker

Beginning: Begin by giving each child one rock to examine using a magnifying glass. On a large piece of chart paper, write down the words that children use to describe their rocks. Draw children's attention to the common attributes that all the rocks possess as well as the differences children mention about their rocks.

Middle: Give each child a small container of rocks and pebbles to examine. Ask the children whether they can find pebbles that are the same in some ways. **Watch** how children group their rocks. Look for children to sort rocks by color, size, shape, or texture, and comment on what you observe. **Repeat the children's descriptive labels** and add new vocabulary words to their descriptions.

End: Ask children to help you add more words about rocks to the chart paper. Invite each child to choose a favorite rock or pebble and tell you about it. Draw attention to the similarities and differences among the children's rocks.

Large-Group Time

KDIs 16, 42

Musical Carpet Squares

Materials:

- Carpet squares for each child and adult plus several extras
- A CD or cassette player
- Recording of lively music without words

Step 1: Sing the "We're gonna shake, shake, shake song" as the easy-to-join activity.

Step 2: Explain to the children that they are going to walk from square to square as you play music. Explain that when the music stops, they should each stop — standing on a carpet square. Be sure both adults are participating with the children, modeling what to do.

Step 3: Play and stop the music. Make sure everyone is standing on a carpet square. Start the music again. Continue, varying the length of time between rounds.

Step 4: Tell the children that this is the last round of play for this activity. Explain that, this time, when the music stops, everyone will put their carpet square in a pile (indicate where) and then go to the next part of the routine.

Other Ideas

Outside Time — KDIs 12, 51 / Meal Conversations — KDIs 12, 41

Outside Time

While interacting and playing with children outside, draw their attention to living and natural things in your outside space. Make comments about grass, trees, flowers, rocks, weeds, bugs, birds, worms, and so forth.

Meal Conversations

While getting ready for the meal, call children using **segmentation** — that is, call them by their name syllables. Do this by calling names (for example, "Gab-ri-ele, pass the juice"; "Ar-leen, take a napkin") to the first two pitches of "Rain, Rain, Go Away." You may want to continue singing your conversations in this two-pitch style for the remainder of the meal.

Home-School Connections

Share the following idea with your children's family members:

Have your child help you the next time you fold laundry. Encourage your child to match socks into pairs, put all the towels together, find all his or her shirts, and so forth.

Did You Know...?

Segmentation is a part of children's growing phonological awareness, or ability to perceive and manipulate various units of sound in language. One way young children hear word sounds in order is by hearing the syllables of names and other common words they hear people calling or singing. For example, they may hear a parent or family member calling "Ty-ler, din-ner!" or singing "Swing low, sweet cha-ri-ot." Young children can begin to hear and say syllables in names and words themselves when the names and words are naturally slowed down and broken into parts by calling or singing.

— Adapted from *Growing Readers Early Literacy Curriculum Teacher Guide,* by Mary Hohmann, page 2

Observations

Record what you saw individual children say and do today. You can use the reproducible sheet on page 178 to make your notes.

Follow-Up Ideas

- Add a basket of pebbles to the toy area, or put pebbles in the sand and water table.
- Write down your own follow-up ideas, using the reproducible sheet on page 179.

DAY 10

Curriculum Content — Key Developmental Indicators (KDIs)*

1. Initiative
2. Planning
4. Problem solving
6. Reflection
11. Community
12. Building relationships
13. Cooperative play
18. Body awareness
22. Speaking
24. Phonological awareness
25. Alphabetic knowledge
26. Reading
29. Writing
32. Counting
35. Spatial awareness
40. Art
41. Music
43. Pretend play
45. Observing
46. Classifying
51. Natural and physical world
57. History

*See the KDIs listed under individual activities.

Greeting Time   KDIs 12, 24, 25, 26, 29, 57

Adult 2: Greet children at the door. When everyone has arrived, join the children and Adult 1 reading books.

Adult 1: Have about 10 books spread out on the floor. Read books with children. (*Note:* This should last no more than 15 minutes.) To the tune of "Mary Had a Little Lamb," sing made-up words, such as

> It's time to put the books away,
> the books away, the books away.
> It's time to put the books away
> and read the message board.

Message Board
Tape a few pebbles to the message board and draw the area sign for the classroom area you've added them to. Help the children read this message that the pebbles have been added to the _____ area.

Draw two simple images of the school with a red circle and diagonal slash over them — the universal "no" symbol. Write *2 no-school days* and help the children interpret the drawings. Remind them that they will stay home for two days and then come back to school.

Planning Time   *Group 1 — KDI 2/Group 2 — KDIs 2, 29, 40*

Group 1: Puppets
Materials: One puppet for the adult and one for children to take turns with

Give one child a puppet. Using a puppet yourself, ask the child to tell her plan to your puppet. When the child has shared her plan, she is free to get started. You can pass the puppet to the next child and repeat the process until all the children have shared their plans.

Group 2: Write or Draw Plans
Ask children to write or draw what they would like to do today. Have the set of area cards laid out on the table. **Expect a range of responses** from the children, including scribbling and telling you their plans, drawing, and writing some words using the cards as a guide. Younger children may find it helpful to go get something they would like to use and draw around it. **Jot down notes** about what each child does with the materials.

Work Time   KDIs 1, 12, 13, 40, 43

When joining children's play, **use the materials in the same way that the children do. Make specific comments** about what you see children doing, **avoiding asking questions.** ("You've used a lot of red paint, a little bit of blue." "You put a car on top of that block.") This will show children you are interested in their work, which will encourage them to want to talk to you about what they are doing.

Day 10

Cleanup Time
KDI 11

Give children a verbal warning 10 minutes and then 5 minutes before the end of work time. At the beginning of cleanup time, remind the children of large-group time yesterday — you might ask, "What did we do when the music stopped? We froze on our carpet square!" Tell them that today for cleanup everyone is going to freeze when they hear the cleanup music stop. Then, when the music starts again, everyone will continue to clean up. Continue playing the game until all the toys are put away.

Recall Time
Group 1 — KDI 6/Group 2 — KDIs 6, 22

Group 1: Hats
Have several hats at the table. One at a time, ask the children to choose their recall hat and point to or tell what they did at work time as they wear their hat.

Group 2: Magic wand
Using a "magic wand" (such as a decorated tube or stick), children can point to what they played with and share what they did. Repeat for all the children in your group.

Small-Group Time
Group 1 — KDIs 45, 46, 51/Group 2 — KDIs 4, 35

Group 1: Looking at Pebbles

Materials:
- Container of small rocks or pebbles for each child
- Magnifying glasses
- A piece of chart paper
- A marker

Beginning: Begin by giving each child one rock to examine using a magnifying glass. On a large piece of chart paper, write down the words that children use to describe their rocks. Draw children's attention to the common attributes that all the rocks possess as well as the differences children mention about their rocks.

Middle: Give each child a small container of rocks and pebbles to examine. Ask the children whether they can find pebbles that are the same in some ways. **Watch** how children group their rocks. Look for children to sort rocks by color, size, shape, or texture, and **comment** on what you observe. **Repeat the children's descriptive labels** and add new vocabulary words to their descriptions.

End: Ask children to help you add more words about rocks to the chart paper. Invite each child to choose a favorite rock or pebble and tell you about it. Draw attention to the similarities and differences among the children's rocks.

Group 2: Puzzles

Materials: For each child, provide a puzzle with the pieces placed in a bag that has the child's name and letter link symbol written on it; also create two to three extra sets.

Beginning: Give each child the base for his or her puzzle (it might be helpful to put the child's name on a small piece of masking tape on the back to help remember who has what puzzle to start with). Ask children what they think they need for this small-group activity. Wait for children to respond "Puzzles!" or "Pieces!" and give them their bags.

Middle: Move around the table from child to child, **making specific comments** on what you see children doing. ("You've got the feet pieces done." "You're trying to find where that piece goes.") Avoid putting the pieces in for children who may need help. Instead, point out similar colors, or shapes. ("This part of your piece is curved — is there a curved part on the puzzle?" "I see your piece is dark blue — are there any other dark blue parts on your puzzle?") If needed, **refer children to other children for help.** ("I think Theresa knows how to do this puzzle; let's ask her.") As children complete their puzzle, they can exchange it for one of the extra puzzles in the middle of the table if they like.

End: Give children a three-minute warning. As they finish up their last puzzle, they can either stack them in the center of the table or put them where they belong in the toy area before they move to the next part of the day.

Day 10

Large-Group Time
KDIs 18, 41

Rowing Boats

Step 1: Sing the "We're gonna shake, shake, shake" song from last week. When all children have joined, sing one more verse and end by having everyone sit down on the floor.

Step 2: Sing "Row, Row, Row Your Boat" with the children. Sing it through again, this time rocking your body forward and backward. Tell the children that you thought it would be fun to row boats with a friend. Start by asking a child if he or she would like to row with you. Sit facing each other and hold hands. Then rock forward and backward with your friend. Ask all the children to find someone to row with. Sing and row with the pairs of friends several times. If the children seem like they could continue with the activity, you might try asking them to now find three people to row with. It may take them a little bit of problem solving to figure out how to make this work! Children might decide to sit

- In a circle of three and rock toward the center and out
- In a circle of three and rock (or sway) side-to-side
- With two children facing each other and a third child in the middle as the "passenger"
- Remember, any safe idea from the children should be supported and encouraged.

Step 3: Tell the children that everyone will sing the song one last time and then row their boats over to the next part of the daily routine.

Other Ideas
Outside Time — KDIs 12, 51/Meal Conversations — KDIs 12, 32

Outside Time
Continue to converse about living and natural things in your outside space. **Make comments** about grass, trees, flowers, rocks, weeds, bugs, birds, worms, and so forth. Provide small cups (recycled containers, etc.) so children can collect more rocks and pebbles, or other natural items if they choose. (*Note:* Some children may prefer to run, ride bikes, climb, and so forth, during this part of the daily routine. This is fine, and it is important to support these children's ideas, too.

Meal Conversations
After children begin eating, invite them to count and compare the things on their plate, saying something like "I wonder how many crackers (or beans or whatever) you have now that you ate one? How many crackers (or beans or whatever) does Drew have?" Children will begin counting and comparing as they continue to eat.

Home-School Connections
Remind families of the importance of reading to their child. Tell them they can borrow a book from your class (if you have a lending library) to read to their child. Create a sign-out sheet for families who want to borrow books and reassure them that it is a positive thing to read the same story several times. Ask them to return the book they borrowed before they check out another book.

Observations

Record what you saw individual children say and do today. You can use the reproducible sheet on page 178 to make your notes.

Follow-Up Ideas

- Add the new "Row, Row, Row Your Boat" song card to the classroom song book.
- Write down your own follow-up ideas, using the reproducible sheet on page 179.

Building on What You've Learned: Week 2 Summary

This week you did the following in your classroom:

- Continued to help children learn the HighScope daily routine in concrete ways
- Continued to use transitions to move from one part of the routine to the next
- Introduced different strategies for cleanup time (moving like robots, freezing on carpet squares)
- Led small-group times that included curriculum content in math and creative representation
- Led large-group times that included curriculum content in movement and music and math
- Incorporated science language and thinking in your interactions with children outside

The children were particularly supported in the following areas:

- Continuing to form relationships with classroom adults
- Continuing to form relationships with other children
- Expressing their plans, choices, and intentions
- Participating in activities that support their development in the curriculum content areas of

  Approaches to Learning
  Social and Emotional Development
  Physical Development and Health
  Language, Literacy, and Communication
  Mathematics
  Creative Arts
  Science and Technology
  Social Studies

You developed your own adult-child interactions skills by using these HighScope interaction strategies (new strategies for this week appear in bolder type):

- Offering children comfort and contact
  - Looking for children in need of comfort and contact
  - Offering reassuring physical contact
  - Offering simple acknowledgments
  - Acknowledging children's feelings
- Participating in children's play
  - Joining play on children's level
  - Playing in parallel with children
  - Using comments and observations about what you saw children doing as openings to enter children's play
  - **Looking for natural openings to begin to play with children**
    - Considering the types of play you observed (exploratory, pretend, constructive, or games) before engaging with children
    - Playing as a partner, letting children retain control

Learn More About...*Small-Group Time*

During small-group time, the same group of children meets each day with the same adult in stable groups. After the adult briefly introduces the activity, children are generally given their own set of materials to work with, sometimes with additional materials or tools for everyone to share. For example, each child may get a lump of play dough and two cookie cutters in a basket, with a larger assortment of cookie cutters in the center of the table to use as desired.

Follow this simple format for successful small-group times:

Beginning:

- Have materials or equipment organized and ready.
- Briefly introduce the small-group time by
    - Handing out the materials or calling attention to the equipment
    - Telling a short story using the materials
    - Posing a problem: "Let's see what would happen if..."
    - Describing the properties of the materials: "In your bag, you'll find some things that are soft and some things that are rough — I wonder what you'll do with them today" (describing yarn and sandpaper).
- Let children begin working immediately.

Middle:

- Observe how children use or examine materials. Listen to what they say.
- Use and examine materials yourself, imitating children.
- Move from child to child and engage in conversations.
- Refer children to each other for problem-solving.
- Use a variety of adult-child interaction strategies (like you use at work time).

End:

- Give children a warning that the activity is coming to an end.
- Make cleaning up materials part of the activity.
- Plan a transition to the next part of your daily routine.

Chapter 3
The Third Week

Getting Ready: Week 3 Overview

Goals for the Third Week
- Add your own messages to the message board, based on observations of children in your classroom.
- Encourage children to start choosing songs to sing at large-group time.
- Implement three literacy-focused small-group times using the samples from the Growing Readers Early Literacy Curriculum that are included in this book.
- Record a minimum of three observations about children per day (each adult does this).

Things to Keep in Mind This Week
Be sure to read each activity plan ahead of time so you will know what materials to prepare.

Daily Routine
- Continue to ask a child to move the daily routine marker to the next part of the routine.
- This week, you will use three sample activities from the Growing Readers Early Literacy Curriculum. Locate the book *Good Night, Gorilla*, by Peggy Rathmann, and an edition of *Mother Goose*; see the Growing Readers activities (pp. 157–175) for detailed information on your small-group times for days 11, 13, and 15.
- For Thursday, have ready a photo, drawing, or painting of a statue for large-group time. If possible, use a statue image from a nearby park or public building, as children may be familiar with it or could go to look at it.
- Continue to add song cards to the classroom song book, use the sign-in sheets, and use the transition songs.
- On Friday, add this to the message board: Two simply drawn images of the school with a red circle and diagonal slash over them — the universal "no" symbol. Write *2 no-school days* and help the children interpret the drawings. Remind them that they will stay home for two days and then come back to school.

Creating Your Own Messages for the Message Board
- As a teaching team, you will select one additional message for the message board, based on your observations of the children. These kinds of messages might inform children of the following:
    - A new material you've added to the classroom and the area it will be in
    - A change in the routine (for example, "You can't go outside because it's raining" — draw the symbol for outside time and add a circle with a slash through it)
    - A change in the teachers (for example, Teacher 2 is sick, so you could write Teacher 2's name and symbol with a circle and slash through it and an arrow pointing to the substitute teacher's name and symbol)
    - A visitor to the classroom (for example, a local dignitary is visiting your program — draw a stick figure adult watching children playing)
    - An issue that continues to emerge from children's play. For example:
        - There is a lot of sand from the sand table spilled on the floor — draw the sand table with dots on the floor and tape up a small whisk broom and dust pan.
        - Children were running through the room and someone got hurt — draw a simple figure of a child crying with the hurt child's symbol underneath and then add a "?" You can ask the children, "Why was _____ crying yesterday?" Wait for their responses, then ask what everyone could remember to do today so no one else gets hurt. Wait for their responses, then ask what they could do if they see someone running. Wait for their responses.

- Children aren't cleaning up — show toys on the floor and a stick figure who is cleaning up with a sad face. Ask the children what this child is doing. Ask "Why is he sad?" and "What could we do to help make him feel happy?"
- Children have left the tops off of the markers and they are getting dried out — tape a dried-out marker without the top to the board, and ask children what this is. Ask a child to see if it will write and then ask, "Why do you think it won't work?" and "What could we do about this problem?"

After Children Leave for the Day

- Record your observations of children and jot down any ideas you want to follow up on. (You can use the reproducible sheets on pp. 178–179 to make your notes.) Each adult should try to record at least three observations.
- Read tomorrow's lesson plans to see what preparations you will need to make before the children arrive.

Some Reminders for This Week

Monday (Day 11)	**Tuesday** (Day 12)	**Wednesday** (Day 13)	**Thursday** (Day 14)	**Friday** (Day 15)
Both Groups: Growing Readers activity (small-group time)	Group 2: Two-inch squares of colored paper for small-group time Family note home: Play music for child	Group 2: "TV" for recall Both Groups: Growing Readers activity (small-group time) Sheet of nursery rhymes to send home	Group 1: Two-inch squares of colored paper for small-group time Statue photo or drawing for large-group time	Family note home: Play follow the leader game — child is the leader Group 1: "TV" for recall Both Groups: Growing Readers activity (small-group time)

DAY 11

Curriculum Content — Key Developmental Indicators (KDIs)*

1. Initiative
2. Planning
6. Reflection
11. Community
12. Building relationships
13. Cooperative play
21. Comprehension
23. Vocabulary
24. Phonological awareness
25. Alphabetic knowledge
26. Reading
28. Book knowledge
29. Writing
32. Counting
35. Spatial awareness
40. Art
43. Pretend play
51. Natural and physical world

*See the KDIs listed under individual activities.

Greeting Time
KDIs 12, 24, 25, 26, 29

Adult 1: Greet children at the door. When everyone has arrived, join the children and Adult 2 reading books.

Adult 2: Have about 10 books spread out on the floor. Read books with children. (*Note:* This should last no more than 15 minutes.) Sing a simple transitional song.

Message Board
Draw your daily routine symbol for cleanup time and draw a question mark (?). Say to the children something like, "Today for cleanup time we are going to do something different — it's a mystery. At cleanup time you'll see what we're going to be doing." (*Note:* HighScope teachers use the ? as a symbol for a question or mystery.) Create your own message.

Planning Time
Group 1 — KDI 2/Group 2 — KDI 2

Group 1: Planning Glasses

Materials: A pair of sunglasses or an old eyeglass frame with lenses removed

Tell the children that there are special planning glasses to wear for planning time today. Give each child a turn looking through the glasses to see something he or she would like to work with. When one child has finished sharing, he or she can leave the group and get started. Repeat this process until all the children have shared their plans.

Group 2: Puzzle
Ahead of time, choose a wooden knob puzzle that you've seen children enjoy playing with. Place a different child's name and letter link symbol on a sticky note on the board under each puzzle piece. At planning time, ask a child to remove a piece. The child whose name is revealed can tell you his plan. That child can then remove the next piece before leaving to get started on his plan. Repeat until all children have planned.

Work Time
KDIs 1, 12, 13, 40, 43

Continue to **join children's play, using the materials in the same way** that the children do. **Avoid asking questions, but instead make specific comments** about what you see children doing. ("You've put on a smock and now you're using the glue and ribbon pieces." "You put the baby to bed and now you're getting her a teddy bear.") This will show children you are interested in their work and will encourage them to want to talk to you about their play.

Day 11

Cleanup Time

KDI 11

After giving the usual 10- and 5-minute warning signals, say to the children something like "Today we are going to have a 'sneaky cleanup.'" Ask children to tiptoe and quietly put away their toys. You should also participate in both cleaning up and being sneaky.

TIP: Planning for cleanup time helps keep children engaged and interested. In these lesson plans, you'll see lots of ideas to help children focus on cleaning up the classroom. Be sure to always plan a strategy for this important time of day. Remember, modeling a light and playful attitude during cleanup time helps children see that this time of day can be fun and productive.

Recall Time

Group 1 — KDI 6/Group 2 — KDI 6

Group 1: Rolling a Ball
After gathering at your table, ask children to walk with you to the floor. Sit down, forming a circle. Roll the ball to a child. That child can tell what he did and then roll the ball to the next child. Continue until all children who want to recall have had a chance to share.

Group 2: Describing and Guessing What You Worked With
Children take turns using a scarf or canvas bag for this recall activity. While everyone else closes their eyes, the first child to have the scarf or bag can go get something she used at work time and hide it in the scarf or bag. The child can give clues about what she did, and when the group guesses it, the child can show her item. Then the next child can take a turn.

Small-Group Time *Group 1 — KDIs 21, 23, 26, 28, 29/Group 2 — KDIs 21, 23, 24, 26*

Group 1: Sample Growing Readers Activity

Connect to *Good Night, Gorilla:* What Things Do You See?

Quick Plan:

- Teacher and children examine and discuss the pictures.
- Children tell the story based on the pictures.
- Children compare pictures on the front and back covers.

(See pp. 158–159 and 164–165 for complete activity and materials.)

Group 2: Sample Growing Readers Activity

Learn Nursery Rhymes: Act Out "Humpty Dumpty" and Other Level 1 Nursery Rhymes

Quick Plan:

- Children listen to and say the nursery rhyme.
- Children act out and say the nursery rhyme.
- Teacher and children discuss nursery rhyme pictures, words, and objects.

(See pp. 166–167 and 172–173 for complete activity and materials.)

Day 11

Large-Group Time

KDIs 24, 32, 40

Marching Ants

Step 1: Start with your easy-to-join activity: Sing the "We're gonna shake, shake, shake" song. When all children have joined, sing one more verse and end by having everyone sit down on the floor.

Step 2: Show the children the song card you made for "The Ants Go Marching One By One." Together, sing the song, using the numbers 1 through 10 in order. Younger children may only want to sing a few verses. As you are singing, have children hold up their fingers (1–10) to show the number they are singing about. After the first few verses, invite the children to make up new rhymes by asking them, for example, "What else can we rhyme with two?" Their responses may result in lines like "The ants go marching two by two, the little one stops to squeeze the glue" (or "tie his shoe"). Expect children to shout out rhymes. Repeat the rhyming words children say and expect that some of the rhymes will not be actual words, for example, *seven/bevin*.

Step 3: As a transition, the children can march like ants to the next part of the daily routine.

Other Ideas

Outside Time — KDIs 12, 51/Meal Conversations — KDIs 12, 35

Outside Time

As you play and interact with the children outside, **look for natural opportunities to make connections between objects and materials and properties.** For example, you might notice a stick outside and make a connection to the wood of the stick and the wood that the climber is made out of. Or you might notice the steel on the trike and make a connection to the steel poles on the swing set.

Meal Conversations

While children are eating, use language that describes the position of things. ("You put your cheese on *top* of your bread." "Your cup is *between* the spoon and the plate." "Jill, you are sitting *across* the table from Gena.")

Observations

Record what you saw individual children say and do today. You can use the reproducible sheet on page 178 to make your notes.

Follow-Up Ideas

- Add the new "The Ants Go Marching One by One" song card to the classroom song book.
- Write down your own follow-up ideas, using the reproducible sheet on page 179.

DAY 12

Curriculum Content — Key Developmental Indicators (KDIs)*

1. Initiative
2. Planning
6. Reflection
11. Community
12. Building relationships
13. Cooperative play
16. Gross-motor skills
18. Body awareness
22. Speaking
23. Vocabulary
24. Phonological awareness
25. Alphabetic knowledge
26. Reading
29. Writing
38. Patterns
40. Art
42. Movement
43. Pretend play
51. Natural and physical world

*See the KDIs listed under individual activities.

Greeting Time
KDIs 12, 24, 25, 26, 29

Adult 2: Greet children at the door. When everyone has arrived, join the children and Adult 1 reading books.

Adult 1: Have about 10 books spread out on the floor. Read books with children. (*Note:* This should last no more than 15 minutes.) Sing a simple transitional song.

Message Board
Draw your daily routine symbol for cleanup time and draw a question mark (?). Ask children if they remember what they did yesterday for cleanup time. Confirm their responses by saying something like "Yes, today we will be doing sneaky cleanup."

Create your own message.

Planning Time
Group 1 — KDI 2/Group 2 — KDI 2

Group 1: Puzzle
Ahead of time, choose a wooden knob puzzle that you've seen children enjoy playing with. Place a different child's name and letter link symbol on a sticky note on the board under each puzzle piece. At planning time, ask a child to remove a piece. The child whose name is revealed can tell you her plan. That child can then remove the next piece before leaving to get started on her plan. Repeat until all children have planned.

Group 2: Planning Glasses
Materials: A pair of sunglasses or an old eyeglass frame with lenses removed

Tell the children that there are special planning glasses to wear for planning time today. Give each child a turn looking through the glasses to see something he or she would like to work with. When one child has finished sharing, he or she can leave the group and get started. Repeat this process until all the children have shared their plans.

Work Time
KDIs 1, 12, 13, 40, 43

While playing as a partner, remember to **refer one child to another** for help or support. This enables children to use their abilities for the benefit of others, recognize each other's strengths, regard each other as valuable resources, and play cooperatively.

Cleanup Time
KDI 11

After giving the usual 10- and 5-minute warning signals, ask children if they remember how they cleaned up yesterday and remind them that they will have a 'sneaky clean-up' again today. Ask children to tiptoe and quietly put away their toys. You should also participate in both cleaning up and being sneaky.

Day 12

Recall Time
Group 1 — KDI 6/Group 2 — KDI 6

Group 1: Describing and Guessing What You Worked With
Children take turns using a scarf or canvas bag for this recall activity. While everyone else closes their eyes, the first child to have the scarf or bag can go get something he used at work time and hide it in the scarf or bag. The child can give clues about what he did, and when the group guesses it, the child can show his item. Then the next child can take a turn.

Group 2: Rolling a Ball
After gathering at your table, ask children to walk with you to the floor. Sit down, forming a circle. Roll the ball to a child. That child can tell what she did and then roll the ball to the next child. Continue until all children who want to recall have had a chance to share.

Did You Know...?
Preschool children are developing mathematical thinking through exploration of materials and their characteristics. Ordering objects — putting things in order according to some graduated attribute — is part of this mathematical thinking. We see children line up the animal figures smallest to largest; the toy cars, bumpiest tires to smoothest tires; and the crayons, lightest to darkest. Children also identify and create patterns, such as red-blue-red-blue on the peg board or big-little-big-little stickers on their artwork. The small-group times on Days 12 and 14 lend themselves to children's mathematical thinking. As the teacher, you can support children's math learning by using the math language suggested in each of the plans. Look for children's spontaneous math play during work time and offer your math support then, too.

Day 12

Small-Group Time

Group 1 — KDIs 23, 40/Group 2 — KDIs 22, 23, 38

Group 1: Shades of Paint

Materials:

For each child, provide

- Three containers of paint: (1) a primary color (for example, each child has red, or each child has blue, or each child has yellow), (2) white, and (3) black
- Paper and paintbrushes
- Paint stirrers, spoons, and eye droppers

Beginning: Show the children the paint and name the color and the white and black. Ask the children what they think will happen when white (or black) is added to the color. Then pour white or black into the primary color, stir, and encourage the children to describe what they see. Tell the children they are going to explore what happens when they add white or black to a color of paint. Use words such as *lighter* and *darker*. Give each child his or her set of painting materials. Encourage the children to experiment on their own, pouring the paint directly from one container into another or mixing paints by using the spoons and droppers. Tell children they can look at what happens to the paint in the containers and/or they can apply the new color to the paper.

Middle: **Observe and comment** along with the children about the changes they see. Focus on how the primary color gets progressively lighter the more white the children add, and how the color gets darker when the children add more black. Encourage children to look at one another's mixed-paint colors and make comparisons. Use vocabulary words such as *light-lighter-lightest* and *dark-darker-darkest*, *paler*, *shade*, *hue*, *tint*, and so forth. Encourage children to look around the room or at their clothing for shades of the primary colors they are transforming and to compare degrees of lightness and darkness.

End: Together with the children, clean up the paints and mixing tools. If children want to keep their papers, label them with the children's names and hang them up to dry. Pick out shades of colors in the children's clothes and shoes to determine the order in which they will proceed to the next activity. For example, you might say, "Anyone wearing dark blue can get washed up now. Next, anyone wearing medium blue (light blue, and so forth)."

Group 2: Frogs on Lily Pads

Materials:

For each child, provide

- Two-inch squares of paper in a variety of colors
- An individual felt board or small carpet piece
- Small plastic frogs or other animal figures

TIP: Small baskets, paper lunchbags, large yogurt containers, and shoeboxes make great containers for individual sets of small-group-time materials.

Beginning: Start by telling the children a story about a frog who crossed a pond by jumping on colored lily pads (use a felt board lying flat on the table for the pond and paper squares for the lily pads). Use a small plastic frog and two colors of paper squares. Arrange the squares by alternating colors in a line across the felt board; for example, red-yellow-red-yellow. As you make the frog "jump," say the color of the square it lands on. Ask the children if they notice anything about the way the "lily pads" are arranged. Modify the story as needed to incorporate animal figures available to you or animals of special interest to the children.

Middle: Give each child a container of colored paper squares, a felt board, and a frog. Ask the children to tell their own story about a frog and lily pads. Watch to see how children arrange the paper on their felt boards. Expect that children may place squares randomly on the board, sort the paper by color, line up the squares in random fashion, or arrange the squares in a specific pattern. **Comment on what you observe children doing.** ("You put all the red lily pads together." "Your frog jumps on yellow, then green, then yellow, then green. What color are you going to put next?")

End: Watch to see whether children make patterns or sort their squares by color. Before cleaning up the materials, ask if children would like to show the ways they arranged the lily pads on their ponds. Listen as children describe their patterns. As you observe, make notes on what children do and say. Ask children to put their paper pieces back in their containers, stack their felt boards in the middle of the table, and put their frogs all in one basket.

Day 12

Large-Group Time
KDIs 16, 18, 42

Fast and Slow Movements

Materials: Recorded music with fast and slow tempos

Step 1: Start with your easy-to-join activity: Sing the "We're gonna shake, shake, shake" song until all the children have joined; then, end by having everyone sit on the floor. Tell children that today everyone is going to be moving to some music but that the music sounds different from what they've heard in class before.

Step 2: Play the slow part of the music and ask the children to move their hands according to how the music sounds. Use words related to time and speed such as *slow, poky, not fast*, and so forth, as you **comment on, acknowledge, and imitate children's actions and extend children's language** while they are moving their hands. Repeat for the fast-tempo music.

Step 3: Play the music with the fast and slow tempos and move together with the children, alerting them to the change in the tempo, if necessary. You might say things like, "Uh oh, it's changing" or "Listen — is it different now?"

Step 4: After the music has ended, ask the children to choose to move their bodies fast or slow as they move to the next part of the daily routine.

Other Ideas
Outside Time — KDIs 12, 51/Meal Conversations — KDIs 12, 22, 23

Outside Time
As you play and interact with the children outside, **look for natural opportunities to make connections between objects and materials and properties.** For example, you might notice a stick outside and make a connection to the wood of the stick and the wood blocks indoors. Or you might notice the rubber on the trike and make a connection to the rubber balls.

Meal Conversations
Talk with children about things they can find outside but not inside (for example, swings, rain, trees, cars, birds, and so forth). Children might expand the conversation by sharing what they like to do with these things outside, and this is fine! **Support children's thoughts by repeating and restating what they share and by acknowledging their contributions.** ("Your mom has the blue van, but your dad's car is black." "You were disappointed because it rained and you couldn't go out on the swings.")

Home-School Connections
Share the following idea with the children's family members:

Play some of your favorite music for your child. You can dance and move with your child, enjoying the time together!

Observations

Record what you saw individual children say and do today. You can use the reproducible sheet on page 178 to make your notes.

Follow-Up Ideas

Write down your own follow-up ideas, using the reproducible sheet on page 179.

DAY 13

Curriculum Content — Key Developmental Indicators (KDIs)*

1. Initiative
2. Planning
6. Reflection
11. Community
12. Building relationships
13. Cooperative play
18. Body awareness

21. Comprehension
22. Speaking
23. Vocabulary
24. Phonological awareness
25. Alphabetic knowledge
26. Reading
28. Book knowledge

29. Writing
40. Art
41. Music
43. Pretend play
46. Classifying

*See the KDIs listed under individual activities.

Greeting Time
KDIs 12, 24, 25, 26, 29

Adult 1: Greet children at the door. When everyone has arrived, join the children and Adult 2 reading books.

Adult 2: Have about 10 books spread out on the floor. Read books with children. (*Note:* This should last no more than 15 minutes.) Sing a simple transitional song.

Message Board
Draw your daily routine symbol for cleanup time; write *cleanup* and *?* and tape a few area cards next to this message. Help the children read this message that, for cleanup time, everyone is going to clean up each of the areas together. Explain that you'll pull out an area card and everyone will work together to clean up that area.

Bring out the classroom song book with three sticky notes attached to it, each having a child's name and letter link symbol written on it. Help children read this message that these three children will choose songs to sing at large-group time. These children may want to take their sticky note and put it on the song they'll sing. (*Note:* This strategy can give children more time to look through the book and choose what they want to sing without the pressure of the large group waiting for them. If the children forget to choose their song ahead of time, that is fine — they can just do so at large-group time).

Planning Time
Group 1 — KDI 2/Group 2 — KDI 2

Group 1: Hula Hoop
Meet in your usual planning place. Tell the children that today everyone is going to move over to the floor to plan. Once on the floor and sitting in a circle, everyone holds on to a hula hoop that is marked in one place with a piece of colorful tape. Everyone sings a short song together and passes the hoop through their hands. The group stops rotating the hoop at the end of the song. The child nearest the tape mark takes a turn sharing his plan. That child can then leave the group and begin his work time. Here is a song idea (to the tune of "Mary Had a Little Lamb"):

> *Now it's time to share our plans,*
>
> *share our plans, share our plans.*
>
> *Now it's time to share our plans.*
>
> *What will you do today?*

Group 2: Train and Train Tracks
Ahead of time, lay out the train tracks in a simple oval design. Place sticky notes with the area names around the tracks. At planning time, children can move the train around the tracks and stop at the station where they would like to work today. **Ask questions to extend children's thinking,** such as who they will work with and what they will use in their plans. After a child has planned, that child can get started on her play. Repeat the process for all the children in your group.

Day 13

Work Time

KDIs 1, 12, 13, 40, 43

As you play as a partner, **refer one child to another for help or support.** This enables children to use their abilities for the benefit of others, recognize each other's strengths, regard each other as valuable resources, and play cooperatively. You might say something like the following to a child:

> "I think Henry knows how to use that computer program. You could ask him how to make it work."

> "I saw Anna stacking those blocks yesterday. Should we see if she can help us make them work now?"

> "Ellie likes to be the baby, have you asked her if she would like to play with you?"

Cleanup Time

KDI 11

After giving the usual 10- and 5-minute warning signals, say to the children something like "Today everyone is going to clean up area by area." Next, pull an area card out of a bag. Everyone can then work together to clean up that area. After the area is cleaned up, pull another area card out of the bag. Repeat for all the areas.

Recall Time

Group 1 — KDIs 6, 46/Group 2 — KDI 6

Group 1: Matching Beads

Materials:

- A string of colored beads
- A cloth bag containing additional beads in the same colors as those on the bead string

Show children the string of colored beads. Ask each child to reach into the bag and take out a bead. Tell the children that when you take off a bead that is the same color as the one they are holding, it will be their turn to share what they did at work time.

Group 2: TV Recall

Ahead of time, cut the middle out of a large box top (the top of a case of computer printer paper works well) to make a large hole. Draw simple buttons on the remaining cardboard on the front. This is your "recall TV set." One at a time, children can hold the box in front of them so their head shows through the hole — thus making them be "on TV." Ask children to share what they did at work time and then pass the TV to the next child. *Note:* You can make this really fun by bringing in an old remote and asking children what channel they are on, and so forth.

Small-Group Time

Group 1 — KDIs 21, 22, 23/Group 2 — KDIs 18, 24, 28

Group 1: Sample Growing Readers Activity

Connect to *Good Night Gorilla*: Try Out Flashlights and Keys

Quick Plan:

- Children guess what objects from the book are in the box.
- Children try out flashlights, keys, and key rings.
- Children show and describe how to use the flashlights or key rings.

(See pp. 160–161 for complete activity and materials.)

Group 2: Sample Growing Readers Activity

Learn Nursery Rhymes: Pat to "Humpty Dumpty" and Other Level 1 Nursery Rhymes

Quick Plan:

- Teacher and children say and pat to four lines of "pat-pat-pat-pat."
- Teacher and children say and pat to nursery rhymes.
- Teacher adds the children's names to the nursery rhymes.

(See pp. 168–169 and 172–175 for complete activity and materials.)

Day 13

Large-Group Time

KDI 41

Singing Songs

Materials: Classroom song book

Step 1: Sing the "We're gonna shake, shake, shake" song until all children have joined; then sing one more verse and end by having everyone sit down on the floor.

Step 2: Bring out the song book with three sticky notes attached to it, each having a child's name and letter link symbol written on it. Tell the class that today these three children will each choose a song from the song book. As these children are picking out their songs, you may want to tap a steady beat on your knees with the rest of the children and chant, "I wonder what they'll pick, I wonder what they'll pick?" Sing the songs chosen by the three children, making sure to include choices of verses from the other children when appropriate.

Step 3: Ask all the children to tiptoe to their next activity.

Other Ideas

Outside Time — KDI 12/Meal Conversations — KDIs 6, 12

Outside Time

Play and interact with the children. **Continue to refer one child to another** for help or support. See today's "Work Time" section for more information on this interaction strategy.

Meal Conversations

During the meal, ask children to just listen to sounds they hear. Children might notice things like the other group talking, chewing noises, someone walking down the hall, the clock ticking, a phone ringing, an airplane flying overhead, a bird outside, and so forth. Continue talking with children about the sounds they hear.

Home-School Connections

Send home a sheet of simple nursery rhymes and share this idea with the children's family members:

Have fun sharing these rhymes (and others that you remember from your childhood) with your child.

Observations

Record what you saw individual children say and do today. You can use the reproducible sheet on page 178 to make your notes.

Follow-Up Ideas

Write down your own follow-up ideas, using the reproducible sheet on page 179.

DAY 14

Curriculum Content — Key Developmental Indicators (KDIs)*

1. Initiative
2. Planning
6. Reflection
11. Community
12. Building relationships
13. Cooperative play
16. Gross-motor skills
21. Comprehension
22. Speaking
23. Vocabulary
24. Phonological awareness
25. Alphabetic knowledge
26. Reading
29. Writing
38. Patterns
40. Art
42. Movement
43. Pretend play
45. Observing

*See the KDIs listed under individual activities.

Greeting Time
KDIs 12, 24, 25, 26, 29

Adult 2: Greet children at the door. When everyone has arrived, join the children and Adult 1 reading books.

Adult 1: Have about 10 books spread out on the floor. Read books with children. (*Note:* This should last no more than 15 minutes.) Sing a simple transitional song.

Message Board
Draw your daily routine symbol for cleanup time; write *cleanup* and *?*, and tape a few area cards next to this message. Help the children read this message that, for cleanup time, everyone is going to clean up by area.

Create your own message.

Planning Time
Group 1 — KDI 2/Group 2 — KDI 2

Group 1: Flashlight
One at a time, have children hold a flashlight and suggest that they shine the light on something they would like to work with. **Comment** on children's plans and **ask open ended questions** to help them extend their ideas. For instance, you might say, "I see your light is on the block area — what will you do there? What will you use in your plan?" After sharing, the child whose turn it is can pass the light to someone else and get started on his plan. Repeat for all children in your group.

Group 2: Tape Recorder
Using a tape recorder, children can take turns recording their work-time plans. **Ask them questions to extend their ideas,** such as who they will work with and what they will use in their plans. Save this tape to use at recall time. After the child whose turn it is has recorded her plan, she can get started on her play.

Work Time
KDIs 1, 12, 13, 21, 22, 23, 40, 43

Focus on having conversations with children. To do this, **respond to children's conversational leads.** When an adult is silent yet attentive, and listens patiently and with interest to ongoing conversations, children will likely address the adult directly or make the first move toward involving him or her in conversations.

Cleanup Time
KDI 11

After giving the usual 10- and 5-minute warning signals, say to the children something like "Today everyone is going to clean up area by area." Next, pull an area card out of a bag. Everyone can then work together to clean up that area. After the area is cleaned up, pull another area card out of the bag. Repeat for all the areas.

Day 14

Recall Time
Group 1 — KDI 6/Group 2 — KDI 6

Group 1: Area Cards and Clothespins

Materials:

- Cards with children's name and letter link symbol on them
- Clothespins
- Area cards

One at a time, show the cards with children's first name and letter link symbol written on them. Ask "Who is this?" When the children respond, give the card and a clothespin to the child whose name/symbol it is and ask him to clip it to the area card corresponding to the area he played in. Ask the child to tell you what he did in that area. As you repeat this activity for all the children, everyone can notice the areas where many children played or just a few children played. Some children may choose to count the clothespins to figure this out.

Group 2: Listen to Our Plans

Listen to the tape recording made at planning time. After listening to one child's plan, see if the children can identify who the planner was. Ask that child whether she actually did that plan or whether she changed it. Be nonjudgmental in your responses. It's okay if children changed their plans or if they wish to recall about something else. Repeat this process until all children have had an opportunity to hear their recording and recall their experiences.

Day 14

Small-Group Time
Group 1 — KDIs 22, 23, 38/Group 2 — KDIs 23, 40, 45

Group 1: Frogs on Lily Pads

Materials:

For each child, provide

- Two-inch squares of paper in a variety of colors
- An individual felt board or small carpet piece
- Small plastic frogs or other animal figures

Beginning: Start by telling the children a story about a frog who crossed a pond by jumping on colored lily pads (use a felt board lying flat on the table for the pond and paper squares for the lily pads). Use a small plastic frog and two colors of paper squares. Arrange the squares by alternating colors in a line across the felt board; for example, red-yellow-red-yellow. As you make the frog "jump," say the color of the square it lands on. Ask the children if they notice anything about the way the "lily pads" are arranged. Modify the story as needed to incorporate animal figures available to you or animals of special interest to the children.

Middle: Give each child a container of colored paper squares, a felt board, and a frog. Ask the children to tell their own story about a frog and lily pads. Watch to see how children arrange the paper on their felt boards. Expect that children may place squares randomly on the board, sort the paper by color, line up the squares in random fashion, or arrange the squares in a specific pattern. **Comment on what you observe children doing.** ("You put all the red lily pads together." "Your frog jumps on yellow then green then yellow then green. What color are you going to put next?")

End: Watch to see whether children make patterns or sort their squares by color. Before cleaning up the materials, ask if children would like to show the ways they arranged the lily pads on their ponds. Listen as children describe their patterns. As you observe, make notes on what children do and say. Ask children to put their paper pieces back in their containers, stack their felt boards in the middle of the table, and put their frogs all in one basket.

Group 2: Shades of Paint

Materials:

For each child, provide

- Three containers of paint: (1) a primary color (for example, each child has red, or each child has blue, or each child has yellow), (2) white, and (3) black
- Paper and paintbrushes
- Paint stirrers, spoons, and eye droppers

Beginning: Show the children the paint and name the color and the white and black. Ask the children what they think will happen when white (or black) is added to the color. Then pour white or black into the primary color, stir, and encourage the children to describe what they see. Tell the children they are going to explore what happens when they add white or black to the color of paint. Use words such as *lighter* and *darker*. Give each child his or her set of painting materials. Encourage the children to experiment on their own, pouring the paint directly from one container into another or mixing paints by using the spoons and droppers. Tell the children they can look at what happens to the paint in the containers and/or they can apply the new color to the paper.

Middle: Observe and comment along with the children about the changes they see. Focus on how the primary color gets progressively lighter the more white the children add, and how the color gets darker when the children add more black. Encourage children to look at one another's mixed-paint colors and make comparisons. Use vocabulary words such as *light-lighter-lightest* and *dark-darker-darkest, paler, shade, hue, tint,* and so forth. Encourage children to look around the room or at their clothing for shades of the primary colors they are transforming and to compare degrees of lightness and darkness.

End: Together with the children, clean up the paints and mixing tools. If children want to keep their papers, label them with the children's names and hang them up to dry. Pick out shades of colors in the children's clothes and shoes to determine the order in which they will proceed to the next activity. For example, you might say, "Anyone wearing dark blue can get washed up now. Next, anyone wearing medium blue (light blue, and so forth)."

Day 14

Large-Group Time
KDIs 16, 42

Statue Music

Materials:

Photo, drawing, or painting of a statue (if possible, one from a nearby park, as children may be familiar with it or could go look at it later)

Recorded music without words

Step 1: Sing the "We're gonna shake, shake, shake" song until all children have joined; then sing one more verse and end by having everyone sit down on the floor.

Step 2: Ask the children if they have ever seen a statue. If possible, have a photo of a statue in a nearby park to show. Tell the children that we can make statues with our bodies by holding them very strong (stiff) and still. Ask the children to stand up and try making a statue along with you. Then ask them if they can change their statue in some way (for example, pick up a leg, move an arm to a different position). Share that you will be putting on some "statue music" (music without words) and that when the music plays, they can move/dance however they want to, but when the music stops, they can make their statue. Play (and occasionally stop) the music, and move and make statues with the children.

Step 3: Tell the children that the next time the music stops they can make a statue and then go to the next activity.

Other Ideas
Outside Time — KDI 12/Meal Conversations — KDIs 12, 22, 23

Outside Time
Play and interact with the children. Practice the interaction strategies that you used during work time.

Meal Conversations
During the meal, play the "I Spy" game by focusing on colors, starting with something on the table (for example, "I spy something red"). Then spy things farther away, and give children hints until they get the answer. ("It's something red, it's in the toy area, it's next to the computer — yes — it's the red peg bin!") Once children are comfortable with the game, they can take turns being the leader and giving clues.

Observations

Record what you saw individual children say and do today. You can use the reproducible sheet on page 178 to make your notes.

Follow-Up Ideas

Write down your own follow-up ideas, using the reproducible sheet on page 179.

DAY 15

Curriculum Content — Key Developmental Indicators (KDIs)*

1. Initiative
2. Planning
6. Reflection
11. Community
12. Building relationships
13. Cooperative play
16. Gross-motor skills
18. Body awareness

21. Comprehension
22. Speaking
23. Vocabulary
24. Phonological awareness
25. Alphabetic knowledge
26. Reading
28. Book knowledge

29. Writing
40. Art
42. Movement
43. Pretend play
45. Observing
57. History

*See the KDIs listed under individual activities.

Greeting Time
KDIs 12, 24, 25, 26, 29, 57

Adult 1: Greet children at the door. When everyone has arrived, join the children and Adult 2 reading books.

Adult 2: Have about 10 books spread out on the floor. Read books with children. (*Note:* This should last no more than 15 minutes.) Sing a simple transitional song.

Message Board
Draw your daily routine symbol for cleanup time, write *cleanup* and *?*, and tape a few area cards next to this message. Help the children read this message that for cleanup time, everyone is going to clean up by area.

Draw two simple images of the school with a red circle and diagonal slash over them — the universal "no" symbol. Write *2 no school days* and help the children interpret the drawings. Remind them that they will stay home for two days and then come back to school.

Planning Time
Group 1 — KDI 2/Group 2 — KDI 2

Group 1: Train and Train Tracks
Ahead of time, lay out the train tracks in a simple oval design. Place sticky notes with the area names around the tracks. At planning time, children can move the train around the tracks and stop at the station where they would like to work today. **Ask questions to extend children's thinking,** such as who they will work with and what they will use in their plans. After a child has planned, that child can get started on his play. Repeat the process for all the children in your group.

Group 2: Hula Hoop
Meet in your usual planning place. Tell the children that today everyone is going to move over to the floor to plan. Once on the floor and sitting in a circle, everyone holds on to a hula hoop that is marked in one place with a piece of colorful tape. Everyone sings a short song together and passes the hoop through their hands. The group stops rotating the hoop at the end of the song. The child nearest the tape mark takes a turn sharing her plan. That child can then leave the group and begin her work time. Here is a song idea (to the tune of "Mary Had a Little Lamb"):

Now it's time to share our plans,

share our plans, share our plans.

Now it's time to share our plans.

What will you do today?

Day 15

Work Time
KDIs 1, 12, 13, 21, 22, 23, 40, 43

Continue to work on having conversations with children. To do this, **respond to children's conversational leads.** When an adult is silent, yet attentive, and listens patiently and with interest to ongoing conversations, the child will likely address the adult directly or make the first move toward involving him or her in conversations.

Cleanup Time
KDI 11

After giving the usual 10- and 5-minute warning signals, tell the children that today everyone is going to clean up area by area. Pull an area card out of a bag. Everyone can then work together to clean up that area. After that area is cleaned up, pull another area card out of the bag. Repeat for all the areas.

Recall Time
Group 1 — KDI 6/Group 2 — KDI 6

Group 1: TV Recall
Ahead of time, cut the middle out of a large box top (the top of a case of computer printer paper works well) to make a large hole. Draw simple buttons on the remaining cardboard on the front. This is your "recall TV set." One at a time, children can hold the box in front of them so their head shows through the hole — thus making them be "on TV." Ask children to share what they did at work time and then pass the TV to the next child. *Note:* You can make this really fun by bringing in an old remote and asking children what channel they are on, and so forth.

Group 2: Matching Beads

Materials:

- A string of colored beads
- A cloth bag containing additional beads in the same colors as those on the bead string

Show children the string of colored beads. Ask each child to reach into the bag and take out a bead. Tell the children that when you take off a bead that is the same color as the one they are holding, it will be their turn to share what they did at work time.

Small-Group Time *Group 1 — KDIs 21, 22, 23, 26, 28/Group 2 — KDIs 21, 22, 23, 26, 28, 29*

Group 1: Sample Growing Readers Activity

Connect to *Goodnight, Gorilla*: What Is in Your House and in the Zoo?

Quick Plan:

- Teacher and children examine and discuss the pictures.
- Children find and discuss familiar objects and toys in the pictures.
- Children choose one favorite object from the pictures.

(See pp. 162–165 for complete activity and materials.)

Group 2: Sample Growing Readers Activity

Learn Nursery Rhymes: Recall "Humpty Dumpty" and Other Level 1 Nursery Rhymes

Quick Plan:

- Children guess nursery rhymes from pictures.
- Children guess nursery rhymes from actions.
- Children guess nursery rhymes from object words.

(See pp. 170–173 for complete activity and materials.)

Day 15

Large-Group Time
KDIs 16, 18, 42

Silent Moves — Visual Processing

Materials: Classroom song book

(*Note:* For information on why visual processing is important to children's development, see p. 101.)

Step 1: Sing the "We're gonna shake, shake, shake" song until all children have joined; then sing one more verse and end by having everyone sit down on the floor. Bring out the song book with two sticky notes attached to it, each having a child's name and letter link symbol written on it. Tell the class that today these two children will each choose a song from the song book. As these children are picking out their songs, you may want to tap a steady beat on your knees with the rest of the children and chant, "I wonder what they'll pick, I wonder what they'll pick?" Put the song book aside.

Step 2: Make direct eye contact with the few children who are there and motion "watch me" (you can do this by mouthing or whispering those words and/or pointing to your eyes and then pointing to yourself). Begin a series of silent moves, stopping after each for children to respond to what they are seeing by imitating your moves. Below are some examples of moves to make.

- Raise both arms above your head. Watch for all children to do this, then stop.
- Put one hand on your lap. Watch for all children to do this, then stop.
- Put your other hand on your lap. Watch for all children to do this, then stop.
- Make your hands "crawl" (using your fingers) down from your lap to your toes. Watch for all children to do this, then stop.
- Put one hand on your tummy. Watch for all children to do this, then stop.
- Put your other hand on your tummy. Watch for all children to do this, then stop.
- Bend one knee. Watch for all children to do this, then stop.
- Bend your other knee. Watch for all children to do this, then stop.

Continue in this fashion, stopping after each significant movement. Depending on how much time this takes, you may want to choose a child to be the one to lead the movements, with stops after each one, as other children follow along and imitate. Allow many children to be leaders as the activity unfolds.

Step 3: When you are ready to finish the large-group time, engage children in one last movement sequence. Then, without saying anything, model a way to walk to the next activity in your daily routine.

Other Ideas
Outside Time — KDIs 12, 45/Meal Conversations — KDIs 6, 12

Outside Time
As you **play and interact** with the children, consider playing the "I Spy" game outside. For example, while you are digging in the sandbox, you might start with something children can easily see. ("I spy something yellow.") Then spy things farther away. Give children hints until they get the answer ("It's something yellow, you can dig with it, it's close to Ava'a foot — Yes! It's the shovel!") Once children are comfortable with the game, they might want to be the leader and give clues.

Meal Conversations
During the meal, **converse with children** about stories that they like. This could be stories from books or stories they have heard. Invite children to recall and talk about the characters in the books and what the characters do.

Home-School Connections
Share this idea with the children's family members:

When it is time for bed, ask your child to be the "leader." You can do this by telling him to decide how you will both walk to bed, and then follow his directions. He may want to wave his hands, walk "wiggly," or march. Make comments like "You are the leader and I am following you."

Day 15

Observations

Record what you saw individual children say and do today. You can use the reproducible sheet on page 178 to make your notes.

Follow-Up Ideas

- You can use silent moves (from large-group time) as a transition activity any time you need to engage the children — for example, while they are taking turns washing their hands before a meal, while they are waiting for everyone to join small- or large-group times, and so on.

- Add the carpet squares to your classroom materials.
- Write down your own follow-up ideas, using the reproducible sheet on page 179.

Building on What You've Learned: Week 3 Summary

This week you did the following in your classroom:

- Recorded three observations about children each day (each adult did this)
- Added your own messages to the message board by looking at your observations about children
- Continued to encourage children's choices at large-group time by letting children choose songs from the song book
- Led small-group times that included curriculum content in language and literacy and math
- Led large-group times that included curriculum content in movement and music, language and literacy, and math
- Incorporated science language and thinking in your interactions with children outside

The children were particularly supported in the following areas:

- Continuing to form relationships with adults and children in their classroom
- Expressing their plans, choices, and intentions
- Participating in activities that supported their development in the curriculum content areas of
    - *Approaches to Learning*
    - *Social and Emotional Development*
    - *Physical Development and Health*
    - *Language, Literacy, and Communication*
    - *Mathematics*
    - *Creative Arts*
    - *Science and Technology*
    - *Social Studies*

You developed your own adult-child interaction skills by using these HighScope interaction strategies (new strategies for this week appear in bolder type):

- Offering children comfort and contact
    - Looking for children in need of comfort and contact
    - Offering reassuring physical contact
    - Offering simple acknowledgments
    - Acknowledging children's feelings
- Participating in children's play
    - Joining play on children's level
    - Playing in parallel with children
    - Using comments and observations about what you saw children doing as openings to enter play
    - Looking for natural openings to begin to play with children
        - Considering the types of play you observed (exploratory, pretend, constructive, or games) before engaging with children
    - Playing as a partner, letting children retain control
- **Conversing with children**
    - **Looking for natural opportunities for conversation**
    - **Responding to children's conversational leads**
- **Encouraging children's problem solving**
    - Referring one child to another

Learn More About...*Recording Observations*

Observations of children (also called *anecdotes*) are a meaningful source of information about children's development and interests. They help adults understand how classroom activities and materials are supporting children's growth, and they are useful to share with families.

Collecting observations about children is part of what HighScope adults do in the classroom; it integrates what they learn about children's needs and interests into their teaching practice. Sometimes adults think that to collect observations they should be removed from children's activities. This is not true! While you interact with children, supporting their play and learning, you can also jot down a few simple sentences about specific things children say and do. Here are a few simple strategies to get you started:

- **Use abbreviations** (for example, the child's initials, HA for house area, SGT for small-group time).
- **Have plenty of note-taking materials on hand** (small pad of paper, sticky notes, index cards, a device for using OnlineCOR Mobile, or whatever works for you and your coteacher).

- **When recording observations, try to write them objectively.** Focus on what the child did or said; be factual and specific. You might find this format helpful:

Beginning — Date the observation occurred. Write down when (during which part of the daily routine) it happened and where it happened (the area of the room). For example, "2/15 At work time, in the block area."

Middle — Write down what the child did and said. Use quotes to document the child's exact language.

End — When applicable, state the outcome.

You may also find it useful to note down the COR Advantage item illustrated in your observation.

For more information on recording observations, see pages 14–15, in the introduction to this book.

Chapter 4
The Fourth Week

Getting Ready: Week 4 Overview

Goals for the Fourth Week
- Record a minimum of four observations about children per day (each adult does this).
- Use problem-solving techniques when conflicts arise in the classroom.

Things to Keep in Mind This Week
- Be sure to read each activity plan ahead of time so you will know what materials you need to prepare.
- Continue to add song cards to the classroom song book, use the sign-in sheets, use transition songs, add your ideas for messages to the children based on your observations.
- See "Learn More About…" on p. 107 for information on using problem-solving with children.

Daily Routine
- Prepare a large, folded-paper book, with a page for each child, to use at recall time on Days 19 and 20. See the recall-time plans for those days for details.
- On Friday, add this to the message board: Two simply drawn images of the school with a red circle and diagonal slash over them — the universal "no" symbol. Write *2 no school days* and help the children interpret the drawings. Remind them that they will stay home for two days and then come back to school.

After Children Leave for the Day
- Record your observations of children and jot down any ideas you want to follow up on.
- Read tomorrow's lesson plans to see what preparations you will need to make before the children arrive.

Some Reminders for This Week				
Monday (Day 16)	**Tuesday** (Day 17)	**Wednesday** (Day 18)	**Thursday** (Day 19)	**Friday** (Day 20)
Group 1: Name and letter-link spinner for planning time Family note home: Blank paper instead of coloring books	Group 2: Name and letter-link spinner for planning time. "Muffet" and "Spider" nametags for large-group time	Add large tubes and small balls to outside time materials (see "Other Ideas" in Day 18)	Group 2: Recall book Family note home: Foil for child to play with	Group 1: Recall book Family note home: Bubbles

DAY 16

Curriculum Content — Key Developmental Indicators (KDIs)*

1. Initiative
2. Planning
4. Problem solving
6. Reflection
11. Community
12. Building relationships
13. Cooperative play
18. Body awareness
21. Comprehension
22. Speaking
23. Vocabulary
24. Phonological awareness
25. Alphabetic knowledge
26. Reading
29. Writing
35. Spatial awareness
36. Measuring
40. Art
43. Pretend play
44. Appreciating the arts
45. Observing
47. Experimenting
48. Predicting
49. Drawing conclusions
51. Natural and physical world

*See the KDIs listed under individual activities.

Greeting Time
KDIs 12, 24, 25, 26, 29

Adult 2: Greet children at the door. When everyone has arrived, join the children and Adult 1 reading books.

Adult 1: Have about 10 books spread out on the floor. Read books with children. (*Note:* This should last no more than 15 minutes.) Sing a simple transitional song.

Message Board
Draw your daily routine symbol for cleanup time, write the word *cleanup*, tape the song card for "Old McDonald Had a Farm" to the board, write "3?" "4?" "5?" "6?" and help children read this message that for cleanup time they will play a guessing game called "How Many Songs Will It Take to Clean Up?" See "Cleanup Time" in this lesson plan for a full description.

Create your own message.

Planning Time
Group 1 — KDI 2/Group 2 — KDI 2

Group 1: Name and Letter-Link-Symbol Spinner
Ahead of time, make a circle out of cardboard and divide it into sections (one section for each child in your group). Put a child's name and letter link symbol in each one of the sections. Attach a spinner (for example, a cardboard arrow attached with something like a brass-plated fastener) to the center of the circle. At planning time, children can take turns spinning the spinner, and when it lands on their name, it is their turn to plan.

Group 2: Simon Says
Play a version of Simon says, using the classroom areas as a way to have children share their plans. For example, you might say, "Simon says if you are going to play in the block area today, put your hand on your nose." Then ask those children who want to play in the block area to put their hands on their nose and say what they want to do. Those children can leave and go play as you do Simon says for another area: "Simon says if you are going to play in the house area, put your fingers on your tummy." Repeat the process until everyone has shared.

Work Time
KDIs 1, 12, 13, 21 22, 23, 40, 43

Continue to **work on conversing with children as a partner.** When you converse with a child,

- Stick to the topic the child wants to talk about.
- Make comments (instead of asking a lot of questions). This allows the child to continue talking without feeling pressured for a response.
- Wait for the child to respond before taking another conversational turn.
- Keep your comments fairly brief.
- If a child doesn't want to converse with you during this time, be respectful of this choice. You may want to move on to another child who does want some support.

Day 16

Cleanup Time
KDI 11

After giving the usual 10- and 5-minute warning signals, tell the children that today everyone will play a guessing game for cleanup time called "How Many Songs Will It Take?" Explain that everyone will sing "Old McDonald Had a Farm" and guess how many verses it will take for the cleanup to be completed. Next, you might say, "Old McDonald has lots of animals that we can sing about in the song. I wonder how many animals it will take us to sing about before we are done cleaning up?"

Recall Time
Group 1 — KDI 6/Group 2 — KDI 6

Group 1: Recall Soup
Tell children that today everyone will make a "recall soup." Set a large pot (or a bucket could be substituted) in the middle of the table and ask a child to go get something small he used at work time to add to the soup. Ask the child to share what he did and then add the item to the pot and give the "soup" a stir. Repeat this process for the other children in your group. At the end, you can review with children the ingredients of your soup.

Group 2: Chairs and Sticky Notes
Ahead of time, write the classroom area symbols on sticky notes. At recall, ask the children to help you put the chairs in a row. Place a sticky note with an area symbol on each of the chair backs. With everyone sitting on the floor, invite the children, one at a time, to go sit in the chair that represents where they played and to share something they did there. Repeat for the other children in your group.

Day 16

Small-Group Time *Group 1 — KDIs 36, 45, 47, 48, 49, 51/Group 2 — KDIs 4, 23, 35*

Group 1: Tube Tunnels

Materials:

For each child, provide

- Wrapping paper or paper towel tubes, some full length and some cut half-length; make sure each child has at least one long and one short tube
- Matchbox cars — at least two per child

Beginning: Show the children the tubes and encourage them to explore and describe them. If no one comments that the tubes are different lengths, point this out to the children. Then give them the cars and tell them the cars will fit in the tubes. Let the children experiment by putting the cars in the tubes. Then tell the children that you wonder how fast the cars can go through the different lengths of tubes. Demonstrate by lifting a long tube and a short tube a small amount at one end and putting a car through each. Ask the children to note which one came out first, which was faster, and how far they each went when they came out the other end.

Middle: Encourage the children to explore different combinations of tube length and position (angle from the floor). Vary the position of the tubes from flat on the floor, to tilted at a small angle, to tilted at a steep angle. Ask the children what they could do make the cars move faster or slower or at the same rate. Together with the children, devise a system for marking how far across the floor the cars roll when they exit the tubes. Encourage the children to observe speed and distance relative to the length and position (angle) of the tube. **Support their observations and extend their vocabulary** with time, distance, and position words such as *fast(er), slow(er), speedy, near, far, angle, steep, flat, raised,* and so on.

End: After a three-minute warning, ask the children to help you return the cars to their container and place the tubes on the table. Ask the children to roll their bodies to the next activity.

Group 2: Dressing Babies or Animals

Materials:

For each child, provide

- A small stuffed animal or doll
- Fabric scraps of various sizes, colors, and textures
- String or yarn lengths
- Masking tape

Beginning: Give each child an animal or doll. Tell the children that these animals/babies want some clothes. Invite children to take their fabric and help their animal or baby get dressed.

Middle: **Comment on what you see children doing.** Use words like *cover, wrap, around, under, sleeve,* and *tie* to describe children's actions. As you move from child to child, **help with any problem solving by referring children to each other.** ("Joseph figured out how to make the yarn stay. You could ask him how he solved the problem.")

End: After a three-minute warning, ask the children to help return any remaining fabric pieces to the bin. Ask the children to help you find a place for the fabric bin in the art area, commenting that they might want to use more fabric at work time tomorrow. Then ask the children to dance to the next part of the daily routine.

Day 16

Large-Group Time

KDI 18

Popcorn!!!

Materials:

- Parachute or large sheet
- Sponges or paper towel balls
- Lively music

Step 1: Sing the "We're gonna shake, shake, shake" song until all children have joined; then sing one more verse and end by having everyone sit down on the floor. Ask children if they've ever made popcorn. Listen as they share their experiences.

Step 2: Spread out the parachute and ask each child to hold on to the handle or the edge. Tell the children to pretend that the parachute is a giant popcorn popper and that you would like them to help you make popcorn. Place many paper towel balls in the middle of the parachute as the "popcorn." Depending on the type of popcorn popper children are familiar with, pretend to add oil or turn on the heat. Put on the music selection and have the children begin shaking the parachute — slowly at first, to represent the sizzling popcorn before it pops.

Step 3: As the music intensifies, the children may begin to increase their shaking so the paper balls pop up in the air. When the balls fly out of the parachute, encourage children to put them back in.

Step 4: Encourage the children to slow their shaking as the music calms down. With children's assistance, gather up the parachute and have the children put the "popcorn" in a separate basket. Tell the children you will leave them in the _____ area for use at work time. Tell the children they can pretend to be popcorn as they move to the next activity.

Other Ideas *Outside Time — KDIs 12, 21, 22, 23/Meal Conversations — KDIs 6, 12, 44*

Outside Time

As you work and play with children outside, continue to **converse with them as a partner.** When you converse with a child,

- Stick to the topic the child wants to talk about.
- Make comments (instead of asking a lot of questions). This allows the child to continue talking without feeling pressured for a response.
- Wait for the child to respond before taking another conversational turn.
- Keep your comments fairly brief.
- If a child doesn't want to converse with you during this time, be respectful of this choice. You may want to move on to another child who does want some support.

Meal Conversations

During the meal, invite children to look around the classroom at their artwork. Talk with them about what media was used to make the artwork. ("I wonder what Yolanda used to make her picture." "How do you think Brent got the beads to stick to his cardboard?") Be sure to **pause and listen** to children's thoughts and comments. **Make extending comments** to help children think about other ways to use materials. ("The beads are all gone. I wonder what else I could use with the glue if I wanted to do a picture like Brent's?")

Home-School Connections

Share the following information with the children's family members:

Instead of buying your child a coloring book, considering giving him or her blank paper to draw on. Any blank paper you have at home will do (including the back of recycled office paper). Also provide crayons or markers. Your child can then make his or her own pictures and drawings. When your child has finished drawing, ask him or her if you can write words on the picture(s) and write the words as your child says them. Read these words back to your child. Display the picture where your child can see it.

Observations

Record what you saw individual children say and do today. You can use the reproducible sheet on page 178 to make your notes.

Follow-Up Ideas

Write down your own follow-up ideas, using the reproducible sheet on page 179.

DAY 17

Curriculum Content — Key Developmental Indicators (KDIs)*

1. Initiative	22. Speaking	36. Measuring
2. Planning	23. Vocabulary	40. Art
4. Problem solving	24. Phonological awareness	43. Pretend play
6. Reflection	25. Alphabetic knowledge	45. Observing
11. Community	26. Reading	47. Experimenting
12. Building relationships	29. Writing	48. Predicting
13. Cooperative play	32. Counting	49. Drawing conclusions
21. Comprehension	35. Spatial awareness	51. Natural and physical world

*See the KDIs listed under individual activities.

Greeting Time
KDIs 12, 24, 25, 26, 29

Adult 1: Greet children at the door. When everyone has arrived, join the children and Adult 2 reading books.

Adult 2: Have about 10 books spread out on the floor. Read books with children. (*Note:* This should last no more than 15 minutes.) Sing a simple transitional song.

Message Board
Draw your daily routine symbol for cleanup time, write the word *cleanup,* tape the song card for "Old McDonald Had a Farm" to the board, write "3?" "4?" "5?" "6?" and help children read this message that again for cleanup time they'll play the guessing game "How Many Songs Will It Take to Clean Up?" See "Cleanup Time" in this lesson plan for a full description.

Create your own message.

Planning Time
Group 1 — KDI 2/Group 2 — KDIs 2, 29

Group 1: Simon Says
Play a version of Simon says, using the classroom areas as a way to have children share their plans. For example, you might say, "Simon says if you are going to play in the block area today, put your hand on your nose." Then ask those children who want to play in the block area to put their hands on their nose and say what they want to do. Those children can leave and go play as you do Simon says for another area: "Simon says if you are going to play in the house area, put your fingers on your tummy." Repeat the process until everyone has shared.

Group 2: Name and Letter-Link-Symbol Spinner
Ahead of time, make a circle out of cardboard and divide it into sections (one section for each child in your group). Put a child's name and letter link symbol in each one of the sections. Attach a spinner (for example, a cardboard arrow attached with something like a brass-plated fastener) to the center of the circle. At planning time, children can take turns spinning the spinner, and when it lands on their name, it is their turn to plan.

Work Time
KDIs 1, 12, 13, 21, 22, 23, 40, 43

Continue to work on conversing with children as a partner. When you converse with a child,

- Stick to the topic the child wants to talk about.
- Make comments (instead of asking a lot of questions). This allows the child to continue talking without feeling pressured for a response.
- Wait for the child to respond before taking another conversational turn.
- Keep your comments fairly brief.
- If a child doesn't want to converse with you during this time, be respectful of this choice. You may want to move on to another child who does want some support.

Day 17

Cleanup Time

KDI 11

After giving the usual 10- and 5-minute warning signals, tell the children that today everyone will play a guessing game for cleanup time called "How Many Songs Will It Take?" Next, you might say, "Yesterday we sang about six animals on Old McDonald's farm during cleanup. Do you think it will take us more animals or fewer animals than yesterday?"

Recall Time

Group 1 — KDIs 6, 29/Group 2 — KDI 6

Group 1: Chairs and Sticky Notes
Ahead of time, write the classroom area symbols on sticky notes. At recall, ask the children to help you put the chairs in a row. Place a sticky note with an area symbol on each of the chair backs. With everyone sitting on the floor, invite the children, one at a time, to go sit in the chair that represents where they played and to share something they did there. Repeat for the other children in your group.

Group 2: Recall Soup
Tell children that today everyone will make a "recall soup." Set a large pot (or a bucket could be substituted) in the middle of the table and ask a child to go get something small she used at work time to add to the soup. Ask the child to share what she did and then add the item to the pot and give the "soup" a stir. Repeat this process for the other children in your group. At the end, you can review with children the ingredients of your soup.

Day 17

Small-Group Time *Group 1 — KDIs 4, 23, 35/Group 2 — KDIs 36, 45, 47, 48, 49, 51*

Group 1: Dressing Babies or Animals

Materials:

For each child, provide

- A small stuffed animal or doll
- Fabric scraps of various sizes, colors, and textures
- String or yarn lengths
- Masking tape

Beginning: Give each child an animal or doll. Tell the children that these animals/babies want some clothes. Invite children to take their fabric and help their animal or baby get dressed.

Middle: **Comment on what you see children doing.** Use words like *cover, wrap, around, under, sleeve,* and *tie* to describe children's actions. As you move from child to child, **help with any problem-solving by referring children to each other.** ("Joseph figured out how to make the yarn stay. You could ask him how he solved the problem.")

End: After a three-minute warning, ask the children to help return any remaining fabric pieces to the bin. Ask the children to help you find a place for the fabric bin in the art area, commenting that they might want to use more fabric at work time tomorrow. Then ask the children to dance to the next part of the daily routine.

Group 2: Tube Tunnels

Materials:

For each child, provide

- Wrapping paper or paper towel tubes, some full length and some cut half length; make sure each child has at least one long and one short tube
- Matchbox cars — at least two per child

Beginning: Show the children the tubes and encourage them to explore and describe them. If no one comments that the tubes are different lengths, point this out to the children. Then give them the cars and tell them the cars will fit in the tubes. Let the children experiment by putting the cars in the tubes. Then tell the children that you wonder how fast the cars can go through the different lengths of tubes. Demonstrate by lifting a long tube and short tube a small amount at one end and putting a car through each. Ask the children to note which one came out first, which was faster, and how far they each went when they came out the other end.

Middle: Encourage the children to explore different combinations of tube length and position (angle from the floor). Vary the position of the tubes from flat on the floor to tilted at a small angle to tilted at a steep angle. Ask the children what they could do make the cars move faster or slower or at the same rate. Together with the children, devise a system for marking how far across the floor the cars roll when they exit the tubes. Encourage the children to observe speed and distance relative to the length and position (angle) of the tube. **Support their observations and extend their vocabulary** with time, distance, and position words such as *fast(er), slow(er), speedy, near, far, angle, steep, flat, raised,* and so on.

End: After a three-minute warning, ask the children to help you return the cars to their container and place the tubes on the table. Ask the children to roll their bodies to the next activity.

Day 17

Large-Group Time
KDIs 24, 25, 43

Songs and a Nursery Rhyme

Materials:

- Classroom song book
- Large pillow
- Bowl
- Spoon
- "Muffet" and "Spider" nametags, each on a string

Step 1: Sing the "We're gonna shake, shake, shake" song until all children have joined; then sing one more verse and end by having everyone sit down on the floor. Bring out the song book with a sticky note having one child's name and letter link symbol written on it. Sing the song that this child chooses.

Step 2: Slowly recite the nursery rhyme "Little Miss Muffet" and ask children to listen for rhyming words while they say the poem with you. Ask children to tell you the rhymes they heard. You can also talk about the words *tuffet, curds,* and *whey,* explaining what they mean.

Step 3: In this step, the group will act out the story. Start by putting the large pillow in the middle of the large-group space as the tuffet. Choose a child to wear the Little Miss (or Mr.) Muffet nametag, sit on the pillow, and pretend to eat with the bowl and spoon. Choose another child to wear the spider nametag and sneak up behind Little Miss Muffet. Little Miss Muffet can then run away. Be aware that sometimes Little Miss Muffet may not run away. For example, Little Miss Muffet may start feeding the spider, may laugh at the spider, may scare the spider back, and so forth. Accept whatever the children decide to do.

Step 4: After many children have had turns as Miss Muffet or the spider, indicate it is the last time to say the rhyme. Dismiss children from large-group time by using their names in a variation of the rhyme:

Along came a spider

And sat down beside her

And frightened Micah *and* Vishnu (use children's names) *away!*

Other Ideas
Outside Time — KDIs 12, 36, 49/Meal Conversations — KDIs 6, 12, 32

Outside Time
Add large tubes (such as gutter flex-spouts from a home improvement store or large packing tubes) and small balls (such as tennis balls or rubber balls) to your materials outside.

Meal Conversations
During the meal, chat with the children about how many people (or animals) live in their home. If possible, once the meal is well underway, you may want to bring out a simple chart that you made ahead of time, with children's names and letter link symbols down one side and a simple stick figure drawing of people (or animals) along the top. After children have shared, you could put tally marks showing how many people (or animals) live in their home. Children may want to count and compare the tally marks.

Observations

Record what you saw individual children say and do today. You can use the reproducible sheet on page 178 to make your notes.

Follow-Up Ideas

- Add the fabric pieces from Group 1's small-group time to the art area.
- Add the "Muffet" and "Spider" nametags from large-group time to the book area so children can reenact the story during work time.
- Write down your own follow-up ideas, using the reproducible sheet on page 179.

DAY 18

Curriculum Content — Key Developmental Indicators (KDIs)*

1. Initiative
2. Planning
6. Reflection
11. Community
12. Building relationships
13. Cooperative play
16. Gross-motor skills
18. Body awareness

21. Comprehension
22. Speaking
23. Vocabulary
24. Phonological awareness
25. Alphabetic knowledge
26. Reading
29. Writing

34. Shapes
35. Spatial awareness
40. Art
42. Movement
43. Pretend play

*See the KDIs listed under individual activities.

Greeting Time
KDIs 12, 24, 25, 26, 29

Adult 2: Greet children at the door. When everyone has arrived, join the children and Adult 1 reading books.

Adult 1: Have about 10 books spread out on the floor. Read books with children. (*Note:* This should last no more than 15 minutes.) Sing a simple transitional song.

Message Board
Tape several fabric scraps to the message board and draw your area symbol for the art area. Help children read this message that the fabric that Group 1 used for small-group time yesterday has been added to the art area. They might want to remember this when they make their plans for work time.

Create your own message.

Planning Time
Group 1 — KDI 2/Group 2 — KDI 2

Group 1: Magnetic Letters

Materials:

- Area cards
- Cookie sheet or other metal surface
- Magnetic letters

Ahead of time, attach the area cards to a cookie sheet or other metal surface. Place a variety of magnetic letters on the table, including the first letter of each child's name. At planning time, individually ask each child to find a letter from his or her name and place it on the area in which he or she would like to work. **Extend children's plans** by asking them about what they will use and who they might play with. *Note:* Children might choose any letter from their name — not just the first letter — and this is fine.

Group 2: Pegs and Pegboards

Materials:

- Area cards
- Pegboard and pegs

Place each area card on a pegboard. Give children pegs and ask them to put them on the pegboard with the area card where they are going to play. If they are making several plans, they may need several pegs. Ask children to share their ideas about what they are going to do. If they've made several plans, talk to them about what they will do first, next, and so forth. After a child has finished planning, he can leave the group and get started on work time.

Day 18

Work Time
KDIs 1, 12, 13, 21, 22, 23, 40, 43

Continue to **work on conversing with children as a partner.** When you converse with a child,

- Stick to the topic the child wants to talk about.
- Make comments (instead of asking a lot of questions). This allows the child to continue talking without feeling pressured for a response.
- Wait for the child to respond before taking another conversational turn.
- Keep your comments fairly brief.
- If a child doesn't want to converse with you during this time, be respectful of this. You may want to move on to another child who does want some support.

Cleanup Time
KDI 11

After giving the usual 10- and 5-minute warning signals, tell the children that today everyone will play "How Many Songs Will It Take?" You can either sing "Old McDonald Had a Farm" again or another song with verses, such as "The Ants Go Marching One by One."

Recall Time
Group 1 — KDI 6/Group 2 — KDI 6

Group 1: "Hot Potato"
Use something soft, such as a beanbag or a sponge, as the hot potato. Pass the hot potato from person to person until the adult says "Stop!" Then the child holding the hot potato can take a turn recalling. Continue the game until everyone has had a chance to recall.

Group 2: Camera
Use an old camera or a box made to look like a camera and ask children to pretend to take a picture of where they played. Include the other children while you ask them for details, such as who else played there, did anyone see what she was doing, who else used those materials, and so forth.

Day 18

Small-Group Time *Group 1 — KDIs 23, 26/Group 2 — KDIs 23, 34, 35, 40*

Group 1: Bubbles! Bubbles! Bubbles!

Materials:

For each child, provide

- A small bowl of water with nontoxic liquid dish soap added
- A straw
- A smock
- Optionally, a tray for each child or newspaper to cover the table (to assist with cleanup)

Beginning: Tell children that for today's small-group time, they'll need to put on a smock. Next, ask children to think about an experience they might have had with blowing (for example, blowing out a birthday candle, blowing dandelion seeds, blowing up a balloon). Together, you all might try taking a deep breath and blowing. Give the children their bowls and straws and invite them to try blowing some more by blowing through the straw.

Middle: **Observe children** as they begin to explore blowing. Some children may need your encouragement to blow (rather than suck in). **Move around the table from child to child.** Notice their excitement as they make bubbles. You can **use descriptive number language** to support their discoveries, including words such as *more, overflowing, enormous, few, several* and *multiple*. Use your bowl and straw to blow bubbles along with the children. This experience might give you other ideas of things to comment on with the children.

End: After a three-minute warning, ask the children to help you clean up by dumping their bubbles in the trash or sink and stacking their bowls. They may also need to wash their hands if they are sticky. Ask children to "blow" themselves to the next part of the daily routine.

Group 2: Foil Sculptures

Materials:

For each child, provide

- Aluminum foil pieces

Additionally, you'll need

- A large piece of paper
- A marker

Beginning: Give each child a piece of aluminum foil to investigate. Write down on the large piece of paper the comments children make about the foil (for example, "It's shiny"; "It's flat"; "It crinkles"). Manipulate a piece of foil the same way you observe children handling the foil.

Middle: Comment on the different shapes the foil is taking. Use words like *twist, form, bend,* and *squeeze* to describe what children are doing. Introduce the word *sculpture* to describe an object that is made by molding, bending, or twisting materials into a specific shape. Ask children if they can *sculpt* their foil into something. Offer children more foil when needed. Twist your foil into a geometric shape and **comment** on what you did. **Listen to children's comments.**

They may say things like

"I turned it into a ball."

"You can squish it smaller."

"My ball is the same size as yours."

"I put a little ball on top of a big ball."

If possible, use a sheet of paper to write down the words you hear children using to describe their work with the foil (such as *squishy, shiny, wrinkly,* and so on). However, don't let creating the list get in the way of interacting with individual children!

End: Give children an opportunity to show each other what they did with the foil. Reread what you have written on the paper and ask the children to give you additional words to describe what they learned about foil that you could add to the list. Display the foil sculptures on a classroom shelf.

Day 18

Large-Group Time

KDIs 16, 18, 42

Sliding/Skating to Music

Materials:

- Two pieces of waxed paper for each child and adult
- Medium-tempo music with no words

Note: Be sure to do this activity on carpeting so the waxed paper will slide.

Step 1: Sing the "We're gonna shake, shake, shake" song until all children have joined; then sing one more verse and end by having everyone sit down on the floor. Introduce the words *skating* and *sliding* to the children. Here is a sample opening:

Adult: "What are some things that skate or slide?"

Child 1: "My uncle skates — he's got these shoes with wheels on them."

Child 2: "Sometimes you fall when you slide on wet grass."

Child 3: "In baseball they slide."

Child 4: "I saw skating on the TV — she was wearing a sparkly dress."

Adult: "You know lots of ways to slide and skate. Today we are going to use these pieces of wax paper so that we can practice sliding and skating. When you get one, try some ways of sliding or skating."

Allow time for exploration with this new material.

Step 2: As children explore using the waxed paper for sliding and skating on the carpet, **join children** in trying out their unique ideas. **Encourage language** concerning the details of their actions:

Adult: "Matthew, I want to try it your way — can you tell me what to do?"

Matthew: "You gotta put the paper under your knee."

Adult: "I am putting it under my knee like you — how do I slide?"

Matthew: "Push with this one." (The adult touches his other knee.)

Adult: "It works; I am doing it like you, Matthew." (The adult slides beside Matthew.)

Shonyah: "I can skate this way." (She shows the adult how she is pushing herself sideways across the carpet.)

Adult: "What could we say about Shonyah's way?"

Nyah: "She is going side to side; I wanna try that!" (Other children copy Shonyah's way of sliding.)

Step 3: After much **acknowledgment of ideas and following children's leads,** bring the movements to a natural stop. Tell children that you will be playing music on the CD player and that they should pick their most favorite way to slide or skate as they listen to the music. Participate with the children, following their ways to skate and slide.

Step 4: As the music comes to an end (or the children show you they are ready to move on), ask the children to skate or slide to the next part of the daily routine. Upon arrival, they can throw their waxed paper in the trash can or give it to the adult.

Other Ideas

Meal Conversations — KDIs 6, 12, 23

Meal Conversations

During the meal, **converse with children** about what they notice about the food they are eating. Children may share about the taste, the texture, what it looks like, if they have it at home, and so forth. You can use vocabulary words like *sweet, salty, sour, tangy, moist, crunchy, squishy, spicy, juicy, warm, chilled, baked, sautéed,* and so forth.

Observations

Record what you saw individual children say and do today. You can use the reproducible sheet on page 178 to make your notes.

Follow-Up Ideas

- Add pieces of foil and waxed paper to the art area.
- Write down your own follow-up ideas, using the reproducible sheet on page 179.

97

DAY 19

Curriculum Content — Key Developmental Indicators (KDIs)*

1. Initiative
2. Planning
6. Reflection
11. Community
12. Building relationships
13. Cooperative play
16. Gross-motor skills
21. Comprehension
22. Speaking
23. Vocabulary
24. Phonological awareness
25. Alphabetic knowledge
26. Reading
29. Writing
34. Shapes
35. Spatial awareness
40. Art
42. Movement
43. Pretend play

*See the KDIs listed under individual activities.

Greeting Time
KDIs 12, 24, 25, 26, 29

Adult 1: Greet children at the door. When everyone has arrived, join the children and Adult 2 reading books.

Adult 2: Have about 10 books spread out on the floor. Read books with children. (*Note:* This should last no more than 15 minutes.) Sing a simple transitional song.

Message Board
Tape a piece of foil and a piece of waxed paper to the message board and draw your area symbol for the art area. Help children read this message that the foil and waxed paper have been added to the art area.

Bring out the classroom song book with two sticky notes attached to it, each having a child's name and letter link symbol written on it. Help children read this message that these two children will select songs to sing at large-group time. These children may want to take their sticky note and put it on the song they'll sing.

Planning Time
Group 1 — KDI 2/Group 2 — KDIs 2, 25

Group 1: Cell Phones
Give a child an old cell phone and have one for yourself. "Call" the child and converse about where he will work and what he will do. Note that children may want to tell you their "number" to call. They will usually give just a single number — often their age! For example, a child might say, "Beth, I'm 4. Call me on my 4 number!" After the child has shared his plan, he can get started. Repeat until all children have planned.

Group 2: Magnetic Letters

Materials:

- Area cards
- Cookie sheet or other metal surface
- Magnetic letters

Ahead of time, attach the area cards to a cookie sheet or other metal surface. Place a variety of magnetic letters on the table, including the first letter of each child's name. At planning time, individually ask each child to find a letter from his or her name and place it on the area in which he or she would like to work. **Extend children's plans** by asking them about what they will use and who they might play with. *Note:* Children might choose any letter from their name — not just the first letter — and this is fine.

Day 19

Work Time
KDIs 1, 12, 13, 40, 43

As you play with children, **be mindful of the questions that you ask, and ask questions sparingly.** Too many closed questions (those that have a right or wrong answer) can actually inhibit children's conversation, but the right *kind* of question can stimulate children's thinking. For example, avoid questions like "What color is this?" or "Which one is longer?" or "How many do I have?" Instead, ask questions about the children's thought process. For example, "How can you tell?" or "What do you think made that happen?" or "What do you think would happen if…?"

Cleanup Time
KDI 11

After giving the usual 10- and 5-minute warning signals, tell the children that today everyone will play "How Many Songs Will It Take?" again. Use your observations about children to choose a song that they will enjoy singing (*Tip:* Choose a song without hand motions or you'll find the children doing the motions instead of cleaning up!)

Recall Time
Group 1 — KDI 6/Group 2 — KDIs 6, 21, 22

Group 1: Camera
Use an old camera or a box made to look like a camera and ask children to pretend to take a picture of where they played. Include the other children while you ask them for details, such as who else played there, did anyone see what she was doing, who else used those materials, and so forth.

Group 2: Group Recall Story

Materials: Recall storybook (see below)

Ahead of time, make a large book out of folded paper (be sure to allow a page for each child in your group). Write these words on the cover: "Recall Story: Once Upon a Work Time…." Inside, write the names and letter link symbols of all the children on each page, leaving room for the children to share what they did. For example:

    Susanna ☼…

    Henry ♥…

At recall time, share the book with the children. Tell them you will write down the words that they tell you for their recall. As children share, fill in their part of the story. After all have contributed, read the whole story together from beginning to end. (*Note:* If you run out of time, you may wish to reread the story for meal conversations.)

Day 19

Small-Group Time

Group 1 — KDIs 23, 34, 35, 40/Group 2 — KDI 40

Group 1: Foil Sculptures

Materials:

For each child, provide

- Aluminum foil pieces

Additionally, you'll need

- A large piece of paper
- A marker

Beginning: Give each child a piece of aluminum foil to investigate. Write down on the large piece of paper the comments children make about the foil (for example, "It's shiny"; "It's flat"; "It crinkles"). Manipulate a piece of foil the same way you observe children handling the foil.

Middle: Comment on the different shapes the foil is taking. Use words like *twist, form, bend,* and *squeeze* to describe what children are doing. Introduce the word *sculpture* to describe an object that is made by molding, bending, or twisting materials into a specific shape. Ask children if they can *sculpt* their foil into something. Offer children more foil when needed. Twist your foil into a geometric shape and **comment** on what you did. **Listen to children's comments.** They may say things like

> "I turned it into a ball."
>
> "You can squish it smaller."
>
> "My ball is the same size as yours."
>
> "I put a little ball on top of a big ball."

If possible, use a sheet of paper to write down the words you hear children using to describe their work with the foil (such as *squishy, shiny, wrinkly,* and so on). However, don't let creating the list get in the way of interacting with individual children!

End: Give children an opportunity to show each other what they did with the foil. Reread what you have written on the paper and ask the children to give you additional words to describe what they learned about foil that you could add to the list. Display the foil sculptures on a classroom shelf.

Group 2: Cutting With Scissors

Materials:

For each child, provide a small basket (or box or tub) containing

- Scissors
- Various paper scraps

Beginning: Tell the children that you've got things for them to cut and put together. Give them their baskets and let them explore the materials.

Middle: **Move around the table from child to child,** observing how they respond to the materials. Expect that some children will cut the paper, some children might snip around the edges of the paper, and some children might just use the tape. All of these explorations are fine. Continue to **work on conversing with children as a partner.**

End: Give children a three-minute warning. Ask them to return the scissors, tape, and extra paper scraps to their proper places in the classroom. Tell children they can take their creations home or choose to display them in the classroom.

TIP: Use either visual silent moves (see p. 81) or verbal silent moves (see p. 101) as an on-the-spot **strategy to help with any transition times.** For example, as children are waiting to wash their hands you might say, "Watch what my hands are doing and see if you can do it." Then put your hands on your head and wait until the children copy, then put your hands on your waist and wait until the children copy, and so forth. Once children become familiar with this game, they can take turns as the leader.

Day 19

Large-Group Time

KDIs 16, 42

Silent Moves — Verbal Processing

Materials: Classroom song book

Step 1: Sing the "We're gonna shake, shake, shake" song until all children have joined; then sing one more verse and end by having everyone sit down on the floor. Bring out the song book with two sticky notes on it, each having a different child's name and symbol on it. Tell the class that today these two children will choose a song from the song book. As these children are selecting their songs, you may want to tap a steady beat on your knees with the rest of the children and chant, "I wonder what they'll pick, I wonder what they'll pick?" After the two children have chosen their songs, put the song book aside.

Step 2: Tell children to listen carefully — that you are going to say some things that they can try to do. Give the children one verbal direction for a physical movement but *don't actually do the movement yourself*. Below are examples.

"*Put your two hands in the air.*"

"*Put one hand on your lap.*"

"*Put the other hand on your lap.*"

"*Put both hands on your feet.*"

After you give the verbal directions, watch for children to do the action. Continue in this fashion, stopping after each significant movement. Depending on how much time this takes, you may want to turn the lead over to a child. Choose one child to lead the movements, with stops after each one, as you and the other children follow. Allow many children to be leaders as the activity unfolds.

Step 3: When you are ready to finish the large-group time, engage in one last movement sequence. Then, verbally tell the children to hop to the next activity in your daily routine.

Did You Know...?

Auditory and visual processing, also known as short-term memory, refers to pieces of information taken in by either the auditory or visual areas of the brain. *Processing* refers to how well the brain understands, interprets, or categorizes information. The large-group activities "Silent Moves — Visual Processing" on Day 15 and "Silent Moves — Verbal Processing" on Day 19 help children to exercise their brains in these important ways.

Other Ideas

Meal Conversations — KDI 24

Meal Conversations

During the meal, invite children to make up rhymes for things on the table. For example, you might say, "Let's play a rhyming game while we eat. I will start and then you can join in." Then you might say something like "*Plate, gate* — that sounds the same" or "*Spoon, moon* — that sounds the same." Accept all answers given.

Home-School Connections

Share this idea with the children's family members:

Give your child a piece of aluminium foil to play with. Watch what your child does with the foil and try imitating your child's actions. Remember that it's okay if your child doesn't "make" anything — he or she can just explore crumpling and shaping the foil.

Observations

Record what you saw individual children say and do today. You can use the reproducible sheet on page 178 to make your notes.

Follow-Up Ideas

- You can use "Silent Moves" (from today's large-group time) as a transition activity any time you need to engage the children — for example, while they are waiting for everyone to wash their hands before a meal, waiting for everyone to join small- or large-group times, and so forth.
- Write down your own follow-up ideas, using the reproducible sheet on page 179.

DAY 20

Curriculum Content — Key Developmental Indicators (KDIs)*

1. Initiative
2. Planning
6. Reflection
11. Community
12. Building relationships
13. Cooperative play
22. Speaking
23. Vocabulary
24. Phonological awareness
25. Alphabetic knowledge
26. Reading
29. Writing
36. Measuring
40. Art
41. Music
43. Pretend play
57. History

*See the KDIs listed under individual activities.

Greeting Time — KDIs 12, 24, 25, 26, 29, 57

Adult 2: Greet children at the door. When everyone has arrived, join the children and Adult 1 reading books.

Adult 1: Have about 10 books spread out on the floor. Read books with children. (*Note:* This should last no more than 15 minutes.) Sing a simple transitional song.

Message Board
Bring out the classroom song book with three sticky notes attached to it, each having a child's name and letter link symbol written on it. Help children read this message that these three children will pick songs to sing at large-group time. These children may want to take their sticky note and put it on the song they'll sing.

Draw two simple images of the school with a red circle and diagonal slash over them — the universal "no" symbol. Write *2 no school days* and help the children interpret the drawings. Remind the children that they will stay home for two days and then come back to school.

Planning Time — Group 1 — KDI 2/Group 2 — KDI 2

Group 1: Pegs and Pegboards

Materials:

- Area cards
- Pegboard and pegs

Place each area card on a pegboard. Give children pegs and ask them to put them on the pegboard with the area card where they are going to play. If they are making several plans, they may need several pegs. Ask children to share their ideas about what they are going to do. If they've made several plans, talk to them about what they will do first, next, and so forth. After a child has finished planning, she can leave the group and get started on work time.

Group 2: Cell Phones
Give a child an old cell phone and have one for yourself. "Call" the child and converse about where she will work and what she will do. Note that children may want to tell you their "number" to call. They will usually give just a single number — often their age! For example, a child might say, "Beth, I'm 4. Call me on my 4 number!" After the child has shared her plan, she can get started. Repeat until all children have planned.

Work Time — KDIs 1, 12, 13, 40, 43

As you play with children, **be mindful of the questions that you ask, and ask questions sparingly.** Too many closed question (those that have a right or wrong answer) can actually inhibit children's conversation, but the right *kind* of question can stimulate children's thinking. For example, avoid questions like "What color is this?" or "Which one is longer?" or "How many do I have?" Instead, ask questions about the children's thought process. For example: "How can you tell?" or "What do think made that happen?" or "What do you think would happen if…?"

Day 20

Cleanup Time — KDI 11

After giving the usual 10- and 5-minute warning signals, tell the children that today everyone will play "How Many Songs Will It Take?" again. Use your observations about children to choose a song that they will enjoy singing (*Tip:* choose a song without hand motions or you'll find the children doing the motions instead of cleaning up!)

Recall Time — *Group 1 — KDIs 6, 22/Group 2 — KDI 6*

Group 1: Group Recall Story

Materials: Recall storybook (see below)

Ahead of time, make a large book out of folded paper (be sure to allow a page for each child in your group). Write these words on the cover: "Recall Story: Once Upon a Work Time…." Inside, write the names and letter link symbols of all the children on each page, leaving room for the children to share what they did. For example:

Susanna ☼…

Henry ♥…

At recall time, share the book with the children. Tell them you will write down the words that they tell you for their recall. As children share, fill in their part of the story. After all have contributed, read the whole story together from beginning to end. (*Note:* If you run out of time, you may wish to reread the story for meal conversations.)

Group 2: "Hot Potato"

Use something soft, such as a beanbag or a sponge, as the hot potato. Pass the hot potato from person to person until the adult says "Stop!" Then the child holding the hot potato can take a turn recalling. Continue the game until everyone has had a chance to recall.

Day 20

Small-Group Time

Group 1 — KDI 40/Group 2 — KDIs 23, 36

Group 1: Cutting With Scissors

Materials:

For each child, provide a small basket (or box or tub) containing

- Scissors
- Various paper scraps

Beginning: Tell the children that you've got things for them to cut and put together. Give them their baskets and let them explore the materials.

Middle: **Move around the table from child to child,** observing how they respond to the materials. Expect that some children will cut the paper, some children might snip around the edges of the paper, and some children might use just the tape. All of these explorations are fine. Continue to **work on conversing with children as a partner.**

End: Give children a three-minute warning. Ask them to return the scissors, tape, and extra paper scraps to their proper places in the classroom. Tell the children they can take their creations home or choose to display them in the classroom.

Group 2: Bubbles! Bubbles! Bubbles!

Materials:

For each child, provide

- A small bowl of water with nontoxic liquid dish soap added
- A straw
- A smock
- Optionally, a tray for each child or newspaper to cover the table (to assist with cleanup)

Beginning: Tell children that for today's small-group time, they'll need to put on a smock. Next, ask children to think about an experience they might have had with blowing (for example, blowing out a birthday candle, blowing dandelion seeds, blowing up a balloon). Together, you all might try taking a deep breath and blowing. Give the children their bowls and straws and invite them to try blowing some more by blowing through the straw.

Middle: **Observe children** as they begin to explore blowing. Some children may need your encouragement to blow (rather than suck in). **Move around the table from child to child.** Notice their excitement as they make bubbles. You can **use descriptive number language** to support their discoveries, including words such as *more, overflowing, enormous, few, several,* and *multiple.* Use your bowl and straw to blow bubbles along with the children. This experience might give you other ideas of things to comment on with the children.

End: After a three-minute warning, ask the children to help you clean up by dumping their bubbles in the trash or sink and stacking their bowls. They may also need to wash their hands if they are sticky. Ask children to "blow" themselves to the next part of the daily routine.

Day 20

Large-Group Time
KDI 41

Singing Songs

Materials: Classroom song book

Step 1: Sing the "We're gonna shake, shake, shake" song until all children have joined; then sing one more verse and end by having everyone sit down on the floor.

Step 2: Introduce a new song to the children.

Step 3: Bring out the song book with three sticky notes placed on it, each having a different child's name and symbol written on it. Tell the class that today these three children will each choose a song from the song book. As these children are selecting their songs, you may want to tap a steady beat on your knees with the rest of the children and chant, "I wonder what they'll pick, I wonder what they'll pick?" Sing the songs chosen by the children, making sure to include verses chosen by the other children when appropriate.

Step 4: Ask the children to choose a way to move to the next activity.

Other Ideas
Outside Time — KDI 12/Meal Conversations — KDI 6

Outside Time
If weather permits, take the leftover bubble solution outside.

Meal Conversations
During the meal, ask children to share what they think they will do over the two no-school days.

Home-School Connections
Share this idea with the children's family members:

Blow bubbles with your child. Bubbles can be made from liquid dish soap diluted with water. Use a variety of objects to blow the bubbles, such as a straw, wire bent into a shape, and so forth. Try asking your child, "What happens if you blow soft or hard?" and "What does the wind do to your bubbles?"

Observations

Record what you saw individual children say and do today. You can use the reproducible sheet on page 178 to make your notes.

Follow-Up Ideas

Write down your own follow-up ideas, using the reproducible sheet on page 179.

Building on What You've Learned: Week 4 Summary

This past week you did the following in your classroom:

- Incorporated a math activity (estimation) as a cleanup-time strategy
- Led small-group times that included curriculum content in math and science and creative representation
- Led large-group times that included curriculum content in movement and music and language and literacy
- Recorded four observations about children each day (each adult did this)

The children were particularly supported in the following areas:

- Continuing to form relationships with adults and children
- Expressing their plans, choices, and intentions
- Participating in activities that supported their development in the broad curriculum content areas of:

   Approaches to Learning
   Social and Emotional Development
   Physical Development and Health
   Language, Literacy, and Communication
   Mathematics
   Creative Arts
   Science and Technology
   Social Studies

You developed your own adult-child interaction skills by using these High/Scope interaction strategies (new strategies for this week appear in bolder type):

- Offering children comfort and contact
    - Looking for children in need of comfort and contact
    - Offering reassuring physical contact
    - Offering simple acknowledgments
    - Acknowledging children's feelings
- Participating in children's play
    - Joining play on children's level
    - Playing in parallel with children
    - Using comments and observations about what you saw children doing as openings to enter play
    - Looking for natural openings to begin to play with children
        - Considering the types of play you observed (exploratory, pretend, constructive, or games) before engaging with children
    - Playing as a partner, letting children retain control
- Conversing with children
    - Looking for natural opportunities for conversation
    - Responding to children's conversational leads
    - **Conversing as a partner with children**
    - **Passing conversational control back to children at every opportunity:**
        - **Sticking to the topics children raise**
        - **Making comments that allow the conversation to continue without pressuring children for a response**
        - **Waiting for children to respond before taking another turn**
        - **Keeping comments fairly brief**
    - **Asking questions responsively:**
        - **Asking questions sparingly**
        - **Relating questions directly to what children are doing**
        - **Asking questions about children's thought process**
- Encouraging children's problem solving
    - Referring one child to another

Learn More About...*Problem-Solving Approach to Conflicts*

Social conflicts are a natural part of a young child's day. HighScope views children's responses to these conflicts as part of their social growth and development. Just as young children are learning new skills in math and literacy, they are also learning new problem-solving skills to deal with interpersonal problems. There are six steps to the problem-solving process:

1. **Approach calmly, stopping any hurtful actions.**

    Place yourself between children, on their level.
    - Watch your tone of voice.
    - Quickly and gently stop any hurting.

2. **Acknowledge children's feelings.**

    For example, you might say, "You look really upset."
    - Place your hands on the disputed object and say, "I'm going to hold this until we figure out the problem." Keep the object in view.
    - Look at each child and use the children's names.
    - Name feelings repeatedly until children are calmer.

3. **Gather information.**

    For example, you might ask, "What's the problem?"
    - Ask "what" not "why."
    - Listen for the details of the problem.

4. **Restate the problem.**

    For example, you might say, "So the problem is…"
    - Restate the details that you hear in children's words.
    - Reframe any hurtful comments; set limits on hurtful actions if necessary, naming the feeling message. ("Name-calling needs to stop. You are feeling very angry.")

5. **Ask for ideas for solutions and choose one together.**

    For example, you might say, "What can we do to solve this problem?"
    - Encourage *children's* ideas for solutions.
    - Ask other children for ideas, if necessary.
    - When ideas are vague, ask "What will that look like?" or "What will you do?"

6. **Be prepared to give follow-up support.**

    For example, you might say, "You solved the problem!"
    - Describe what the child did that worked, with details.
    - Check back to make sure the solution is still working.

Use these six steps throughout the day, when conflicts arise. Record observations about children in these situations using *COR Advantage Item H. Conflict resolution* as a guide.

For more information about problem solving, see *You Can't Come to My Birthday Party! Conflict Resolution With Young Children*, by Betsy Evans, available from HighScope Press.

TIP: While you are learning the six steps for problem solving, give yourself some visual support. Teachers have found these strategies useful:

- Write out the six steps and post them in your classroom.
- If you wear a work identification badge, write the six steps on a small card and slip them behind your ID so you can just flip the badge over to see the steps.
- Laminate the six steps to the back of a classroom clipboard (if you use the clipboard for attendance, notes about children, etc).

Chapter 5
The Fifth Week

Getting Ready: Week 5 Overview

Goals for the Fifth Week
- Record a minimum of five observations about children per day (each adult does this).
- Identify the curriculum content illustrated in each of your observations.
- Implement three literacy-focused small-group times using the samples from the Growing Readers Early Literacy Curriculum that are included in this book.
- Use your observations of children to develop plans specific to your children. This week you will plan a large-group time and a cleanup-time strategy and you will also modify a planning-time strategy.

Things to Keep in Mind This Week

Daily Routine
- Identify the curriculum content illustrated in each of your observations about children. Write down the curriculum content after you record your observation — for example,

    At work time, in the block area, Gina touched and counted, "1, 2, 3, 4 blocks." — BB. Counting.

- Be sure to read each activity plan ahead of time so you know what materials you need to prepare.
- This week, you will use three sample activities from the Growing Readers Early Literacy Curriculum. Locate the book *Good Night, Gorilla*, an edition of Mother Goose, and the Growing Readers activities (see pp. 157–175) for use in your small-group times on days 21, 23, and 25.
- On Day 22, you will plan the large-group time. Using your observations about children, you will choose a large-group time activity from the past weeks that you think children will enjoy doing again. See "Follow-Up Ideas" in Day 21 (p. 112) for more information.
- On Day 25, you will choose a character or animal based on your children's interests as part of a cleanup strategy. As a teaching team, review your observations of children. What have you noted that children enjoy playing or pretending? Choose something that you've seen children enjoy and use that idea as a way to clean up. For example, you might pretend to be cars and drive the toys to where they belong, or babies and talk in high voices, or bunnies and hop to put the toys away. Add your idea to the lesson plan for cleanup time. Be sure to share your strategy with the children by adding it to the message board.
- On Friday, add this to the message board: Two simple images of the school with a red circle and diagonal slash over them — the universal "no" symbol. Write *2 no school days* and help the children interpret the drawings. Remind them that they will stay home for two days and then come back to school.
- Continue to add your own message to the message board at greeting time.

Other
Continue to add song cards to the classroom song book.

After Children Leave for the Day
- Record your observations of children and jot down any ideas you want to follow up on.
- Read tomorrow's lesson plans to see what preparations you will need to make before the children arrive.

Lesson Plans for the First 30 Days

Some Reminders for This Week

Monday (Day 21)	**Tuesday** (Day 22)	**Wednesday** (Day 23)	**Thursday** (Day 24)	**Friday** (Day 25)
Both groups: Growing Readers activity (small-group time) Family note home: Read with your child Use your observations to plan large-group time for tomorrow		Draw a large, simple classroom diagram or map that Group 1 will use today and Group 2 will use Friday at planning time Make large area signs to lay on the floor that Group 2 will use today and Group 1 will use Friday at planning time Both groups: Growing Readers activity (small-group time) Prepare shapes for large-group time activity	Family note home: Look at a family photo album with your child Use your observations about children to plan the cleanup strategy for tomorrow	Both groups: Growing Readers activity (small-group time) Adult 1: Use your observations about children to plan small-group time for day 26 (see "Small-Group Time" in Day 26 for more information)

DAY 21

Curriculum Content — Key Developmental Indicators (KDIs)*

1. Initiative
2. Planning
6. Reflection
11. Community
12. Building relationships
13. Cooperative play
16. Gross-motor skills
21. Comprehension
22. Speaking
23. Vocabulary
24. Phonological awareness
25. Alphabetic knowledge
26. Reading
28. Book knowledge
29. Writing
35. Spatial awareness
40. Art
42. Movement
43. Pretend play

*See the KDIs listed under individual activities.

Greeting Time
KDIs 12, 24, 25, 26, 29

Adult 1: Greet children at the door. When everyone has arrived, join the children and Adult 2 reading books.

Adult 2: Have about 10 books spread out on the floor. Read books with children. (*Note:* This should last no more than 15 minutes.) Sing a simple transitional song.

Message Board
Draw your daily routine symbol for cleanup time, write the word *cleanup*, and tape a bucket or bag to this message. Help the children read this message that for cleanup time they can pick a container and gather things to put away. See "Cleanup Time" in this lesson for a full description.

Create your own message.

Planning Time
Group 1 — KDI 2/Group 2 — KDI 2

Group 1: Planning Bus

Materials: Small pieces of paper or light cardboard or card stock to use as "bus tickets"

Ahead of time, set up the children's chairs in a line like bus seats. At planning time, give each child a "bus ticket" and tell the children they can get on the planning bus. The child who sits in the first seat can tell his plan and then give you the ticket, take his chair and put it back where it came from, and get started on his plan. Continue planning with the child now sitting in the front seat. Repeat until all children have planned.

Group 2: Area Cards and Animal Figures

Materials:
- Set of animal figures
- Area cards

Ahead of time, look at your notes about children and then choose a set of animal figures that your children seem to enjoy playing with. As you start this activity, lay the area cards out on the table. Give each child an animal figure. Individually ask children to place their figure on the card representing the area in which they would like to work. Help children extend their plans by asking them for details about what will they use, who else might be involved, and so forth.

Work Time
KDIs 1, 12, 13, 40, 43

Continue to work on the types of questions that you ask children. In addition to questions about children's thought process, **ask questions that relate directly to what children are doing,** as such questions may stimulate discussion. For example, you might ask one or more of the following questions: "How can you tell? "What do you think made that happen?" "What do you think would happen if…?" Avoid asking questions that you already know the answer to. Always remember to **limit the amount of questions you ask and respect children's responses** to them.

Day 21

Cleanup Time — KDI 11

After giving the usual 10- and 5-minute warning signals, tell the children they can use cleanup buckets (or bags or large yogurt containers) to help them clean up. Invite children to use the small buckets (or other containers) to collect things that need to be put away. When children have some things in their container, they can put those items away. Remember to keep a light, playful attitude throughout cleanup time.

Recall Time — *Group 1 — KDIs 29, 40/Group 2 — KDI 6*

Group 1: Write or Draw

Materials:

For each child, provide

- A piece of paper
- A pencil or several crayons

Additionally, have on hand

- Area cards

Give each child a piece of paper and either a pencil or several crayons. Ask the children to draw or write what they did at work time. Also have the area cards at the table so that children can copy area names if they wish. (*Note:* Younger children may just get something they played with and draw around it.)

Group 2: Bell

Materials:

- Cards with children's names and letter link symbols
- A bag
- A bell or shaker

Ahead of time, put the children's cards with their names and letter link symbols in a bag. One at a time, pull a child's name out of the bag. This will help decide whose turn it is. Give that child a small bell or shaker. While the rest of the children close their eyes and put their head on the table, the child whose turn it is goes to an area he or she played in and rings the bell. The rest of the group then guesses where that child played by listening to the direction the sound is coming from. The child then returns to the table and shares what he or she did in that area. Repeat the activity for the other children in your group.

Small-Group Time — *Group 1 — KDIs 21, 22, 23, 26, 28, 29/Group 2 — KDIs 21, 22, 23, 26, 28*

Group 1: Sample Growing Readers Activity

Learn Nursery Rhymes: Act Out "Humpty Dumpty" and Other Level 1 Nursery Rhymes

Quick Plan:

- Children listen to and say the nursery rhyme.
- Children act out and say the nursery rhyme.
- Teacher and children discuss nursery rhyme pictures, words, and objects.

(*See pp. 166–167 and 172–173* for complete activity and materials.)

Group 2: Sample Growing Readers Activity

Connect to *Good Night, Gorilla*: What Things Do You See?

Quick Plan:

- Teacher and children examine and discuss the pictures.
- Children tell the story based on the pictures.
- Children compare pictures on the front and back covers.

(*See pp. 158–159 and 164–165 for complete activity and materials.*)

Day 21

Large-Group Time
KDIs 16, 42

Pretend Dancing

Materials: Lively music with no words

Step 1: Sing the "We're gonna shake, shake, shake" song until all children have joined; then sing one more verse and end by having everyone sit down on the floor.

Step 2: Ask children to watch and imitate what you are doing. First, pretend to play a guitar, then ask children what everyone is doing. Wait for their responses. Repeat this process, but this time pretend to play the drums. Next, lay on your back and move your feet in the air. Ask children what they think you are doing — wait for their responses. If no one guesses, tell them that you are doing pretend dancing! Ask children to spread out and join you, reminding them that they have to be careful not to have their feet touch another child's body. Tell them that when you put on the music, they can begin dancing. Play lively music without words and join the children in pretend dancing, moving your feet around in the air.

Step 3: When the music is over, ask children to dance to the next part of the day.

Other Ideas
Outside Time — KDIs 12, 35/Meal Conversations — KDIs 21, 22

Outside Time

As you work and play with children outside, use language that focuses on the position and direction of things. You might say things like

"You're climbing around Ian."

"I'm underneath you."

"You're running toward your Mom."

Meal Conversations

During the meal, invite children to play "the special word game" with you. Tell children that when they hear the special word, they can tap their finger on the table. Tell them what the word is and then begin saying different words until you say the special word. ("The special word is *pumpkin*. When you hear *pumpkin*, tap your finger on the table. Ready? *Cherries, watermelon, pears, grapes, pineapples, bananas, **pumpkin**.*") Continue playing the game, changing the special word. Let children be the leaders — choosing the special word and then saying the string of words.

Home-School Connections

Share the following idea with the children's family members:

Read a book to your child. If it's a book you've read to your child before, pause from time to time to see if yor child can fill in some parts of the story.

Observations

Record what you saw individual children say and do today. You can use the reproducible sheet on page 178 to make your notes.

Follow-Up Ideas

- Look at your observations of the children. Choose a large-group-time activity from the past weeks that children enjoy doing and repeat the activity tomorrow. For example, you might choose
    - Musical Carpet Squares from Day 9
    - Rowing Boats from Day 10
    - Fast and Slow Movements from Day 12
    or some other activity from a previous day.
- Write down other follow-up ideas, using the reproducible sheet on page 179.

TIP: As you record observations about children, you may find it useful to briefly **note the curriculum content area** illustrated by your anecdotes. Post several lists of the KDIs around your classroom. These quick references will help you remember the content you want to look for and support while you scaffold the children's play.

DAY 22

Curriculum Content — Key Developmental Indicators (KDIs)*

1. Initiative
2. Planning
6. Reflection
11. Community
12. Building relationships
13. Cooperative play
24. Phonological awareness
25. Alphabetic knowledge
26. Reading
29. Writing
32. Counting
36. Measuring
38. Patterns
40. Art
43. Pretend play
57. History

*See the KDIs listed under individual activities.

Greeting Time
KDIs 12, 24, 25, 26, 29

Adult 2: Greet children at the door. When everyone has arrived, join the children and Adult 1 reading books.

Adult 1: Have about 10 books spread out on the floor. Read books with children.

(*Note:* This should last no more than 15 minutes.) Sing a simple transitional song.

Message Board
Draw your daily routine symbol for cleanup time, write *cleanup*, and tape a bucket or bag to the board next to this message. Help the children read this message that for cleanup time they can pick a container and gather things to put away. See "Cleanup Time" in this lesson plan for a full description.

Create your own message.

Planning Time
Group 1 — KDI 2/Group 2 — KDI 2

Group 1: Area Cards and Animal Figures

Materials:
- Set of animal figures
- Area cards

Ahead of time, look at your notes about children and then choose a set of animal figures that your children seem to enjoy playing with. As you start this activity, lay the area cards out on the table. Give each child an animal figure. Individually ask children to place their figure on the card representing the area in which they would like to work. Help children extend their plans by asking them for details about what will they use, who else might be involved, and so forth.

Group 2: Planning Bus

Materials: Small pieces of paper or light cardboard or card stock to use as "bus tickets"

Ahead of time, set up the children's chairs in a line like bus seats. At planning time, give each child a "bus ticket" and tell the children they can get on the planning bus. The child who sits in the first seat can tell her plan and then give you the ticket, take her chair and put it back where it came from, and get started on her plan. Continue planning with the child now sitting in the front seat. Repeat until all children have planned.

Work Time
KDIs 1, 12, 13, 40, 43

Continue to work on the types of questions that you ask children. In addition to questions about children's thought process, ask questions that relate directly to what children are doing, as such questions may stimulate discussion. For example, you might ask one or more of the following questions: "How can you tell?" "What do you think made that happen?" "What do you think would happen if…?" Avoid asking questions that you already know the answer to. Always remember to **limit the amount of questions you ask and respect children's responses** to them.

Day 22

Cleanup Time

KDI 11

After giving the usual 10- and 5-minute warning signals, tell the children they can use cleanup buckets (or bags or large yogurt containers) to help them clean up. Invite children to use the small buckets (or other containers) to collect things that need to be put away. When children have some things in their container, they can put these items away. Remember to keep a light, playful attitude throughout cleanup time.

Recall Time

Group 1 — KDI 6/Group 2 — KDIs 29, 40

Group 1: Bell

Materials:

- Cards with children's names and letter link symbols
- A bag
- A bell or shaker

Ahead of time, put the children's cards with their names and letter link symbols in a bag. One at a time, pull a child's name out of the bag. This will help decide whose turn it is. Give that child a small bell or shaker. While the rest of the children close their eyes and put their head on the table, the child whose turn it is goes to an area he or she played in and rings the bell. The rest of the group then guesses where that child played by listening to the direction the sound is coming from. The child then returns to the table and shares what he or she did in that area. Repeat the activity for the other children in your group.

Group 2: Write or Draw

Materials:

For each child, provide

- A piece of paper
- A pencil or several crayons

Additionally, have on hand

- Area cards

Give each child a piece of paper and either a pencil or several crayons. Ask the children to draw or write what they did at work time. Also have the area cards at the table so that children can copy area names if they wish. (*Note:* Younger children may just get something they played with and draw around it.)

Day 22

Small-Group Time

Group 1 — KDI 40 / Group 2 — KDIs 32, 36, 38

Group 1: Exploring Clay

Materials:

For each child, provide

- A hunk of clay
- A tongue depressor or clay tool
- A clay mat
- A small dish of water
- A smock

Beginning: Let the children know that they will need to put on a smock. Give each child a hunk of clay and clay mat and say something like "Today we are going to work with the clay." Be sure to have a hunk of clay for yourself.

Middle: Move around the table from child to child, observing what they are doing with the clay. Try using your clay in the same way as the children. Partway through, you might need to bring out the water to help soften the clay. Add the tongue depressor as a backup material only if needed. Use your conversation techniques as you interact and support children's discoveries (see pp. 3–6 in the introduction to this book).

End: Give children a three-minute warning and ask them to put all their clay in the clay tub. Cover the tub with a wet towel. Remind the children that the clay will be in the art area if they want to use it at work time tomorrow.

Group 2: Bear Families

Materials:

For each child, provide

- Plastic counting bears in three colors and sizes or other small figures that can be sorted by two or more attributes (for example, color, size, type of animal)
- Small blocks to introduce as a backup material

Beginning: Tell the children a very short story about a family of bears. Set out a pile of red bears that are different sizes. Ask the children if they recognize something that is the same about all the bears in the family. Introduce a blue bear and say that the blue bear is looking for a family, too. Ask how you should make a family for that bear. Children may suggest that you make a collection of blue bears. Follow the children's idea and make a pile of blue bears. As a continuation of the story, say that the baby bears want to play together and put the smallest bears together. Tell the children that they will get some bears and that you're wondering how they might go together.

Middle: Give each child a basket of bears to sort. Some children may repeat parts of the story as they sort their bears. Watch to see which children sort their bears by color, size, or both attributes. Listen for children to use comparison words like *same/different, more/less,* and *bigger/smaller.* Some children may put their bears in order (seriate them) from largest to smallest. Some may count their bears. Encourage those children who are interested in counting the bears in their piles to determine which pile has the most or least. Some children may put bears into random piles, line them up, or begin pretend play with them. After a few minutes, give children some small blocks to use with their bears.

End: Give children a three-minute warning. At the end of small-group time, put three baskets in the middle of the table. Ask the children to sort their bears into the baskets by color. Tell the children that the bears will be available to use during work time.

115

Day 22

Large-Group Time
Your KDIs: _____

Your Idea From Previous Activities
Step 1: Sing the "We're gonna shake, shake, shake" song until all children have joined; then sing one more verse and end by having everyone sit down on the floor.

Step 2: Implement your plan based on previous activities (see "Follow-Up Ideas" on p. 112 from Day 21). Your plan is to

Step 3: Invent your own transition to suggest children use to get to the next part of the daily routine.

Other Ideas
Outside Time — KDIs 12, 40/Meal Conversations — KDIs 12, 32, 57

Outside Time
If weather permits, add materials that children can use to draw or write with outside. These might include chalk, paper, and crayons, or even just water and paintbrushes.

Meal Conversations
During the meal, converse with children about their ages. Talk about how old they are, who is younger or older, and the ages of their siblings (if they know). Try to **use comments and then pause,** rather than ask a lot of questions — this will encourage more language from the children:

Adult: "Shannon, you said you are four but your baby is just a baby." (The adult pauses.)

Shannon: "Yes, he's just little." (The adult listens and pauses.)

Micah: "My baby's bigger now. She's two."

Adult: "Two is getting bigger." (The adult pauses.)

Koby: "Yeah, but not as big as me — I'm three!"

Observations

Record what you saw individual children say and do today. You can use the reproducible sheet on page 178 to make your notes.

Follow-Up Ideas

Write down your own follow-up ideas, using the reproducible sheet on page 179.

DAY 23

Curriculum Content — Key Developmental Indicators (KDIs)*

1. Initiative
2. Planning
6. Reflection
11. Community
12. Building relationships
13. Cooperative play
16. Gross-motor skills
17. Fine-motor skills
18. Body awareness
21. Comprehension
22. Speaking
23. Vocabulary
24. Phonological awareness
25. Alphabetic knowledge
26. Reading
28. Book knowledge
29. Writing
35. Spatial awareness
40. Art
42. Movement
43. Pretend play

*See the KDIs listed under individual activities.

Greeting Time
KDIs 12, 24, 25, 26, 29

Adult 1: Greet children at the door. When everyone has arrived, join the children and Adult 2 reading books.

Adult 2: Have about 10 books spread out on the floor. Read books with children. (*Note:* This should last no more than 15 minutes.) Sing a simple transitional song.

Message Board
Draw your daily routine symbol for cleanup time and write *cleanup*. Draw your classroom's light switch, with the switch in the "on" position, and an arrow pointing to another drawing of the light switch in the "off" position. Help the children read this message that today everyone is going to clean up with no lights. See "Cleanup Time" in this lesson plan for a full description.

Create your own message.

Planning Time
Group 1 — KDIs 2, 35/Group 2 — KDI 2

Group 1: Classroom Map
Ahead of time, on a large piece of paper, draw a simple map of the classroom consisting primarily of the area signs and names. Give each child a small car, and one at a time, ask the children to drive their car to the area on the map where they'd like to work. Ask for details about what they will be doing. Repeat for all the children in your group.

Group 2: Buckets and Beanbags

Materials:
- Area signs
- One bucket for each area sign
- A beanbag, sponge, or soft ball

Ahead of time, choose a place in the classroom that has a larger open space. Lay out large area signs on the floor and place a bucket by each. Meet at your usual table and then say to the children something like "Today we are having planning time in the _____ area." One at a time, give the children a beanbag, sponge, or soft ball and ask them to drop it in the bucket next to the sign of the area where they would like to work. Ask the children to share details of their plans, such as who they will work with and what they will use in their plan. Once a child has planned, he or she can get started with play. Repeat for all the children in your group.

Day 23

Work Time
KDIs 1, 12, 13, 40, 43

When playing with the children, avoid praising them (for example, with language like "good job" or "good girl" or "I like the way you..."). Instead, **use encouragement strategies** by asking children to describe their efforts, ideas, and work. Our goal is to have children evaluate their own work, which will help develop their self-esteem.

You might say things like

"What can you tell me about your picture?"

"How did you build this spaceship?"

"I see you put a lot of animals on the top of your blocks. What will you do next?"

Cleanup Time
KDI 11

After giving the usual 10- and 5-minute warning signals, say to the children something like "Today we're going to clean up in the dark!" (Only do this if you have windows or natural lighting so that the room is still safe.) Turn off a set of lights and invite children to help you find things to put away. Children will often enjoy combining this with "sneaky cleanup" from Day 11.

Recall Time
Group 1 — KDI 6/Group 2 — KDI 6

Group 1: Dolls
Give each child a stuffed animal or doll and have one for yourself. One at a time, ask children to recall their work-time activities to your stuffed animal or doll. Another option would be to ask children to tell their recall to another child's animal or doll and listen while their partner shares his or her recall.

Group 2: Name and Letter-Link-Symbol Spinner
Use the name and letter-link-symbol spinner that you made for planning time last week (see Day 16, p. 86). Once again have children spin the spinner; when it lands on their name, it is their turn to share what they did at work time.

Small-Group Time
Group 1 — KDIs 18, 24, 28/Group 2 — KDIs 21, 22, 23

Group 1: Sample Growing Readers Activity

Learn Nursery Rhymes: Pat to "Humpty Dumpty" and Other Level 1 Nursery Rhymes

Quick Plan:

- Teacher and children say and pat to four lines of "pat-pat-pat-pat."
- Teacher and children say and pat to nursery rhymes.
- Teacher adds the children's names to the nursery rhymes.

(See pp. 168–169 and 174–175 for complete activity and materials.)

Group 2: Sample Growing Readers Activity

Connect to *Good Night Gorilla:* Try Out Flashlights and Keys

Quick Plan:

- Children guess what objects from the book are in the box.
- Children try out flashlights, keys, and key rings.
- Children show and describe how to use the flashlights or key rings.

(See pp. 160–161 for complete activity and materials.)

Large-Group Time

KDIs 16, 17, 42

Musical Shapes

Materials:

- Large geometric shapes (circle, rectangle, triangle) cut out of heavy felt or paper
- Lively marching music

Note: Make sure you only use one color for all the shapes (i.e., all red or all blue) so that children focus on the shape and not the color.

Step 1: Sing the "We're gonna shake, shake, shake" song until all children have joined; then sing one more verse and end by having everyone sit down on the floor. Explain to the children that they are going to walk from shape to shape as you play music, and that when the music stops, they should each stop (stand) on the nearest shape. Explain that you will then tell them what to do, depending on the shape they are standing on.

Step 2: Play and stop the music. Make sure everyone is standing on a shape. Then say something like "Everyone standing on a square, clap your hands." After a few rounds of this, encourage the children to suggest the actions. ("What should everyone standing on a circle do now?") When you are sure the children understand the game, add "not" statements, such as, "If you are *not* on a circle, put your thumb on your nose" and "If your shape does *not* have a curved part, shake one foot."

Step 3: Tell children to remember the look of this last shape they are standing on. Then ask them to transition to the next activity using this shape; for example, "If you are on a square, bring me your shape and go to *(the next activity),*" and so on.

> **TIP:** You can use other "not" or "no" statements throughout the day. For example, when sending children to the next part of your daily routine, you might say, "If you are *not* a boy, you can go and get your jacket on" or "If you are *not* wearing velcro shoes, you can go to your planning group."

> **Did You Know...?**
>
> Day 23's large-group time helps children begin to explore classification through "not" and "no" language. Dealing with absent characteristics ("does not have curved parts") calls upon two developing capacities in young children — forming mental images and thinking about two things at once. These are complex thought processes for preschoolers. For example, to understand the statement, "If your shape does *not* have a curved part, shake one foot," a child has to form a mental image of curved parts of shapes and then think about the shape they have to see if it does *not* have that curve. These are important concepts for both early math and early science learning.

Other Ideas

Outside Time—KDIs 12, 42/Meal Conversations—KDIs 6, 12

Outside Time

If weather permits, consider taking music outside. While many children may still want to run, climb, ride, and throw, you may find some children will enjoy moving and dancing to the music. Keep this time informal and unstructured. Remember that moving to music is just another choice for children.

Meal Conversations

During the meal, name a food that the children are eating and invite the children to make up a story about that food. For example, you might start by saying "We're having broccoli today. Let's make up a broccoli story together. Once upon a time, there was a tall stalk of broccoli...." Be sure to pause to allow children to share their ideas about what happens in the story.

Day 23

Observations

Record what you saw individual children say and do today. You can use the reproducible sheet on page 178 to make your notes.

Follow-Up Ideas

- Add large shapes (from large-group time) to an area of your room.
- Write down your own follow-up ideas, using the reproducible sheet on page 179.

DAY 24

Curriculum Content — Key Developmental Indicators (KDIs)*

1. Initiative
2. Planning
6. Reflection
11. Community
12. Building relationships
13. Cooperative play
21. Comprehension
22. Speaking
23. Vocabulary
24. Phonological awareness
25. Alphabetic knowledge
26. Reading
29. Writing
32. Counting
36. Measuring
38. Patterns
40. Art
41. Music
43. Pretend play

*See the KDIs listed under individual activities.

Greeting Time
KDIs 12, 24, 25, 26, 29

Adult 2: Greet children at the door. When everyone has arrived, join the children and Adult 1 reading books.

Adult 1: Have about 10 books spread out on the floor. Read books with children. (*Note:* This should last no more than 15 minutes.) Sing a simple transitional song.

Message Board
Draw your daily routine symbol for cleanup time and write *cleanup*. Draw your classroom's light switch with the switch in the "on" position and an arrow pointing to another drawing of the light switch in the "off" position. Help the children read this message that today everyone is going to clean up with no lights. See "Cleanup Time" in this lesson for a full description.

Bring out the classroom song book with three sticky notes attached to it, each having a child's name and letter link symbol written on it. Help children read this message that these three children will choose songs to sing at large-group time. These children may want to take their sticky note and put it on the song they'll sing.

Planning Time
Group 1 — KDI 2/Group 2 — KDI 2

Group 1: Tape Recorder
Using a tape recorder, children take turns recording their work-time plans. **Ask them questions to extend their ideas,** such as who they will work with and what they will use in their plans. After the child whose turn it is has recorded his plan, he can get started on his play. Save the tape to use at recall time.

Group 2: Flashlight
One at a time, have children hold a flashlight and suggest that they shine the light on something they would like to work with. **Comment** on children's plans and ask **open ended questions** to help them extend their ideas. For instance, you might say, "I see your light is on the block area — what will you do there? What will you use in your plan?" After sharing, the child whose turn it is can pass the light to someone else and get started on her plan. Repeat for all children in your group.

Work Time
KDIs 1, 12, 13, 40, 43

When playing with the children, avoid praising them (for example, with language like "good job" or "good girl" or "I like the way you…"). Instead, **use encouragement strategies by making specific comments** about what you see children doing. Some examples:

"I see you have painted a lot of blue dots at the top and here are red lines on the bottom."

"You put all the blue duplos on the bottom and the red duplos on the next row."

This strategy helps to give children nonjudgmental support when they seek adult acknowledgments.

121

Day 24

Cleanup Time
KDI 11

After giving the usual 10- and 5-minute warning signals, say to the children something like "Today we're going to clean up in the dark!" (Only do this if you have windows or natural lighting so that the room is still safe.) Turn off a set of lights and invite children to help you find things to put away. Children will often enjoy combining this with "sneaky cleanup" from Day 11.

Recall Time
KDIs 6, 21/Group 2 — KDIs 6, 29

Group 1: Listen to Our Plans
Listen to the tape recording made at planning time. After listening to one child's plan, see if the rest of the children can identify who the planner was. Ask that child whether he did that plan or whether he changed it. Be nonjudgmental in your responses. It's okay if children changed their plans or if they wish to recall about something else. Repeat this process until all children have had an opportunity to hear their recording and recall their experiences.

Group 2: Area Cards and Clothespins

Materials:

- Cards with children's name and letter link symbol on them
- Clothespins
- Area cards

One at a time, show the cards with children's first name and letter link symbol written on them. Ask "Who is this?" When the children respond, give the card and a clothespin to the child whose name/symbol it is and ask her to clip it to the area card corresponding to the area she played in. Ask the child to tell you what she did in that area. As you repeat this activity for all the children, everyone can notice the areas where many children played or just a few children played. Some children may choose to count the clothespins to figure this out.

Day 24

Small-Group Time

Group 1 — KDIs 32, 36, 38/Group 2 — KDI 40

Group 1: Bear Families

Materials:

For each child, provide

- Plastic counting bears in three colors and sizes or other small figures that can be sorted by two or more attributes (for example, color, size, type of animal)
- Small blocks to introduce as a backup material

Beginning: Tell the children a very short story about a family of bears. Set out a pile of red bears that are different sizes. Ask the children if they recognize something that is the same about all the bears in the family. Introduce a blue bear and say that the blue bear is looking for a family, too. Ask how you should make a family for that bear. Children may suggest that you make a collection of blue bears. Follow the children's idea and make a pile of blue bears. As a continuation of the story, say that the baby bears want to play together and put the smallest bears together. Tell the children that they will get some bears and that you're wondering how they might go together.

Middle: Give each child a basket of bears to sort. Some children may repeat parts of the story as they sort their bears. Watch to see which children sort their bears by color, size, or both attributes. Listen for children to use comparison words like *same/different, more/less,* and *bigger/smaller.* Some children may put their bears in order (seriate them) from largest to smallest. Some may count their bears. Encourage those children who are interested in counting the bears in their piles to determine which pile has the most or least. Some children may put bears into random piles, line them up, or begin pretend play with them. After a few minutes, give children some small blocks to use with their bears.

End: Give children a three-minute warning. At the end of small-group time, put three baskets in the middle of the table. Ask the children to sort their bears into the baskets by color. Tell the children that the bears will be available to use during work time.

Group 2: Exploring Clay

Materials:

For each child, provide

- A hunk of clay
- A tongue depressor or clay tool
- A clay mat
- A small dish of water
- A smock

Beginning: Let the children know that they will need to put on a smock. Give each child a hunk of clay and clay mat and say something like "Today we are going to work with the clay." Be sure to have a hunk of clay for yourself.

Middle: Move around the table from child to child, observing what they are doing with the clay. Try using your clay in the same way as the children. Partway through, you might need to bring out the water to help soften the clay. Add the tongue depressor as a backup material only if needed. Use your conversation techniques as you interact and support children's discoveries (see pp. 3–6 in the introduction to this book).

End: Give children a three-minute warning and ask them to put all their clay in the clay tub. Cover the tub with a wet towel. Remind the children that the clay will be in the art area if they want to use it at work time tomorrow.

Day 24

Large-Group Time

KDIs 24, 41

Rhyming With "Down By the Bay"

Materials: Classroom song book

Step 1: Sing the "We're gonna shake, shake, shake" song until all children have joined; then sing one more verse and end by having everyone sit down on the floor. Bring out the song book with two sticky notes attached to it, each having a different child's name and letter link symbol written on it. Tell the class that today these two children will each choose a song from the song book. As these children are picking out their songs, you may want to tap a steady beat on your knees with the rest of the children and chant, "I wonder what they'll pick, I wonder what they'll pick?" Sing the songs chosen by the two children, making sure to include choices of verses from the other children when appropriate.

Step 2: Begin a conversation that has a rhyme in it. Example: "There is something I wanted to SAY, we all came to school TODAY!" Point out the rhyming words. Ask children to think of other rhyming words. **Listen** to input from children and **acknowledge** their ideas and attempts at rhyming.

Step 3: Let children know that they will be working with a song that gives them a chance to make a rhyme and think of something fun to say. Think of the tune and tempo of the song before beginning to sing. Set a beat by patting your knees, encouraging children to join in with the beat-keeping as they listen. Begin singing the song "Down By The Bay":

Down by the bay, where the watermelons grow.

Back to my home, I dare not go.

For if I do, My mother would say:

*"Did you ever see a **spider**, getting much **wider**?"*

Down by the bay.

Be sure to emphasize and slow down when you get to the rhyming words at the end. Talk about the two rhyming words, repeating them slowly. If necessary, model another rhyme as you go through the song one more time. As children begin to understand the rhyming task in the song, ask them for rhyming suggestions. Their rhymes may not make "adult sense"; however, children are nonetheless developing their skill at creating them. (Examples: "Have you ever seen a *tiger* — doing a *biger*?" "Have you ever seen a *lizard* walking on a *tizard*?")

Step 4: To transition the children from this activity to another part of the daily routine, play a name rhyming game. Start the game by saying to children "If you hear your name in the song, you can go to *the next part of the daily routine*." Sing just the last line of the song and rhyme children's names as they transition. Examples:

Did you ever see a Liam? I think I see 'im.

Did you ever see Jimmy doing a shimmy?

Did you ever see Sue tying her shoe?

✓ Other Ideas

Outside Time — KDI 12/Meal Conversations — KDIs 12, 22, 23

Outside Time

Think about ways to **encourage, rather than praise** children's efforts outside. Examples:

"You tried and tried and you made a basket!"

"Ruthie, you've been waiting so patiently for a turn on the bike. I think Elmer is almost done."

"Elmer, you heard Ruthie ask about a turn on the bike, and you gave her the one you were using."

Meal Conversations

During the meal, play the "I Spy" game using shapes (for example, by saying "I spy something round" or "I spy something in the shape of a circle"). Start with something clearly visible on the table, then "spy" something farther away. Keep giving children hints until they guess the object. Once children catch on to the game, they can be the leaders.

Home-School Connections

Share this idea with the children's family members:

Go through your family photo album with your child and talk about your family. Share what you liked to do when you were a child and who the people in the photo are. Make comments like "This is Uncle Boo when he was a baby" or "When I was a little boy, I liked to play with balls, too."

Observations

Record what you saw individual children say and do today. You can use the reproducible sheet on page 178 to make your notes.

Follow-Up Ideas

- Add the clay to the art area.
- Add a song card for "Down By the Bay" to the classroom song book.
- Look at your observations about children. What do you see that children enjoy playing or pretending? Choose something you've seen children enjoy and use that idea as a way to clean up tomorrow. For example, everyone could pretend to be cars and drive the toys to where they belong, or to be bunnies and hop to put toys away. Add your idea to tomorrow's lesson plan for cleanup time.
- Use the strategy of rhyming with children's names to choose children for jobs or to transition children to other times of the day.
- Write down your own follow-up ideas, using the reproducible sheet on page 179.

DAY 25

Curriculum Content — Key Developmental Indicators (KDIs)*

1. Initiative
2. Planning
6. Reflection
11. Community
12. Building relationships
13. Cooperative play
21. Comprehension
22. Speaking
23. Vocabulary
24. Phonological awareness
25. Alphabetic knowledge
26. Reading
28. Book knowledge
29. Writing
35. Spatial awareness
40. Art
41. Music
43. Pretend play
49. Drawing conclusions
51. Natural and physical world
56. Geography
57. History

*See the KDIs listed under individual activities.

Greeting Time
KDIs 12, 24, 25, 26, 29, 57

Adult 1: Greet children at the door. When everyone has arrived, join the children and Adult 2 reading books.

Adult 2: Have about 10 books spread out on the floor. Read books with children. (*Note:* This should last no more than 15 minutes.) Sing a simple transitional song.

Message Board
Tape a baggie with a piece of clay inside it to the message board and draw the area sign for the art area. Help the children read this message that the clay has been added to the art area.

Draw two simple images of the school with a red circle and diagonal slash over them — the universal "no" symbol. Write *2 no school days* and help the children interpret the drawings. Remind them that they will stay home for two days and then come back to school.

Planning Time
Group 1 — KDI 2/Group 2 — KDIs 2, 35, 56

Group 1: Buckets and Beanbags

Materials:

- Area signs
- One bucket for each area sign
- A beanbag, sponge, or soft ball

Ahead of time, choose a place in the classroom that has a larger open space. Lay out large area signs on the floor and place a bucket by each. Meet at your usual table and then say to the children something like "Today we are having planning time in the _____ area." One at a time, give the children a beanbag, sponge, or soft ball and ask them to drop it in the bucket next to the sign of the area where they would like to work. Ask the children to share details of their plans, such as who they will work with and what they will use in their plan. Once a child has planned, he or she can get started with play. Repeat for all the children in your group.

Group 2: Classroom Map

Ahead of time, on a large piece of paper, draw a simple map of the classroom consisting primarily of the area signs and names. Give each child a small car, and one at a time, ask the children to drive their car to the area on the map where they'd like to work. Ask for details about what they will be doing. Repeat for all the children in your group.

Day 25

Work Time

KDIs 1, 12, 13, 40, 43

When playing with the children, avoid praising them (for example, with language like "good job" or "good boy" or "I like the way you…). Instead, **use encouragement strategies by making specific comments** about what you see children doing. Some examples:

"You ran around the climber, and now you're going up the slide."

"You asked Marissa for a turn on the computer, and she said, 'Sure!'"

This strategy helps to give children nonjudgmental support when they seek adult acknowledgment.

Cleanup Time

KDI 11

For this cleanup time activity, use your observations of children and choose a character or an animal (such as dogs, dinosaurs, babies, or kittens) that you know the children enjoy pretending to be. Give children a verbal warning 10 minutes and then 5 minutes before the end of work time. At the beginning of cleanup time, say to children something like "Today we're going to clean up like _____." Invite them to share how they think this character or animal might move and sound. You can make this really fun by moving and talking like this character/animal yourself.

Recall Time

Group 1 — KDI 6/Group 2 — KDI 6

Group 1: Name and Letter-Link-Symbol Spinner

Use the name and letter-link-symbol spinner that you made for planning time last week (see Day 16, p. 86). Once again have children spin the spinner; when it lands on their name, it is their turn to share what they did at work time.

Group 2: Dolls

Give each child a stuffed animal or doll and have one for yourself. One at a time, ask children to recall their work-time activites to your stuffed animal or doll. Another option would be to ask children to tell their recall to another child's animal or doll and listen while their partner shares his or her recall.

Small-Group Time *Group 1 — KDIs 21, 22, 23, 24, 26, 28/Group 2 — KDIs 21, 22, 23*

Group 1: Sample Growing Readers Activity

Learn Nursery Rhymes: Recall "Humpty Dumpty" and Other Level 1 Nursery Rhymes

Quick Plan:

- Children guess nursery rhymes from pictures.
- Children guess nursery rhymes from actions.
- Children guess nursery rhymes from object words.

(See pp. 170–173 for complete activity and materials.)

Group 2: Sample Growing Readers Activity

Connect to *Good Night, Gorilla:* What Is in Your House and in the Zoo?

Quick Plan:

- Teacher and children examine and discuss the pictures.
- Children find and discuss familiar objects and toys in the pictures.
- Children choose one favorite object from the pictures.

(See pp. 162–165 for complete activity and materials.)

Day 25

Large-Group Time

KDIs 24, 41

Singing Songs

Materials: Classroom song book

Step 1: Sing the "We're gonna shake, shake, shake" song until all children have joined; then sing one more verse and end by having everyone sit down on the floor.

Step 2: In the song book, turn to the "Down By the Bay" song card used in yesterday's large-group time and sing some verses with the children. Make sure to use the children's rhyming ideas.

Step 3: Show the children the front of the song book after you have placed two or three sticky notes on it, each having a child's name and letter link symbol written on it. Tell the class that today these three children will each choose a song from the song book. As these children are picking out their songs, you may want to tap a steady beat on your knees with the rest of the children and chant, "I wonder what they'll pick, I wonder what they'll pick?" Sing the songs chosen by the three children, making sure to include choices of verses from the other children when appropriate.

Step 4: Ask the children to choose a way to move to their next activity.

Other Ideas

Outside Time — KDIs 12, 49, 51

Outside Time
As you play and interact with children, converse about changes you might see in nature in your outside space. Make comments about grass, snow, ice, trees, flowers, rocks, weeds, bugs, birds, worms, and so forth. You might say things like the following:

"It's starting to get colder — the leaves are falling off the trees."

"The grass is getting really long — it feels damp to me today."

"We used to see bugs in this dirt, but I can't find any now that it's cold."

Meal Conversations
Together with the children, create a story that recalls some of their experiences at large-group time. You might start by saying "Let's make up a story about what we like to do at large-group time. Once upon a time, there were some children. They came to school and they loved large-group time. At large-group time, they...." Be sure to let children contribute to the story. Children might want to include their favorite songs, rhymes, movement activities, and so on.

Observations

Record what you saw individual children say and do today. You can use the reproducible sheet on page 178 to make your notes.

Follow-Up Ideas

- Look at your observations about children. What do you see that children enjoy playing or pretending? Choose one of these interests and use that idea as a way to clean up tomorrow.
- **Adult 1:** Look at your observations about children and select art materials you think they would enjoy using for a collage activity during your small-group time on Day 26.
- Write down your own follow-up ideas, using the reproducible sheet on page 179.

Building on What You've Learned: Week 5 Summary

This past week you did the following in your classroom:

- Recorded five observations about children each day (each adult did this)
- Identified the curriculum content illustrated in each of your observations of children
- Used strategies to keep children engaged at cleanup time
- Implemented three literacy-focused small-group times using sample activities from the Growing Readers Early Literacy Curriculum
- Led small-group times that included curriculum content in math and creative representation
- Led large-group times that included curriculum content in music and movement, language and literacy, and math
- Planned a large-group time based on your observations of children

The children were particularly supported in the following areas:

- Continuing to form relationships with adults and children
- Expressing their plans, choices, and intentions
- Participating in activities that supported their development in the broad curriculum content areas of
    - *Approaches to Learning*
    - *Social and Emotional Development*
    - *Physical Development and Health*
    - *Language, Literacy, and Communication*
    - *Mathematics*
    - *Creative Arts*
    - *Science and Technology*
    - *Social Studies*

You developed your own adult-child interactions skills by using these HighScope interaction strategies (new strategies for this week appear in bolder type):

- Offering children comfort and contact
    - Looking for children in need of comfort and contact
    - Offering reassuring physical contact
    - Offering simple acknowledgments
    - Acknowledging children's feelings
- Participating in children's play
    - Joining play on children's level
    - Playing in parallel with children
    - Using comments and observations about what you saw children do as openings to enter play
    - Looking for natural openings to begin to play with children
        - Considering the types of play you observed (exploratory, pretend, constructive, or games) before engaging with children
    - Playing as a partner, letting children retain control
- Conversing with children
    - Looking for natural opportunities for conversation
    - Responding to children's conversational leads
    - Conversing as a partner with children
    - Passing conversational control back to children at every opportunity:
        - Sticking to the topics children raise
        - Making comments that allow the conversation to continue without pressuring children for a response
        - Waiting for children to respond before taking another turn
        - Keeping comments fairly brief
    - Asking questions responsively
        - Asking questions sparingly
        - Relating questions directly to what children are doing
        - Asking questions about children's thought process
- Encouraging children's problem solving
    - Referring one child to another
- **Using encouragement instead of praise**
    - **Participating in children's play**
    - **Encouraging children to describe their efforts, ideas, and products**
    - **Repeating and restating children's words**

Learn More About...*COR Advantage*

COR Advantage, the latest version of High-Scope's Child Observation Record (COR) is an observation-based assessment instrument that provides systematic assessment of young children's knowledge and abilities in all areas of development. Using COR Advantage is a continuous process. Throughout the year, adults record their observations about children in the form of anecdotal notes and use them to score the instrument. Using such notes and other relevant portfolio items, adults score their entries on a scale of 0 to 7 to reflect each child's current level of development, from infancy through kindergarten.

For example, for **COR Advantage Item R. Writing,** the eight levels of development are as follows (two examples of the behavior follow each level statement):

Level 0. Child grasps objects.
- 8/22 Chase reached for a rubber ring and picked it up.
- 6/25 Vivian picked up a clothespin, dropped it, and picked it up again.

Level 1. Child makes marks on a writing surface.
- 7/15 During group time, Kenyon made faint marks on his paper with a crayon.
- 12/4 During group time, Daphne dabbed her paintbrush on the paper.

Level 2. Child scribbles.
- 4/6 During choice time, Daniela used a crayon to scribble back and forth, covering most of her paper.
- 7/18 During outside time, Archie used the sidewalk chalk to make loopy scribbles on the pavement.

Level 3. Child writes discrete letterlike forms.
- 11/2 Upon arrival, Orion wrote an *O* by his name and letter-link symbol on the sign-in sheet.
- 3/15 During work time in the art area, Brianna wrote lines and circles on a piece of notebook paper. She said, "This is my grocery list."

Level 4. Child writes five or more recognizable letters or numerals.
- 1/12 Upon arrival, Elizabeth wrote "ELiBEH" by her name and letter-link symbol on the sign-in sheet.
- 2/16 At work time in the house area, Ling wrote "LING 4." She said, "This is my name, and I'm four!"

Level 5. Child combines letters to form words (other than his or her name) for a purpose.
- 5/24 During choice time in the block area, Sadik asked his teacher how to write the word *open*. As she said the letters, he wrote them on the sign for his boat.
- 6/19 During work time in the art area, Jenna drew a heart and wrote, "HPE BRDA MOM" (for "Happy Birthday Mom").

Level 6. Child writes a sentence, separating the words with spaces.
- 9/18 During morning work, Elena drew a picture of an animal in her journal. She wrote, "We wnt to the zu [We went to the zoo]."
- 12/1 During writer's workshop, Sanford wrote, "I like ice cream," using his finger to hold a space between each word.

Level 7. Child uses writing conventions (in English) by writing several sentences from left to right in horizontal lines.
- 4/14 During center time, Ephram wrote a story of four sentences. When he ran out of room on one line, he went on to the next, moving his pencil to the beginning of the next line in his notebook.
- 1/31 During choice time, Lanie wrote her ideas on the dry-erase board. She wrote several sentences in the small space, moving to the beginning of a new line each time she came to the end of the board, and put a period after each sentence.

By periodically reviewing anecdotes, teachers can make sure they have all the information they need for each child in all the COR Advantage areas of development. If they notice a gap, they may pay special attention to that child or area over the next few days to collect the missing information. To accurately use COR Advantage, training by a designated HighScope trainer or from a HighScope online training course is necessary.

Chapter 6
The Sixth Week

Getting Ready: Week 6 Overview

Goals for the Sixth Week
- Record a minimum of six observations about children per day (each adult does this).
- Identify the curriculum content illustrated in each of your observations.
- Use your observations about children to develop plans specific to your children.
- Identify the possible curriculum content in activities you planned.

Things to Keep in Mind This Week
- This week, you'll rely on your observations about children to individualize your plans for selected activities throughout the daily routine.
- For each activity you plan, identify the possible curriculum content likely to be present and write it by your activity plan.
- Continue to add song cards to the classroom song book, use the sign-in sheets, and use the transition songs.
- Continue to add a message specific to your classroom to the message board.
- On Friday, add this to the message board: Two simply drawn images of the school with a red circle and diagonal slash over them — the universal "no" symbol. Write *2 no school days* and help the children interpret the drawings. Remind them that they will stay home for two days and then come back to school.

After Children Leave for the Day
- Record your observations of children and jot down any ideas you want to follow up on.
- Read tomorrow's lesson plans to see what preparations you will need to make before the children arrive.

Some Reminders for This Week

Monday (Day 26)	**Tuesday** (Day 27)	**Wednesday** (Day 28)	**Thursday** (Day 29)	**Friday** (Day 30)
Group 2: Plan your small-group time for tomorrow Family note home: Read and discuss a book with your child	Use your observations about children to complete Wednesday's plans Identify the curriculum content in your planned activities Family note home: Bath ideas	Use your observations about children to complete Thursday's plans Identify the curriculum content in your planned activities	Use your observations about children to complete Friday's plans Identify the curriculum content in your planned activities	Use the blank planning sheets on pages 180–182 and your observations about children to complete your lesson plans for Monday Identify the curriculum content in your planned activities Family note home: Recall your day with your child

131

DAY 26

Curriculum Content — Key Developmental Indicators (KDIs)*

1. Initiative
2. Planning
6. Reflection
11. Community
12. Building relationships
13. Cooperative play
21. Comprehension
24. Phonological awareness
25. Alphabetic knowledge
26. Reading
29. Writing
31. Number words and symbols
32. Counting
40. Art
41. Music
42. Movement
43. Pretend play
46. Classifying

*See the KDIs listed under individual activities.

Greeting Time
KDIs 12, 24, 25, 26, 29

Adult 2: Greet children at the door. When everyone has arrived, join the children and Adult 1 reading books.

Adult 1: Have about 10 books spread out on the floor. Read books with children. (*Note:* This should last no more than 15 minutes.) Sing a simple transitional song.

Message Board

Draw your daily routine symbol for cleanup time, write *cleanup*, and draw the character you've chosen to use for cleanup time. (See "Cleanup Time" in this lesson for a full description of what you will be doing.) Help the children read this message that for cleanup time, everyone is going to clean up like _____.

Bring out the classroom song book with three sticky notes attached to it, each having a child's name and letter link symbol written on it. Help children read this message that these three children will choose songs to sing at large-group time. These children may want to take their sticky note and put it on the song they'll sing.

Planning Time
Group 1 — KDI 2/Group 2 — KDIs 2, 42

Group 1: Little Mouse With a String

Materials: A string for each child

Remind the children of the book *Good Night, Gorilla*, showing them a page with the mouse and the string. One at a time, give the children a string and ask them to be the little mouse from the story. Ask them to take the string and tie it to something that they will work with and bring it back to the table to share with you. After sharing their ideas about what they would like to do, children can get started on their plans. Repeat for all the children in your group.

Group 2: Planning Paths

Materials: Large area signs

Lay out the large area signs on the floor in a path formation in a large open space. Meet at your usual table and then say to the children something like "Today we are having planning time in the _____ area." With everyone sitting down on the floor in that area, share that today everyone is going to plan by moving down the planning path. Invite children, one at a time, to hop or jump down the path and stop on an area sign indicating the area in which they would like to work. After telling you their plan, the children might want to hop the rest of the way down the path and then get started. Make sure all children have a chance to plan. (*Note:* It's okay if children want to hop to several areas as they may now be making several plans.)

Day 26

Work Time
KDIs 1, 12, 13, 40, 43

When playing with children, **offer ideas or suggestions within the scope of their play.** When used carefully, these extensions can challenge young children's thinking to expand the depth and content of their play — furthering their understanding. **Be sure these ideas stay within children's play theme and don't change the content or focus of the play.** Always respect children's reactions to your ideas.

Here are some examples of how simple extensions can open up a whole new world of ideas for children: For many days, Stan and April make a large fire truck and then sit in it — you might build a house and pretend it catches on fire. Or, for many days, Nigel and Shondra pretend to be kittens. You might take one of the "kittens" and notice that it's not feeling well and suggest that perhaps it needs to see the veterinarian.

Cleanup Time
KDIs 11, 43

For this cleanup time activity, use your observations of children and choose a character or an animal (such as dogs, dinosaurs, babies, or kittens) that you know the children enjoy pretending to be. Give children a verbal warning 10 minutes and then 5 minutes before the end of work time. At the beginning of cleanup time, say to children something like "Today we're going to clean up like _____." Invite them to share how they think this character or animal might move and sound. You can make this really fun by moving and talking like this character/animal yourself.

Recall Time
Group 1 — KDIs 6, 32/Group 2 — KDIs 6, 40

Group 1: Cups and Figures

Materials:

- Toy figures
- Area cards
- A large cup to go with each area card

Choose figures that your children currently enjoy working with (for example, dinosaurs, people figures, plastic bugs). Place an area card by each cup. One at a time, give children a figure and ask them to drop it in the cup indicating the area where they worked and to share details of what they did. Repeat for all the children in your group. At the end, you may wish to include the children in counting how many figures are in each cup. Together, you can decide which area had the most children and which had the fewest.

Group 2: Play dough

Give each child a small hunk of play dough. Ask children to make something they did at work time. Move from child to child and invite them to share their recall with you. It's okay if you don't recognize what children are making — they will tell you about what they did. (*Note:* if you have children who have difficulty with this, you may want to tell them they can get something they played with and press it into the play dough.)

Day 26

Small-Group Time

Group 1 — KDI 40/Group 2 — KDIs 25, 31, 46

Group 1: Collage: Art Material and Glue

Use your observations of the children in your small group to select art materials for this collage activity. These could be ribbon scraps, paper pieces, yarn, buttons, small pebbles, recyclables, wrapping paper scraps, glitter, and so on. Select three to four different materials based on your children's interests. Also, think about your children's level of development or the learning area that you'd like to support — this will guide your interactions with the children.

Materials:

For each child, provide

- A sturdy cardboard base
- A basket with collage items
- A container of glue

For everyone, provide extras of your selected materials.

Beginning: Give each child a basket of materials; invite the children to see what they can do with them.

Middle: Move around the room observing how each child is using the materials. Be sure to add the extra materials to the middle of the table if needed. Let your chosen developmental experience area guide the language that you use to support children's work. You could also change your focus specifically for each child.

End: Give children a three-minute warning and remind them where they can place their collages to dry. Invite children to help resort any extra collage materials into their respective bins. Then ask children to choose how they would like to move to the next part of the daily routine.

Group 2: Letter and Number Parts

Materials:

For each child, provide

- Large letters (both upper- and lowercase) and numbers — for example, written in marker on posterboard or construction paper or made of wood, cardboard, stencils, or cutouts
- Paper and writing materials for children interested in writing or tracing the letters and numbers

Additionally, you will need chart paper divided into three columns and headed as follows: One with a straight mark and the word *straight,* one with a curved mark and the word *curved,* and one with both straight and curved marks and the words *straight and curved.*

Beginning: Tell the children they are going to look at written letters and numbers to see which ones have straight parts and which ones have curved parts, adding that some may have both. Show them what you mean by *straight* by picking out a letter or number and tracing the straight part with your finger; show them where you've made a straight line on the chart pad. Do the same with a curved part. Let the children begin to explore the letters and numbers, inviting them to examine and feel the parts. Encourage children to name the letters and numbers and/or supply the names for them.

Middle: As the children explore, supply letter and number names. Comment on the parts (using vocabulary words such as *straight, round, circle, half-circle, lines, curves, up and down, sideways, point*). As children say whether each letter/number has straight and/or curved parts, write that letter or number in the corresponding column on the chart paper. Encourage children who are interested in doing so to write or trace the numbers and letters on the chart or their own papers and to comment on their characteristics.

End: Together, count the letters and numbers in each column. Write down the totals and talk about which group has more, less, or the same. Store the letters and numbers in an area chosen by the children for their use at work time.

Day 26

Large-Group Time

KDI 41

Singing Songs

Materials: Classroom song book

Step 1: Sing the "We're gonna shake, shake, shake" song until all children have joined; then sing one more verse and end by having everyone sit down on the floor.

Step 2: Show the children the front of the song book after you have placed three sticky notes on it, each having a child's name and letter link symbol written on it. Tell the class that today these three children will each choose a song from the song book. As these children are picking out their songs, you may want to tap a steady beat on your knees with the rest of the children and chant, "I wonder what they'll pick, I wonder what they'll pick?" Sing the songs chosen by the three children, making sure to include choices of verses from the other children when appropriate.

Step 3: Ask the children to choose a way to move to their next activity.

Did You Know...?

For large-group time, **children have been singing with you and your coteacher,** not a recording. There are many reasons why it's important that *you* are the musical source of singing in your classroom. By singing without recorded music, you can

- Slow down the tempo of the song so the children can keep up with you.
- Adjust the pitch higher or lower so children can sing comfortably. Remember, children's natural singing voices are in a higher range than are most adults' voices.
- Take into consideration the ability level of your group. Most recordings have many complicated verses and motions that preschoolers can't do. When you are in control of the song, you may decide to sing just the first verse with your children.
- Pause at the end of a phrase of an action song, giving children a chance to do the movements.
- Modify the song based on the interests and ideas of your children. When singing "Old MacDonald Had a Farm" to a recording, the recording provides the animals that you'll sing about. When you are in control of the singing, you can let children choose the creatures they want to sing about, including dinosaurs and robots!

Remember, a recording can't do any of the things mentioned above. If you already have recordings of children's songs, you can use them to teach yourself songs you like, away from the classroom. Then you can sing the songs with the children yourself, adjusting the tempo and lyrics to your group. Remember, children will be encouraged to sing when they see and hear it modeled and enjoyed by you.

— Adapted from Weikart, P. S., Haraksin, L., & Hutson-Brandhagen, J. (2008). *Making Connections: Movement, Music, & Literacy.* Ypsilanti, MI: HighScope Press.

Day 26

✓ Other Ideas — *Outside Time — KDIs 12, 25, 31/Meal Conversations — KDIs 6, 12, 21*

Outside Time
As you play and interact with children outdoors, look for opportunities to draw attention to letters and numbers visible from your playground. For example, you might say,

> *"I can see the letters S-T-O-P on that stop sign."*
>
> *"This twig looks like the letter Y."*
>
> *"The tire looks like a zero."*

Meal Conversations
During the meal, let the children know that you will describe something on the table and they can guess what it is. ("It is soft." Children guess. "It is small or tiny." Children guess. "It is green." Children guess peas.) Once children get the idea of the game, they can be the leaders and give the clues.

Home-School Connections
Remind the children's family members to read to their child. Also share this idea with the children's families:

If appropriate, you might talk about how the book characters might be feeling. For example, you might say, "How do you think the lost duck feels?" or "Look at his face — he's feeling really angry."

👁 Observations

Record what you saw individual children say and do today. You can use the reproducible sheet on page 178 to make your notes.

➡ Follow-Up Ideas

- **Adult 2:** Look at your observations about children and select art materials you think they would enjoy using for a collage activity for tomorrow's small-group time.

- Write down your own follow-up ideas, using the reproducible sheet on page 179.

DAY 27

Curriculum Content — Key Developmental Indicators (KDIs)*

1. Initiative
2. Planning
6. Reflection
11. Community
12. Building relationships
13. Cooperative play
24. Phonological awareness
25. Alphabetic knowledge
26. Reading
29. Writing
31. Number words and symbols
32. Counting
35. Spatial awareness
40. Art
43. Pretend play
46. Classifying
50. Communicating ideas

*See the KDIs listed under individual activities.

Greeting Time
KDIs 12, 24, 25, 26, 29

Adult 1: Greet children at the door. When everyone has arrived, join the children and Adult 2 reading books.

Adult 2: Have about 10 books spread out on the floor. Read books with children. (*Note:* This should last no more than 15 minutes.) Sing a simple transitional song.

Message Board
Draw your daily routine symbol for cleanup time and write *cleanup*. Also draw a pair of eyes looking. (See "Cleanup Time" in this lesson plan for a full description of what you will be doing.) Help the children read this message that for cleanup time everyone is going to clean up by playing "I Spy" and looking for things to put away.

Create your own message.

Planning Time
Group 1 — KDI 2/Group 2 — KDI 2

Group 1: Planning Paths

Materials: Large area signs

Lay out the large area signs on the floor in a path formation in a large open space. Meet at your usual table and then say to the children something like "Today we are having planning time in the _____ area." With everyone sitting down on the floor in that area, share that today everyone is going to plan by moving down the planning path. Invite children, one at a time, to hop or jump down the path and stop on an area sign indicating the area in which they would like to work. After telling you their plan, children might want to hop the rest of the way down the path and then get started. Make sure all children have a chance to plan. (*Note:* It's okay if children want to hop to several areas as they may now be making several plans.)

Group 2: Little Mouse With a String

Materials: A string for each child

Remind the children of the book *Good Night, Gorilla*, showing them a page with the mouse and the string. One at a time, give the children a string and ask them to be the little mouse from the story. Ask them to take the string and tie it to something that they will work with and bring it back to the table to share with you. After sharing their ideas about what they would like to do, they can get started on their plans. Repeat for all the children in your group.

137

Day 27

Work Time
KDIs 1, 12, 13, 40, 43

When playing with children, **offer ideas or suggestions within the scope of their play.** When used carefully, these extensions can challenge young children's thinking to expand the depth and content of their play — furthering their understanding. **Be sure these ideas stay *within* children's original play theme and don't change the content or focus of the play.** Always respect children's reactions to your ideas. Here is an example of how you can extend a child's idea: After observing Kayra building the same structure with the Lincoln Logs for several days, you might join her and add another room to a similar structure that you build. Watch for her reactions to your idea.

Cleanup Time
KDIs 11, 50

After giving the usual 10- and 5-minute warning signals, say to the children something like "Today we're going to play 'I spy' for cleanup time." Both adults can give smaller groups of children clues about what to put away. ("I spy something that's white....You can scoop with it...and it rhymes with *beasuring bups.* Yes! The measuring cups!") After children get the idea of the game, they might enjoy giving clues to each other.

Recall Time
Group 1 — KDIs 6, 40, 50/Group 2 — KDIs 6, 32

Group 1: Play dough
Give each child a small hunk of play dough. Ask children to make something they did at work time. Move from child to child and invite them to share their recall with you. It's okay if you don't recognize what children are making — they will tell you about what they did. (*Note:* if you have children who have difficulty with this, you may want to tell them they can get something they played with and press it into the play dough.)

Group 2: Cups and Figures

Materials:

- Toy figures
- Area cards
- A large cup to go with each area card

Choose figures that your children currently enjoy working with (for example, dinosaurs, people figures, plastic bugs). Place an area card by each cup. One at a time, give children a figure and ask them to drop it in the cup indicating the area where they worked and to share details of what they did. Repeat for all the children in your group. At the end, you may wish to include the children in counting how many figures are in each cup. Together, you can decide which area had the most children and which had the fewest.

Small-Group Time

Group 1 — KDIs 25, 31, 46/Group 2 — KDI 40

Group 1: Letter and Number Parts

Materials:

For each child, provide

- Large letters (both upper- and lowercase) and numbers — for example, written in marker on posterboard or construction paper or made of wood, cardboard, stencils, or cutouts
- Paper and writing materials for children interested in writing or tracing the letters and numbers

Additionally, you will need chart paper divided into three columns and headed as follows: One with a straight mark and the word *straight*, one with a curved mark and the word *curved*, and one with both straight and curved marks and the words *straight and curved*.

Beginning: Tell the children they are going to look at written letters and numbers to see which ones have straight parts and which ones have curved parts, adding that some may have both. Show them what you mean by *straight* by picking out a letter or number and tracing the straight part with your finger; show them where you've made a straight line on the chart pad. Do the same with a curved part. Let the children begin to explore the letters and numbers, inviting them to examine and feel the parts. Encourage children to name the letters and numbers and/or supply the names for them.

Middle: As the children explore, supply letter and number names. Comment on the parts (using vocabulary words such as *straight, round, circle, half-circle, lines, curves, up and down, sideways, point*). As children say whether each letter/number has straight and/or curved parts, write that letter or number in the corresponding column on the chart paper. Encourage children who are interested in doing so to write or trace the numbers and letters on the chart or their own papers and to comment on their characteristics.

End: Together, count the letters and numbers in each column. Write down the totals and talk about which group has more, less, or the same. Store the letters and numbers in an area chosen by the children for their use at work time.

Group 2: Collage: Art Material and Glue

Use your observations of the children in your small group to select art materials for this collage activity. These could be ribbon scraps, paper pieces, yarn, buttons, small pebbles, recyclables, wrapping paper scraps, glitter, and so on. Select three to four different materials based on your children's interests. Also, think about your children's level of development or the learning area that you'd like to support — this will guide your interactions with the children.

Materials:

For each child, provide

- A sturdy cardboard base
- A basket with collage items
- A container of glue

For everyone, provide extras of your selected materials.

Beginning: Give each child a basket of materials; invite the children to see what they can do with them.

Middle: Move around the room, observing how each child is using the materials. Be sure to add the extra materials to the middle of the table if needed. Let your chosen developmental experience area guide the language that you use to support children's work. You could also change your focus specifically for each child.

End: Give children a three-minute warning and remind them where they can place their collages to dry. Invite children to help resort any extra collage materials into their respective bins. Then ask children to choose how they would like to move to the next part of the daily routine.

Day 27

Large-Group Time

KDI 24

Nursery Rhyme: "Hickory, Dickory, Dock"

Materials: A percussion instrument, such as a triangle or wood block

Step 1: Sing the "We're gonna shake, shake, shake" song until all children have joined; then sing one more verse and end by having everyone sit down on the floor.

Step 2: In preparation for saying the nursery rhyme "Hickory, Dickory, Dock" with the children, go through the motions first. Ask children to find a way to make their fingers scamper up. Then ask them to find a way to make their fingers run back down. Practice doing this a few times.

Step 3: Now layer on the rhyme. Say "Hickory, Dickory, Dock" with the children. When you say the phrase "The mouse ran up the clock," pause and wait for the children to wiggle their fingers up toward the ceiling like a mouse scampering up the clock. When you say the phrase "The clock struck one," have one child strike the triangle (or wood block or other percussion instrument) while the other children wiggle their fingers back down to their laps. Continue the last phrase of the rhyme.

Step 4: After saying the rhyme a few times, tell the children that you are going to change the words *hickory*, *dickory*, and *dock* so they all start with the /b/ sound. Children can identify that the letter *B* makes the /b/ sound. Say the new version of the rhyme, "bickory, bickory, bock." Continue using different letter sounds and having children take turns striking the triangle.

Step 5: Transition to the next part of the daily routine by asking children to move like mice.

Other Ideas *Outside Time — KDIs 12, 25, 31/Meal Conversations — KDIs 12, 35*

Outside Time
As you play and interact with children outdoors, look for opportunities to draw attention to letters and numbers visible from your playground. For example, you might say,

"I can see the letters C-H-I-L-D on our school's sign."

"The railing slats look like both an 1 and an I."

"The sidewalk makes an L."

Meal Conversations
During the meal, talk with children about where they are sitting. Use descriptive words like *between, in the middle, on the side, beside, across, next to*, and so on. You might start by saying "There's lots of ways we could describe where we're sitting...."

Home-School Connections
Share this idea with the children's family members:

Tonight when you bathe your child, give him or her a variety of plastic materials in several sizes to play with. You might try measuring spoons, measuring cups, or margarine tubs and yogurt containers with lids. Comment on how your child fits these things together. While your child is washing, talk about what he or she does first, second, and third. ("You washed your face first, then you washed your toes second, and after that, the third thing you washed was your legs.")

Observations

Record what you saw individual children say and do today. You can use the reproducible sheet on page 178 to make your notes.

Follow-Up Ideas

Use your observations of children to complete tomorrow's plan, using the reproducible sheets on pages 179–182.

DAY 28

Curriculum Content — Key Developmental Indicators (KDIs)*

1. Initiative
2. Planning
6. Reflection
11. Community
12. Building relationships
13. Cooperative play
16. Gross-motor skills
24. Phonological awareness
25. Alphabetic knowledge
26. Reading
29. Writing
40. Art
42. Movement
43. Pretend play
50. Communicating ideas

*See the KDIs listed under individual activities.

Greeting Time
KDIs 12, 24, 25, 26, 29

Adult 2: Greet children at the door. When everyone has arrived, join the children and Adult 1 reading books.

Adult 1: Have about 10 books spread out on the floor. Read books with children. (*Note:* This should last no more than 15 minutes.) Sing a simple transitional song.

Message Board
Draw your daily routine symbol for cleanup time, write *cleanup*, and draw a pair of eyes. Help the children read this message that today everyone is going to play "I spy" at cleanup time. See "Cleanup Time" in this lesson plan for a full description.

Create your own message.

Planning Time
Group 1 — KDI 2/Group 2 — KDIs 2, 29, 40

Group 1: Character Based on Children's Interests
Look at your notes about the children. Choose an animal or character that the children have shown an interest in (for example, a dog, cat, dinosaur). Ask each child to tell his or her plans using the voices and movements of the character you've chosen. ("Robot Carolyn, can you tell us your plan today?")

Group 2: Planning Stories

Materials:

For each child, provide

- A stapled blank book (see below)
- Crayons

Additionally, you will need the small area cards.

Ahead of time, for each child, prepare a simple stapled book with the child's name and letter link symbol on the cover. At planning time, pass out the books to the children. Give them crayons and tell them that, inside the book, they can write or draw their planning story about what they want to do today. It's helpful to have the small area cards on the table in case children wish to include writing in their plans by copying individual letters or the area names. As children finish with their stories, they can tell you about what they wrote or drew. Some children may want you to take dictation of what they say. After all children have planned, set aside these books because you will use them again for recall time today.

Day 28

Work Time
KDIs 1, 12, 13, 40, 43; plus your own curriculum content ideas:

Ahead of time, with your teaching team, look at your observations of children and choose a content area that you don't have any observation on. (See the introduction for information on content areas and page 130 for information on COR Advantage assessment items.) Together, brainstorm language you could use to support this content area with the children. During work time, look for opportunities to make comments using these words when interacting with children. For example, you could use words that describe similarities and differences (Science and Technology, KDI 46. Classifying; *COR Advantage Item BB. Observing and classifying*) when children are building with blocks, using scoops and buckets at the water table, creating a collage in the art area, or even making pretend meals in the house area.

Cleanup Time
KDIs 11, 50

After giving the usual 10- and 5-minute warning signals, say to the children something like "Today we're going to play 'I spy' for cleanup time." Both adults can give smaller groups of children clues about what to put away. ("I spy something that's white....You can scoop with it...and it rhymes with *beasuring bups*. Yes! The measuring cups!") After children get the idea of the game, they might enjoy giving clues to each other.

Recall Time
Group 1 — KDIs 6, 29, 40/Group 2 — KDIs 6, 29, 40

Group 1: Recall Two Things
Give each child a sheet of paper with the numbers 1 and 2 on it (see below). Tell them they can write or draw two things they did at work time.

Sarah explained her recall picture by saying (1) she played with John and (2) they made soup for their babies in the house area.

Group 2: Recall Stories
Using the same books that you used at planning time, give children crayons and invite them to write or draw recall stories. It's helpful to have the small area cards on the table in case children wish to include writing by copying individual letters or the area names in their recall stories. As children finish with their stories, they can tell you about what they wrote or drew. Some children may want you to take dictation of what they say. Children can take these books home and "read" them to their families.

> **TIP:** Here's another way to use a **planning (or recall) book**. When you make the book, be sure it has about 10 pages. You can use it as a planning or recall book periodically, over the course of your program year. Be sure to date each page. At the end of the year, you'll have a nice record of the child's drawing and writing development to share with families at your year-end conference.

Day 28

Small-Group Time
Groups 1 & 2 — Your curriculum content ideas:

Group 1: Unexplored Material
Use your observations of children in your small group to choose a material from your classroom that children haven't been playing with. You can use small-group times as a way to reintroduce the material to children. If, several days after this small-group time you still notice that children are not using the material, you may choose to remove it from the classroom and add a new material in its place.

Materials: For each child, provide a set of the unexplored material you have chosen.

Beginning: Tell children that yesterday, after they went home, you were straightening up the classroom when your found this (the material you have chosen) on the shelf in the _____ area. Explain to the children that you thought they might like to see what they could do with the material for today's small-group time.

Middle: Give children time to explore the material; also use it yourself. **Move from child to child and make comments about what you see children doing** with the material. Refer to similarities and differences in how children are playing. ("Ella and BJ are both stacking, but Naveh has made a long pattern.") Try out the different ways that children are using the material, following their leads.

End: Ask the children to help you put the material back in its container. Ask them to come with you as you put it back on the shelf in the _____ area (so they'll know where the material is in case they want to use it in the future). Ask children to move "very wiggly" to the next part of the daily routine.

Group 2: Unseen Content Areas
Use your observations of children in your small-group time to select a curriculum content area or a specific KDI that you haven't seen children involved in. (See the introduction to this book for more on content categories and KDIs.) For this small-group time, choose materials that lend themselves to the KDIs belonging to that content area; for example, crayons for drawing and painting pictures (Creative Arts), instruments for moving to music (Creative Arts), shells and ice cube trays for sorting objects (Science and Technology), different sized twigs and rubber bands for comparing properties (Science and Technology), people figures and unit blocks for pretending (Creative Arts), beanbags and buckets for moving with objects (Physical Development and Health), and so on.

Materials: For each child, provide a set of your selected materials.

Beginning: Give each child a set of materials and make a simple opening statement, describing what they might do with the materials.

Middle: Observe how children respond to the materials and **use the language related** to your chosen unseen content area and KDIs. Use the materials yourself, imitating what children do. **Be sure to follow the children's leads.** It's okay if children use the materials in ways that you hadn't imagined.

End: Ask children to help put away the materials. Together, choose a way to move to the next part of your routine.

Day 28

Large-Group Time

KDIs 16, 25, 42

Dancing With Letters

Materials:

- Large wooden or plastic letters (enough for each child and adult)
- Carpet squares
- Music without words

Step 1: Sing the "We're gonna shake, shake, shake" song until all children have joined; then sing one more verse and end by asking children to get a carpet square and sit on it. Say to children something like "Today we're going to dance on our carpet square with letters." Pass out one letter to each child (if possible give each child a letter that's in his or her name).

Step 2: Play the music and model things children might do with their letter, such as

- Dancing with the letter in front of them
- Dancing with the letter held up high
- Putting the letter on the carpet square and jumping over it

Step 3: Ask children for ideas on how everyone can dance with their letters; use the children's ideas. Remember that not all children may want to follow your ideas or other children's ideas — they may want to carry out their own ideas on their carpet square. This is okay.

Step 4: Tell children that this is the last dance and that when the music stops they can put their letter back in the container and dance to the next part of the daily routine.

Other Ideas

Outside Time/Meal Conversations: Your curriculum content ideas:

Outside Time
Continue using language from unseen content areas (see "Work Time" in today's lesson plan).

Meal Conversations
During the meal, converse with children about who they played with during work time and what they did together. Talk to children about working together and how they solved problems with what they were doing. If a child says that he did not play with anyone, offer an acknowledgment by saying something like "You chose to do something by yourself today, Henry."

Observations

Record what you saw individual children say and do today. You can use the reproducible sheet on page 178 to make your notes.

Follow-Up Ideas

- Add the letters and numbers you've been using this week to the art area or toy area.
- Write down other follow-up ideas, using the reproducible sheet on page 179.

DAY 29

Curriculum Content — Key Developmental Indicators (KDIs)*

Add your own possible KDIs based on your ideas about today's lesson plan.

Greeting Time

Adult 1: Greet children at the door. When everyone has arrived, join the children and Adult 2 reading books.

Adult 2: Have about 10 books spread out on the floor. Read books with children. (*Note:* This should last no more than 15 minutes.) Sing a simple transitional song.

Your curriculum content ideas:

Message Board
Tape a few of the letters and numbers used in yesterday's large-group time to the message board and draw the area sign for the art area or toy area — wherever you choose to add these materials. Help the children read this message that the letters and numbers have been added to the _____ area.

Create your own message.

Planning Time

Groups 1 & 2: Your curriculum content ideas:

Group 1: Building Toy

Materials:
- Building toy with many pieces
- Area cards

Choose a building toy that the children in your classroom enjoy working with (for example, Legos, Bristle Blocks, small wooden blocks). Lay the area cards out on the table and place a larger sized building toy base or piece by each. Give each child a building toy piece. As children tell you their plans, they can add their piece to the base next to the area card identifying the area in which they would like to work. As more children make their plans, you can involve the other children by commenting on the size of the growing structures. ("The art area building is really getting large, and the house area building is tiny.")

Group 2: Character Based on Children's Interests

Look at your notes about the children. Choose an animal or character that the children have shown an interest in (for example, a robot, dog, cat, dinosaur). Ask each child to tell his or her plans using the voices and movements of the character you've chosen. ("Robot Carolyn, can you tell us your plan today?")

Work Time

Your curriculum content ideas:

Ahead of time, with your teaching team, look at your observations of children and choose a content area that you don't have any observation on. (See the introduction to this book for information on content areas and COR categories and assessment items.) Together, brainstorm language you could use to support this content area with the children. During work time, look for opportunities to make comments using these words when interacting with children. For example, you could use comparison words (Science and Technology, KDI 46. Classifying; *COR Advantage Item BB. Observing and classifying*) when children are building with blocks, using scoops and buckets at the water table, creating a collage in the art area, or even making pretend meals in the house area.

145

Day 29

Cleanup Time

Your curriculum content ideas:

After giving the usual 10- and 5-minute warning signals, say to the children something like "Today we need strong children for cleanup time." Invite children to see how many things they can carry and put away. Most children will count how many things they are holding in their hands. Some children might be able to count the total number of things they put away. Accept either idea as you assist the children in putting away the toys.

Recall Time

Groups 1 & 2: Your curriculum content ideas:

Group 1: Map

Materials:

- Classroom map
- Toy cars

For this activity you will use the simple map of the classroom consisting primarily of the area signs and names that you used for planning time in Days 23 and 25. Give each child a small toy car and, one at a time, ask the children to drive their car to the area on the map showing where they worked. Extend their recall by asking them about the details of what they did. Include other children in the discussion by asking whether they saw the recalling child working there.

Group 2: Recall Two Things

Give each child a sheet of paper with the numbers 1 and 2 on it (see below). Tell them they can write or draw two things they did at work time.

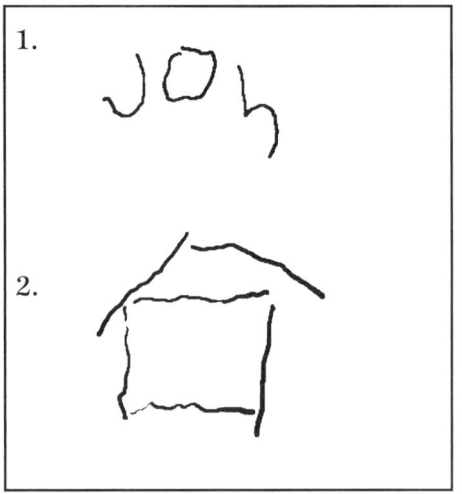

Sarah explained her recall picture by saying (1) she played with John and (2) they made soup for their babies in the house area.

Small-Group Time

Groups 1 & 2: Your curriculum content ideas:

Group 1: Unseen Content Areas

Use your observations of children in your small-group time to select a curriculum content area or a specific KDI that you haven't seen children involved in. (See the introduction to this book for more on content categories and KDIs.) For this small-group time, choose materials that lend themselves to the KDIs belonging to that content area; for example, crayons for drawing and painting pictures (Creative Arts), instruments for moving to music (Creative Arts), shells and ice cube trays for sorting objects (Science and Technology), different sized twigs and rubber bands for comparing properties (Science and Technology), people figures and unit blocks for pretending (Creative Arts), beanbags and buckets for moving with objects (Physical Development and Health), and so on.

Materials: For each child, provide a set of your selected materials.

Beginning: Give each child a set of materials and make a simple opening statement, describing what they might do with the materials.

Middle: Observe how children respond to the materials and **use the language related** to your chosen unseen Content area and KDIs. Use the materials yourself, imitating what children do. **Be sure to follow the children's leads.** It's okay if children use the materials in ways that you hadn't imagined.

End: Ask children to help put away the materials. Together, choose a way to move to the next part of your routine.

Group 2: Combining Materials: Small Building Toys and Figures

You may find it helpful to use your observations of the children in your small group in choosing a set of small building toys for this activity. Choose a building toy you have seen children using, such as Legos, Duplos, Bristle Blocks, or Lincoln Logs. Also select figures that children have shown an interest in (such as small people, dinosaurs, or farm animals) for children to combine with the building toys.

Materials: For each child, provide a small container of building toys as well as several figures to be added later during the activity.

Beginning: Ask children to close their eyes and listen as you snap or connect a few pieces of the building toys together. Ask if they can guess what it is. Give the children their baskets of materials and tell them they can play with their builders. Also have a basket for yourself. Watch what children do with the builders and imitate their actions.

Middle: Move around the table from child to child, **making specific comments** on what you see children doing. ("You've stacked all your pieces into a tower." "You're using the red brick over here and the yellow bricks on this side.") Avoid asking children what they made (perhaps they are exploring and don't have anything particular in mind — this is okay). Instead you might say, "Tell me about what you are doing." Halfway through this small-group time, add the animals or other figures to the middle of the table, saying something like "Some of you might want to use these with your builders." Some children may, others may not. This is okay.

End: Give children a three-minute warning. After three minutes, ask them to take apart their structures, sorting the builders and the figures back into their containers. Ask the children to move like their favorite figure to the next activity.

Day 29

Large-Group Time

Your curriculum content ideas:

Your Idea from Previous Activities

Step 1: Sing the "We're gonna shake, shake, shake" song until all children have joined; then sing one more verse and end by having everyone sit down on the floor.

Step 2: Implement your plan based on previous activities. Your plan is to…

Step 3: Invent your own transition that children can use to get to the next part of the daily routine.

Other Ideas

Your curriculum content ideas:

Meal Conversations
During the meal, invite the children to join you in making up silly same-sound sentences starting with names. Use names children know, and come up with simple sentences and *alliterative phrases* (phrases with words having the same beginning sounds). For example, you might say, "Karla kicked kangaroos" or "David drove dinosaurs." Continue, pausing at the end of each phrase and letting children come up with ideas.

Adult: "Mary made…"

Child: "Messes!"

Adult: "Nita needs…"

Child: "Necklaces!"

Children may or may not offer words that start with the same beginning sounds. Accept children's ideas, but if you find this happening often, you may want to add the sound hint:

Adult: "Mary made …/m/…/m/…"

Child: "Monkeys!"

Observations

Record what you saw individual children say and do today. You can use the reproducible sheet on page 178 to make your notes.

Follow-Up Ideas

Use your observations of children to complete tomorrow's plan, using the reproducible sheets on pages 179–182.

DAY 30

Curriculum Content — Key Developmental Indicators (KDIs)*

Add your own possible KDIs based on your ideas about today's lesson plan.

Greeting Time

Your curriculum content ideas:

Adult 2: Greet children at the door. When everyone has arrived, join the children and Adult 1 reading books.

Adult 1: Have about 10 books spread out on the floor. Read books with children. (*Note:* This should last no more than 15 minutes.) Sing a simple transitional song.

Message Board

Create your own message.

Draw two simple images of the school with a red circle and diagonal slash over them — the universal "no" symbol. Write *2 no school days* and help the children interpret the drawings. Remind them that they will stay home for two days and then come back to school.

Planning Time

Groups 1 & 2: Your curriculum content ideas:

Group 1: Planning Stories

Materials:

For each child, provide

- A stapled blank book (see below)
- Crayons

Additionally, you will need the small area cards.

Ahead of time, for each child, prepare a simple stapled book with the child's name and letter link symbol on the cover. At planning time, pass out the books to the children. Give them crayons and tell them that, inside the book, they can write or draw their planning story about what they want to do today. It's helpful to have the small area cards on the table in case children wish to include writing in their plans by copying individual letters or the area names. As children finish with their stories, they can tell you about what they wrote or drew. Some children may want you to take dictation of what they say. After all these children have planned, set aside these books because you will use them again for recall time today.

Group 2: Building Toy

Materials:

- Building toy with many pieces
- Area cards

Choose a building toy that the children in your classroom enjoy working with (for example, Legos, Bristle Blocks, small wooden blocks). Lay the area cards out on the table and place a larger sized building toy base or piece by each. Give each child a building toy piece. As children tell you their plans, they can add their piece to the base next to the area card identifying the area in which they would like to work. As more children make their plans, you can involve the other children by commenting on the size of the growing structures. ("The art area building is really getting large, and the house area building is tiny.")

Day 30

Work Time

Your curriculum content ideas:

With your teaching team, ahead of time, look at your observations of children and choose a content area that you don't have any observation on. Together, brainstorm language you could use to support this content area with the children. During work time, look for opportunities to make comments using these words when interacting with children. For example, you could use position and direction words (Mathematics, KDI 35. Spatial awareness) when children are building with blocks, using scoops and buckets at the water table, creating a collage in the art area, or even making pretend meals in the house area.

Cleanup Time

Your curriculum content ideas:

Review the cleanup strategies that you've tried so far and choose one to repeat today. After giving the usual 10- and 5-minute warning signals, say to the children something like "Today we will clean up by _____."

Recall Time

Groups 1 & 2: Your curriculum content ideas:

Group 1: Recall Stories
Using the same books that you used at planning time, give children crayons and invite them to write or draw recall stories. It's helpful to have the small area cards on the table in case children wish to include writing by copying individual letters and the area names in their recall stories. As children finish with their stories, they can tell you about what they wrote or drew. Some children may want you to take dictation of what they say. Children can take these books home and "read" them to their families.

Group 2: Map

Materials:

- Classroom map
- Toy cars

For this activity, you will use the simple map of the classroom consisting primarily of the area signs and names that you used for planning time in Days 23 and 25. Give each child a small toy car and, one at a time, ask the children to drive their car to the area on the map showing where they worked. Extend their recall by asking them about the details of what they did. Include other children in the discussion by asking whether they saw the recalling child working there.

Day 30

Small-Group Time

Groups 1 & 2: Your curriculum content ideas:

Group 1: Combining Materials: Small Building Toys and Figures

You may find it helpful to use your observations of the children in your small group in choosing a set of small building toys for this activity. Choose a building toy you have seen children using, such as Legos, Duplos, Bristle Blocks, or Lincoln Logs. Also select figures that children have shown an interest in (such as small people, dinosaurs, or farm animals) for children to combine with the building toys.

Materials:

For each child, provide a small container of building toys as well as several figures to be added later during the activity.

Beginning: Ask children to close their eyes and listen as you snap or connect a few pieces of the building toys together. Ask if they can guess what it is. Give the children their baskets of materials and tell them they can play with their builders. Also have a basket for yourself. Watch what children do with the builders and imitate their actions.

Middle: Move around the table from child to child, **making specific comments** on what you see children doing. ("You've stacked all your pieces into a tower." "You're using the red brick over here and the yellow bricks on this side.") Avoid asking children what they made (perhaps they are exploring and don't have anything particular in mind — this is okay.) Instead you might say, "Tell me about what you are doing." Halfway through this small-group time, add the animals to the middle of the table, saying something like "Some of you might want to use these with your builders." Some children may, others may not. This is okay.

End: Give children a three-minute warning. After three minutes, ask them to take apart their structures, sorting the builders and the figures back into their containers. Ask the children to move like their favorite figure to the next activity.

Group 2: Unexplored Material

Use your observations of children in your small group to choose a material from your classroom that children haven't been playing with. You can use small-group times as a way to reintroduce the material to children. If, several days after this small-group time you still notice that children are not using the material, you may choose to remove it from the classroom and add a new material in its place.

Materials:

For each child, provide a set of the unexplored material you have chosen.

Beginning: Tell children that yesterday, after they went home, you were straightening up the classroom when your found this (the material you have chosen) on the shelf in the _____ area. Explain to the children that you thought they might like to see what they could do with the material for today's small-group time.

Middle: Give children time to explore the material; also use it yourself. **Move from child to child and make comments about what you see children doing** with the material. Refer to similarities and differences in how children are playing. ("Ella and BJ are both stacking, but Naveh has made a long pattern.") Try out the different ways that children are using the material, following their leads.

End: Ask the children to help you put the material back in its container. Ask them to come with you as you put it back on the shelf in the _____ area (so they'll know where the material is in case they want to use it in the future). Ask children to move "very wiggly" to the next part of the daily routine.

Day 30

Large-Group Time

Your curriculum content ideas:

Beanbag Toss

Materials:

For each child and adult, provide

- A beanbag or sponge
- A receptacle, such as small bucket or bin, shoebox, large yogurt container, or the like

Step 1: Sing the "We're gonna shake, shake, shake" song until all children have joined; then sing one more verse and end by having everyone sit down on the floor. Give each child a beanbag and a bucket (or other receptacle) and encourage the children to toss their beanbag into their bucket.

Step 2: As children work with the beanbags, **partner with individual children** as they work at their own levels. Some children may need more encouragement, and some children may benefit from suggestions for more challenging ways of tossing:

"When I can't get it in, I move my bucket closer. That's a way to solve this problem."

"Evan, you seem to be able to get your beanbag inside this bucket many times. Have you tried to aim for it if the bucket is farther away?"

Step 3: Bring the activity to a natural close, encouraging children to try one more toss. Then, begin to collect the buckets. Place a large container for the beanbags in the center of the area and encourage children to put the beanbags away by tossing them into the large container. Then ask children to hop to the next part of the daily routine.

Other Ideas

Meal Conversations: Your curriculum content ideas:

Meal Conversations

During the meal, talk with the children about the kinds of food they are eating and what foods they like to eat. Be nonjudgmental in your responses, adding your own comments to extend children's thinking. ("Some people do like candy. I also love apples — they are very crunchy.")

Home-School Connections

Share this idea with the children's family members:

Recall with your child about what you do during the day. You might start this recall session by saying "I'd like to recall my day with you." If you have a job outside the home, you might tell your child what your job is like and what specific tasks you do. If you work inside the home, you can talk about all the different things you do during the day.

Observations

Record what you saw individual children say and do today. You can use the reproducible sheet on page 178 to make your notes.

Follow-Up Ideas

Write down your own follow-up ideas, using the reproducible sheet on page 179.

Building on What You've Learned: Week 6 Summary

This past week you did the following in your classroom:
- Recorded six observations about children each day (each adult did this)
- Identified the curriculum content illustrated in each of your observations of children
- Used your observations of the children in your classroom to develop specific plans for them
- Identified the possible curriculum content in the activities you planned

The children were particularly supported in the following areas:
- Building on their relationships with classroom adults and other children
- Expressing their plans, choices, and intentions
- Participating in activities that supported their development in the broad curriculum content areas of
    Approaches to Learning
    Social and Emotional Development
    Physical Development and Health
    Language, Literacy, and Communication
    Mathematics
    Creative Arts
    Science and Technology
    Social Studies

You developed your own adult-child interaction skills by using these HighScope interaction strategies (new strategies for this week appear in bolder type):
- Offering children comfort and contact
    - Looking for children in need of comfort and contact
    - Offering reassuring physical contact
    - Offering simple acknowledgments
    - Acknowledging children's feelings
- Participating in children's play
    - Joining play on children's level
    - Playing in parallel with children
    - Using comments and observations about what you saw children doing as openings to enter play
    - Looking for natural openings to begin to play with children
        - Considering the types of play you observed (exploratory, pretend, constructive, or games) before engaging with children
    - Playing as a partner, letting children retain control
    - Referring one player to another
    - Suggesting new ideas within ongoing play situations
        - Offering suggestions within the play theme
- Conversing with children
    - Looking for natural opportunities for conversation
    - Responding to children's conversational leads
    - Conversing as a partner with children
    - Passing conversational control back to children at every opportunity:
        - Sticking to the topics children raise
        - Making comments that allow the conversation to continue without pressuring children for a response
        - Waiting for children to respond before taking another turn
        - Keeping comments fairly brief
    - Asking questions responsively:
        - Asking questions sparingly
        - Relating questions directly to what children are doing
        - Asking questions about children's thought process
- Encouraging children's problem solving
    - Referring one child to another
- Using encouragement instead of praise
    - Participating in children's play
    - Encouraging children to describe their efforts, ideas, and products
    - Repeating and restating children's words
    - **Using language that supports unseen areas of COR Advantage**

Learn More About...*Creating Your Own Lesson Plans for Your Children*

Now that you've gotten a taste of HighScope by using our lesson plans, you can create your own! First, create your own lesson plan form. Our advice? The simpler the better — simply use the format found in this book and modify it to follow your own daily routine.

Once your have your lesson plan form, you're ready to start the planning process. If at all possible, plan with your teaching team.

Together with your teaching team, look at your observations about children, then ask yourself these questions:

- What did I see children doing today?
- What do their actions tell me about...
  - Their development level?
  - Their interests?
- How can I provide materials and interact with children to support their play and learning?

Here is an example of how this planning process can work:

First, consider children's developmental levels. **→ Dev. level →** Jenna speaks in one- or two-word responses.

Then identify children's interests. **→ Interests →** The children really enjoy using the cardboard tubes that a parent donated to the classroom.

Put the two together to come up with a lesson plan idea. **→ Plan Idea →** For the children's planning time, I'll ask them to look through a tube and tell what they want to do at work time.

Plan and use adult support strategies to make the activity appropriate for the developmental range of all the children in your group. **→ Dev. range →** Jenna uses one- or two-word phrases and Henry uses a compound subject or object in sentences.

→ My strategy → With children like Jenna, who can point or say a few words about what they want to do or play with, I can use comments to acknowledge what they say.

→ My strategy → With children like Henry, I can ask them to share more details about their plan:

- What else will they use?
- Are they going to work with anyone else?
- Do they think they'll do this for all of work time?
- Do they want to make a second plan?

Adults also consider specific curriculum content areas (KDIs and COR Advantage Items) and classroom materials when creating lesson plans.

Other HighScope Resources

If you liked the activities presented in this book, you can find more in the following HighScope publications:

"I'm Older Than You. I'm Five!" Math in the Preschool Classroom, Second Edition, by Ann S. Epstein and Suzanne Gainsley

This book presents 50 early math activities for preschoolers. The activities build on children's natural interests and offer children the time and freedom to construct and reflect on math ideas. Aligned with the National Council of Teachers of Mathematics, the activities in this book will help children gain competence in the early math content area.

50 Large-Group Activities for Active Learners, by Christine Boisvert and Suzanne Gainsley

This book presents 50 engaging large-group activities that stimulate children's creativity, help them learn skills and concepts, and introduce them to a wide range of new and thought-provoking experiences. The book also contains valuable ideas for action songs, group storytelling, movement activities, and cooperative games and projects.

Small-Group Times to Scaffold Early Learning, by HighScope Early Childhood Staff

This book presents 52 small-group activities based on five curriculum content areas: language, literacy, and communication; mathematics; science and technology; the creative arts (art and music); and physical development and health. This book includes step-by-step instructions for each activity, suggestions for how to adapt the activity and materials for children with special needs, and content-area summaries describing how children master concepts and develop skills in each domain. Easy-to-read charts outline examples of what children at different developmental levels may say and do during activities, with suggestions for how adults can support children at each of these levels.

Explore and Learn Quick Cards: 80 Activities for Small Groups, by Michelle Graves

Each of these 80 handy and easy-to-use cards contains practical suggestions and detailed descriptions to help teachers create active-learning small groups. The set of cards includes four dividers that organize the activities according to children's interests, new materials, curriculum content areas, and community experiences. Also included in this set are cards that offer tips and suggestions for planning successful small-group times. The three-hole-punched cards are also conveniently sized to fit hanging files in the HighScope Teacher Resources Box or a file cabinet.

Fee, Fie, Phonemic Awareness: 130 Prereading Activities for Preschoolers, by Mary Hohmann

This book focuses on *phonemic awareness* — identified by reading experts as an essential skill that prepares children for reading. The 130 phonemic awareness activities in the book are based on the latest scientific evidence about what children need to become confident and successful readers and writers.

Letter Links: Alphabet Learning With Children's Names, by Andrea DeBruin-Parecki and Mary Hohmann

Letter Links is all about the alphabetic principle from a child development point of view. It highlights the importance of using symbols in preschool along with printed letters. *Letter Links* uses children's natural interest in learning to write their own name as an entryway to teaching them letter recognition skills, letter-sound correspondence, and letter/word writing by using nametags and letter-linked images. (You can also learn about Letter Links Online at the HighScope website, www.highscope.org.)

Find out more about these and other products at the HighScope online store, accessible from the Foundation's Web site at *www.highscope.org*. You can also find classroom materials to support active learning, such as adult-child interaction posters, daily routine cards, area signs, and work-in-progress signs.

References

Evans, B. (2002). *You Can't Come to My Birthday Party! Conflict Resolution With Young Children.* Ypsilanti, MI: HighScope Press.

HighScope Educational Research Foundation. (1996). *Adult-child interaction* (participant guide, 2nd ed.). Ypsilanti, MI: HighScope Press.

HighScope Educational Research Foundation. (2010). *Growing Readers Early Literacy Curriculum* (GRC) Second Edition. Ypsilanti, MI: HighScope Press.

HighScope Educational Research Foundation. (2014). *COR Advantage 1.5 scoring guide.* Ypsilanti, MI: HighScope Press.

Hohmann, M., and Tangorra, J. (Eds.). (2007). *Let's talk literacy: Practical readings for preschool teachers.* Ypsilanti, MI: HighScope Press.

Hohmann, M. (2010). *Growing Readers Early Literacy Curriculum teacher guide.* Ypsilanti, MI: HighScope Press.

Weikart, P. S., Haraksin, L., & Hutson-Brandhagen, J. (2008). *Making connections: Movement, music, & literacy.* Ypsilanti, MI: HighScope Press.

Chapter 7
Sample Growing Readers Activities

Lesson Plans for the First 30 Days

SMALL-GROUP ACTIVITY

22 Connect to *Good Night, Gorilla*: What Things Do You See?

Level One

CONTENT AREA: **Comprehension**
TOPIC: **Connection**

Literacy Learning Focus
Children observe, describe, and comment on what they see in *Good Night, Gorilla* and use this information to create a simple story line.

> **Quick Plan**
> - Teacher and children examine and discuss the pictures.
> - Children tell the story based on the pictures.
> - Children compare pictures on the front and back covers.

Materials
- A copy of *Good Night, Gorilla* by Peggy Rathmann—number the pages in pencil or with sticky notes and make page 1 the title page and page 36 the page with the copyright information
- *Good Night, Gorilla* Vocabulary Card

Hint: The **copyright** states the legal rights of the publication. Elements usually include the word *copyright,* the copyright symbol: ©, and the name of the copyright holder. In this book the copyright information appears on a page in the back; in other books it may appear on a page in the front.

Beginning
1. Gather in a comfortable spot where you and the children can cluster as close to *Good Night, Gorilla* as possible. Put the book on the floor, front cover up, so that the children can easily touch and take a leisurely look at the pictures.
2. Begin by saying something like "**Today we're going to read the book called *Good Night, Gorilla.* The person who wrote this book and drew the pictures is Peggy Rathmann. What do you see on the cover?**" Listen to and acknowledge the children's observations. If they haven't figured it out, let them know that the little creature holding the key is the gorilla mentioned in the title. If they notice the puffin in the lower left-hand corner, let them know that it is the special icon or picture that stands for the company who made (published) the book.
3. Turn to the title page, a two-page spread. Ask the children to tell you what they see. They may (or may not) notice that the writing is the same on both the title page and the cover. Therefore, they may need to spend some time flipping back and forth between the title page and the cover. If the children remark on the banana that's hanging mysteriously in the upper right-hand corner of the picture on the title page, you might say, "**Let's watch and see if we see a banana again in another picture.**"

Middle
4. Turn to the first two pages of the story and ask the children to tell you what they see. Give children plenty of time to look at the book and then to describe what they see. Listen to and support their observations and add your own from time to time. For example, a conversation about the first two pages of the story might begin in the following manner:

Teacher:	We can tell what's happening in this story by looking at the pictures. There are lots of things to see in the pictures.
Child 1:	Balloon!
Child 2:	There's that tire.
Child 3:	*(Points to the flashlight)* What's this?
Child 4:	A light...a light...to see.
Teacher:	He's holding a flashlight so he can see in the dark.
Child 4:	Yeah! A flashlight!
Child 5:	He's got a hat.

Copyright © 2010 HighScope® Educational Research Foundation C61

Copyright © 2012 HighScope® Educational Research Foundation. The owner of this book has permission to copy this page for its use in the classroom.

Lesson Plans for the First 30 Days

Child 6: And keys.

Child 1: *(Points to a patch on the zookeeper's arm)* Blood.

Child 6: A funny pocket.

Teacher: It does look like a funny pocket with a blood-red line on it. Under the red line it says *Zoo*. It's a patch on the sleeve of the zookeeper's uniform that tells people that he works at the zoo.

5. Before turning the page, summarize what the children have seen and include the words the zookeeper is saying. For example, depending on what your children notice and say, you might say, "Okay, in this picture we've seen toys and things in the gorilla's cage with the red bars, such as a balloon, a tire swing, a mouse, some bananas, some trees, a bike, a book, and a tiny gorilla. Outside the cage we've seen the moon, the zookeeper, the zookeeper's patch that says *Zoo*, his keys, his flashlight, and the yellow beam of light from the flashlight. The zookeeper is saying 'Good night, Gorilla.'"

6. Repeat steps 4 and 5 until you reach the end of the story. Give the children plenty of time to examine the pictures and comment on what they see. Comment on objects and parts of objects the children overlook or may not know the names of. (For a list of the objects in *Good Night, Gorilla*, see the *Good Night, Gorilla* Vocabulary Card.)

End

7. Finally, look at the back cover of the book and the last two pages that include the book's dedication and copyright information. Again, ask the children what they see. Listen for or invite them to notice that the back cover includes pictures that also appear on the first two pages of the story. Flip back and forth between the back cover and pages 2 and 3 during this conversation.

8. Let children know that *Good Night, Gorilla* will be in the book area for them to look at whenever they want.

Follow-Up

As you read more picture books with children during other parts of the day, encourage them to examine and talk about what they see in the pictures.

Related Small-Group Times

Connection activities 23 and 24

Copyright © 2010 HighScope® Educational Research Foundation

Copyright © 2012 HighScope® Educational Research Foundation. The owner of this book has permission to copy this page for its use in the classroom.

Lesson Plans for the First 30 Days

SMALL-GROUP ACTIVITY

23 Connect to *Good Night, Gorilla:* Try Out Flashlights and Keys

Level One

CONTENT AREA: **Comprehension**
TOPIC: **Connection**

Literacy Learning Focus
Children connect *Good Night, Gorilla* to their own lives as they use objects from the story.

> **Quick Plan**
> - Children guess what objects from the book are in the box (see **Materials** for more information).
> - Children try out flashlights, keys, and key rings.
> - Children show and describe how to use the flashlights or key rings.

Materials
- ☆ A copy of *Good Night, Gorilla* by Peggy Rathmann
- ☆ A box for each child (or for every two children, depending on the number of flashlights you can gather)
- ☆ Each box should contain the following:
  - ✔ Real keys of any sort and size
  - ✔ Pipe cleaners (or flexible pieces of wire)
  - ✔ A flashlight

Beginning
1. Gather in a comfortable spot where children have enough room to maneuver boxes, flashlights, pipe cleaners, and keys. Place *Good Night, Gorilla* where children can easily see the cover.
2. Show the children the pile of boxes you have for them and ask them to guess what things from *Good Night, Gorilla* are in the boxes. Listen to and acknowledge children's guesses.
3. Open one box so the children can see the flashlight, keys, and pipe cleaners for them to try out and explore. If they wonder why you have included a pipe cleaner (or wire), let them know you thought they might be able to think of a way to make it into a ring to hold their keys like the zookeeper's key ring.
4. Pass out the boxes so children can open them and discover ways to use the flashlights and keys they contain.

Middle
5. Watch and listen to the children as they figure out how to turn their flashlights on and off and shine them about the room. Comment on what you see and hear. For example, you might have the following conversation:

    Child: Look! It's moving!
    Teacher: I see! You're shining the beam of light on the ceiling!
    Child: On there!
    Teacher: You can shine the beam of light on the door...on the doorknob. Whoops! There it goes to the floor.
    Child: On my hand!
    Teacher: Now you're shining a circle of light on your hand!

6. Watch and listen to the children as they work with their keys and pipe cleaners (or wire). Comment on what you see and hear. For example, you might have the following exchange:

    Child: They're on.
    Teacher: You put your keys on your pipe cleaner.
    Child: *(Bends over to search for a belt loop, finds one, works to string the pipe cleaner with keys through the loop, and finally looks up in frustration)*
    Teacher: Is there a way I can help?
    Child: Hold this.
    Teacher: *(Holds one end of the pipe cleaner)*

Copyright © 2010 HighScope® Educational Research Foundation

C63

Copyright © 2012 HighScope® Educational Research Foundation. The owner of this book has permission to copy this page for its use in the classroom.

Child: *(Twists one pipe cleaner end around the end the teacher is holding)* There!

Teacher: Now you're wearing your ring of keys on your belt—just like the zookeeper wears his keys!

Child: *(Turns to another child)* Hey Keegan, look! Key ring!

End

7. Ask the children to keep their flashlights and put their keys and pipe cleaners back in their boxes.

8. Let the children know that the flashlights and keys will be in the house area (or wherever you decide to store them) to play with at other times of the day.

9. Dismiss children by asking each one, in turn, to show and describe something he or she can do with the flashlight. Then have children put them back in their boxes and go to the next part of the classroom daily routine. Relate children's actions to actions in the story when feasible.

Follow-Up

If children focus mostly on the flashlights, you may wish to repeat this small-group time just using the keys and pipe cleaners or wire. As children use the flashlights and keys at other times of the day, look for opportunities to talk with them about what they are doing.

Related Small-Group Times

Connection activities 22 and 24

Lesson Plans for the First 30 Days

SMALL-GROUP ACTIVITY

24 Connect to *Good Night, Gorilla*: What Is in Your House and in the Zoo?

Level One

CONTENT AREA: **Comprehension**
TOPIC: **Connection**
SMALL-GROUP ACTIVITY 24

Literacy Learning Focus
Children connect *Good Night, Gorilla* to their own lives as they look for and talk about toys, objects, and furnishings in the story that remind them of toys, objects, and furnishings from their own homes and neighborhoods.

Quick Plan
- Teacher and children examine and discuss the pictures.
- Children find and discuss familiar objects and toys in the pictures.
- Children choose one favorite object from the pictures.

Materials
- A copy of *Good Night, Gorilla* by Peggy Rathmann
- *Good Night, Gorilla* Vocabulary Card

Beginning
1. Gather in a comfortable spot where you and the children can cluster as close to *Good Night, Gorilla* as possible. Put the book on the floor, front cover up, so that the children can easily touch and examine the pictures.

2. Begin by saying something like "Today, let's look for pictures of things in *Good Night, Gorilla* that are like real things you see or play with at home or at someone else's house. Let's look on the cover. What do you see that's like something you've seen or played with?" Pause for the children to gather their ideas. Listen to and acknowledge their contributions.

   If no one offers an idea, you might point to the key the gorilla is holding and say one of the following statements (then pause, listen to, and acknowledge children's contributions): "I have a key to the door of my house." "My brother has a belt (hat, shirt) like the zookeeper's." "I have a small flashlight on my key chain." "We have flashlights in our classroom."

Middle
3. Turn to the first two pages of the story. To begin the conversation, make a comment. For example, you might say, "Hmm. I wonder what you see on this page that's like something you have or you play with." Give children plenty of time to look at the pages and then to make a connection to and talk about something they see in the picture. Listen to and support their observations and add your own from time to time. For example, a conversation about the connections the children make with the objects on the first two pages of the story might begin in the following manner:

   Teacher: I bet there are some things in this picture that you play with or have at your house.
   Child 1: My cousin has a bike, a big one.
   Child 2: *(Points out the window to the playground)* Trikes.
   Teacher: Jamison's cousin has a big bike, and outside at our school we have trikes or tricycles, which are bikes with three wheels, like the trike in the gorilla's cage!
   Child 2: *(Points to the gorilla's bike)* Where ride?
   Child 3: Uh, oh! He's gonna crash in there!
   Teacher: It does look crowded in the gorilla's cage. There's not much room for riding a tricycle.
   Child 4: Maybe he rides in a big cage.
   Child 5: I ride at my grandma's.

Copyright © 2010 HighScope® Educational Research Foundation   C65

Copyright © 2012 HighScope® Educational Research Foundation. The owner of this book has permission to copy this page for its use in the classroom.

Teacher:	So, we have trikes at school, Jamison's cousin has a big bike, and Yvonne has a trike at her grandma's like the tricycle the gorilla has in his cage. It looks like the gorilla might have to ride his bike carefully in his cage so he doesn't crash into things, or maybe he rides in another big cage.
Child 6:	Maybe he just keeps it there.
Teacher:	I see. Maybe he just keeps his trike in the cage like we keep our trikes in the shed.
Child 6:	Yeah, we take 'em out to ride.

4. Repeat step 3 for each pair of facing pages. Take your time on each two-page spread so the children have plenty of time to examine the pictures and comment on the connections they make between things they see on the page and their own life experiences with similar objects. (As you talk with the children, keep in mind the list of object names on the *Good Night, Gorilla* Vocabulary Card.)

End

5. After the last two pages of the story, close the book and say something like "**We saw lots of things in *Good Night, Gorilla* that we already knew something about!**"

6. Dismiss the children by giving each child, in turn, the opportunity to find something in the book that is like something he or she has seen or played with. Or, dismiss the children by naming the color of the animals' cages: Turn to the first two-page spread and say something like "**Anyone wearing red like the gorilla's cage can go to (the next part of the classroom daily routine).**" Pause for the children to respond. Turn to the next two-page spread and say something like "**Anyone wearing pink like the elephant's cage can go to....**" Continue through the other pages as needed.

Follow-Up

As you read more picture books with children during other parts of the day, encourage them to look at the pictures and talk about objects they see that are like things they themselves have seen or played with.

Related Small-Group Times

Connection activities 22 and 23

VOCABULARY
Good Night, Gorilla

Objects

Use some of these **nouns** (words that name people, places, things, events, and ideas) in conversations with children each time you look at and talk about *Good Night, Gorilla*.

Animals	***Colors***	***Furnishings***	peel
armadillo	black	alarm clock	shadow
brush	brown	awning	sky
elephant	dark green	bedpost	trees
giraffe	gray	bedside dresser (or	
gorilla	green	bureau)	***Neighborhoods***
hoof	green-yellow	bedstead	lawn
horns	lavender	blanket	path
hyena	light blue	carpet	sidewalk
lion	light green	cord	sign
mane	light pink	curtains (also drapes)	signpost
mouse	light yellow	designs	streetlights
paw	midnight blue	doorknob	walkway
shell	orange	drawer	
spots	pitch black	finial	***Tools***
tail	purple	footboard	beam of light
toes	red	fringe	flashlight
tongue	red-orange	handrails	key ring
trunk	tan	headboard	keys
tuft (tail tip)	turquoise	lamp	rope
tusk	white	patterns	
vulture	yellow	photo gallery	***Toys***
		photographs	Babar (toy)
Clothing and People	***Dwellings***	picture frames	baby bottle
belt loop	arch	pillow	ball
belt	archway	reading light	balloon
brim	bars	shade	basket
buckle	baseboard	shade pulls	Ernie (armadillo toy)
hat	bedding (grass, straw)	stem	handlebars
husband	cage	stripes	pacifier (has many
mustache	cave	wallpaper	names)
nametag	door	window shades	pedals
nightcap	enclosure		pull toy
nightgown	house	***Nature***	seat
partner	keyhole	bamboo tree	string
patch	lock	banana	stuffed toy
pocket	pen	bone	tire
shirt	porch	branch	tire swing
slippers	porch light	bunch	tricycle
tie	roof	bushes	wheels
uniform	stairs	flowers	
visor	steps	grass	*More vocabulary*
wife	stoop	moon	*words follow on the*
zookeeper	tiles	moonlight	*back of this card.*
	wall	night	
	window	peanuts	
	windowsill		
	zoo		

Copyright © 2010 HighScope® Educational Research Foundation. The owner of this copy of the curriculum has permission to copy this card for its use in the classroom.

V11

Copyright © 2012 HighScope® Educational Research Foundation. The owner of this book has permission to copy this page for its use in the classroom.

Lesson Plans for the First 30 Days

Actions

Use some of these **verbs** (words that express action, existence, or occurrence) in conversations with children each time you look at and talk about *Good Night, Gorilla*.

Gorilla Actions
balance
carry
climb
copy
cover
crawl
creep
cross
drag
enter
eye
feel
fit
follow
grab
grasp
grin
hang
hide
hold
hush
imitate
lead
lean
leave
lie
look
lower
march
open
play
point
quiet
reach
return
scoot
sit
sleep
smile
snatch
sneak
snuggle
speak
stand
step
stop
stretch
swing
tiptoe
touch
turn
unlock
wait
wake up
yawn

Human Actions
bend
carry
check
climb
close (eyes)
dangle
enter
escort
fall asleep
hold
lean
make (the rounds)
patrol
perch
pull
reach
return
shine
sit
sit up
sleep
speak
stretch
take off
tiptoe
turn off
turn on
undress
walk
watch
yawn

Mouse Actions
balance
bite
carry
climb
cross
drag
enter
follow
gnaw
haul
hide
hoist
lean
let down
lie down
lift
look
lower
perch
pull
raise
rest
return
sit
sleep
speak
stand
strain
struggle
tug
tunnel
walk
watch
work
yank

Other Animal Actions
bend
cross
curl up
enter
follow
grasp
hold
hover
join
leave
lick
lie down
lift
line up
lumber
parade
pause
raise
return
roost
signal
sit
sleep
smile
speak
step
step on
stroll
wait
walk
watch

Ideas

Use some of these words connected to the ideas of *surprise*, *bedtime*, and *plans* in conversations with children as you look at and talk about *Good Night, Gorilla*.

Surprise
amaze
amazement
anticipate
anticipation
astonish
astonishment
expect
plan
suspect
unexpected
wonder
wondering
wonderment

Bedtime
active
awake
cuddle
drowsy
energetic
fast asleep
nestle
patient
persistent
sleepy
sound asleep
tired
wakeful
worn out

Plans
change
choice
choose
conclude
consider
decide
decision
determine
idea
intend
intention
think

Copyright © 2010 HighScope® Educational Research Foundation. The owner of this copy of the curriculum has permission to copy this card for its use in the classroom. V12

Copyright © 2012 HighScope® Educational Research Foundation. The owner of this book has permission to copy this page for its use in the classroom.

Lesson Plans for the First 30 Days

SMALL-GROUP ACTIVITY

1 Learn Nursery Rhymes: Act Out "Humpty Dumpty" and Other Level One Nursery Rhymes

Level One — CONTENT AREA: **Phonological Awareness** — TOPIC: **Rhyming** — SMALL-GROUP ACTIVITY 1

Literacy Learning Focus
Children build a repertoire of level one nursery rhymes by hearing, saying, and acting out nursery rhymes and by looking at and discussing related illustrations.

Quick Plan
- Children listen to and say the nursery rhyme.
- Children act out and say the nursery rhyme.
- Teacher and children discuss nursery rhyme pictures, words, and objects.

Hint: Level One Nursery Rhymes are nursery rhymes with rhyming words close together, that is, nursery rhymes with two words that rhyme within a single line or a group of four beats of the nursery rhyme—for example, "Jack and *Jill* went up the *hill*."

Materials
- ☆ A book (or books) of *Mother Goose* nursery rhymes
- ☆ Bookmarks or sticky notes marking your chosen level one nursery rhymes; for example, "Hickory, Dickory, Dock," "Humpty Dumpty," "Jack and Jill," and "Three Little Kittens" (see **Follow-Up** for a list of other level one nursery rhymes)
- ☆ Props related to nursery rhymes; for example, a large block (for a wall)—for "Humpty Dumpty"; a clock—for "Hickory, Dickory, Dock"; a mound of pillows (for a hill)—for "Jack and Jill"; and a bucket, mittens, and a pie tin—for "Three Little Kittens"
- ☆ *Mother Goose* Vocabulary: Level one Nursery Rhymes Card

Beginning
1. Gather in a comfortable spot on the floor where children can cluster around you and the *Mother Goose* nursery rhymes. Make sure children have plenty of room to move.
2. Begin by saying something like "**Today we're going to say and act out some** *Mother Goose* **nursery rhymes, and then we'll look at the pictures that go with them.**" Listen to and acknowledge children's comments and ideas about nursery rhymes and the character, Mother Goose.

Middle
3. Start with the first nursery rhyme you have selected and say something like "**Here's 'Humpty Dumpty.'**" Say the "Humpty Dumpty" nursery rhyme to the children with enjoyment and expression. Before you say it a second time, invite the children to join in and say the words they know. Afterward, listen to and support any comments they make about the nursery rhyme.
4. Bring out the related prop (or props)—in this case, a large block to stand for a wall—and say something like "**Here's Humpty Dumpty's wall. Let's see who can be Humpty Dumpty and fall off the wall while we say the nursery rhyme!**" Invite the children to take turns acting out "Humpty Dumpty" while everyone else says the nursery rhyme.
5. Bring out the *Mother Goose* book and turn to the page with "Humpty Dumpty." Together with the children, look at the illustration and invite children to talk about what they see. Support their observations and add your own related

Copyright © 2010 HighScope® Educational Research Foundation PA7

Copyright © 2012 HighScope® Educational Research Foundation. The owner of this book has permission to copy this page for its use in the classroom.

Lesson Plans for the First 30 Days

comments. When feasible, take the opportunity to explain new words in the nursery rhyme and to identify objects with names the children may not know that appear in the illustrations. For example, you might have a conversation like the following about the "Humpty Dumpty" illustration:

Child 1: *(Points to the bunny)* A bunny.
Teacher: Yes, there is a bunny with a fluffy white tail sitting next to the wall.
Child 2: Fluffy! That's funny!
Teacher: It is a funny word to say—fluffy. A fluffy bunny.

Listen to and support children's observations. Anticipate that some children will be interested in talking about who or what Humpty Dumpty is.

Hint: When you **use more than one** *Mother Goose* **book** for this activity, the children will enjoy talking about the similarities and differences in the way the book illustrators have imagined and drawn Humpty Dumpty.

6. Repeat steps 3–5 for the other level one nursery rhymes you have selected. Take your time. If you don't get through all the nursery rhymes, come back to them at another small-group time. (For new words in the set of nursery rhymes listed below, see the *Mother Goose* Vocabulary: Level One Nursery Rhymes Card.)

End

7. Let the children know that the *Mother Goose* book will be in the book area for them to look at during the day.

8. Dismiss the children one by one to the next part of the classroom daily routine by inviting each child to choose one of the nursery rhymes and point to and talk about what he or she likes in the illustration.

Follow-Up

Repeat this small-group activity until you have worked through the level one nursery rhymes listed below, along with any other nursery rhymes, poems, or children's stories with rhyming words close together.

Level One Nursery Rhymes

To find the page of a nursery rhyme in the *Mother Goose* book you are using, turn to the book's index.

Related Small-Group Times

Rhyming activities 2 and 3

Copyright © 2010 HighScope® Educational Research Foundation

PA8

vCopyright © 2012 HighScope® Educational Research Foundation. The owner of this book has permission to copy this page for its use in the classroom.

Lesson Plans for the First 30 Days

SMALL-GROUP ACTIVITY

2 Learn Nursery Rhymes: Pat to "Humpty Dumpty" and Other Level One Nursery Rhymes

Level One — Phonological Awareness — Rhyming — SMALL-GROUP ACTIVITY 2

Literacy Learning Focus
Children build a repertoire of level one nursery rhymes by hearing, saying, and patting to the nursery rhymes.

> **Quick Plan**
> - Teacher and children say and pat to four lines of "pat-pat-pat-pat."
> - Teacher and children say and pat to nursery rhymes.
> - Teacher adds the children's names to the nursery rhymes.

Hint: Level One Nursery Rhymes are nursery rhymes with rhyming words close together, that is, nursery rhymes with two words that rhyme within a single line or a group of four beats of the nursery rhyme—for example, "Jack and *Jill* went up the *hill*."

Materials
- ☆ A book (or books) of *Mother Goose* nursery rhymes
- ☆ Bookmarks or sticky notes marking your chosen level one nursery rhymes; for example, "Hickory, Dickory, Dock," "Humpty Dumpty," "Jack and Jill," and "Three Little Kittens" (see **Follow-Up** for a list of other level one nursery rhymes)
- ☆ *Mother Goose* Vocabulary: Level One Nursery Rhymes Card
- ☆ How to Pat to a Nursery Rhyme Activity Support Card

Beginning
1. Gather in a comfortable spot on the floor where children can cluster around you. Begin by saying something like "**See if you can try doing what I'm doing with my hands.**" With both hands lightly pat your thighs 16 times (counting internally to yourself, not out loud), then stop. Do this several times until all or most of the children have joined in patting their thighs.

2. Next, say something like "**Try saying what I'm saying while we pat.**" (Pat on each underlined word.) Do this several times.

   <u>Pat</u> <u>pat</u> <u>pat</u> <u>pat</u>
   <u>Pat</u> <u>pat</u> <u>pat</u> <u>pat</u>
   <u>Pat</u> <u>pat</u> <u>pat</u> <u>pat</u>
   <u>Pat</u> <u>pat</u> <u>pat</u> <u>pat</u>

Middle
3. Place the *Mother Goose* book where everyone can see the cover and say something like "**Today we're going to say some of the nursery rhymes we've been learning and pat to them.**"

4. Open to "Humpty Dumpty" and say something like "**Here's the nursery rhyme about Humpty Dumpty who falls off the wall, breaks, and can't be put back together again.**" Pause to give the children a chance to look at and talk about the Humpty Dumpty illustration. Listen to and support their comments and ideas.

5. Gently pat both hands on your knees or thighs and invite the children to join you in saying the nursery rhyme and patting to "Humpty Dumpty." (Again, pat on each underlined syllable or word.)

   <u>Hump</u>-ty <u>Dump</u>-ty <u>sat</u> on a <u>wall</u>;
   <u>Hump</u>-ty <u>Dump</u>-ty <u>had</u> a great <u>fall</u>.
   <u>All</u> the king's <u>hor</u>-ses and <u>all</u> the king's <u>men</u>
   <u>Could</u>-n't put <u>Hump</u>-ty to-<u>geth</u>-er a-<u>gain</u>.

   After you have said the nursery rhyme once in this manner, and the children have joined in on some of the words, say something like "**That was fun! Let's do it again!**" Say the nursery rhyme and pat to it again.

Copyright © 2010 HighScope® Educational Research Foundation   PA9

Copyright © 2012 HighScope® Educational Research Foundation. The owner of this book has permission to copy this page for its use in the classroom.

Lesson Plans for the First 30 Days

Hint: Don't be surprised if children focus on patting and say only a few words of the nursery rhyme. Gradually, as their experience with patting to familiar nursery rhymes grows, **children's ability to coordinate patting with speaking will improve.**

6. Invite the children to select another nursery rhyme they know from the pages you marked. Then repeat steps 4 and 5 for that nursery rhyme. When completing step 5, pat to the stressed, or accented syllables in each line of the nursery rhyme. (See the How to Pat to a Nursery Rhyme Activity Support Card for assistance with patting.) Repeat step 6 as long as the children continue to select nursery rhymes. Use and talk about new words as they arise. (See the *Mother Goose* Vocabulary: Level One Nursery Rhymes Card.)

End

7. Let children know that the *Mother Goose* book will be in the book area for them to look at during the day.

8. Dismiss the children one by one to the next part of the classroom daily routine by adding a child's name to one of the nursery rhymes. Pat to the nursery rhyme as you say it. For example,

> <u>Hump</u>-ty **Dump**-ty <u>sat</u> on a <u>wall</u>;
> <u>Hump</u>-ty **Dump**-ty <u>had</u> a great <u>fall</u>.
> <u>All</u> **Danny's** <u>hor</u>-ses and <u>all</u> **Danny's** <u>men</u>
> <u>Could</u>-n't put <u>Hump</u>-ty to-<u>geth</u>-er a-<u>gain</u>.

The following are examples of other verses to use:

> <u>Hick</u>-o-ry, <u>dick</u>-o-ry <u>dock</u>. ____ **Fi**-<u>ona</u> ran <u>up</u> the <u>clock</u>…
>
> **Max** and **Jill** went <u>up</u> the <u>hill</u>…
>
> **Graham's** little <u>kit</u>-tins <u>lost</u> their <u>mit</u>-tens…
>
> <u>Lit</u>-tle **Darla** **Tit**-tle-mouse <u>lived</u> in a <u>lit</u>-tle house…
>
> <u>An</u>-na-**Down**-<u>Dil</u>-ly has <u>come</u> to <u>town</u>…
>
> <u>Hey</u>, diddle, <u>did</u>-dle, **Bing** and the <u>fid</u>-dle…
>
> <u>Lit</u>-tle **Caitlin** <u>Hor</u>-ner <u>sat</u> in a <u>cor</u>-ner…
>
> <u>Old</u> **Dubai** <u>Hub</u>-bard <u>went</u> to the <u>cup</u>-board…
>
> <u>El</u>-ber **Sprat** could <u>eat</u> no <u>fat</u>…

> <u>Ros</u>-a-lina **Lock**-et <u>lost</u> her (his) <u>pock</u>-et…
>
> **Sa**-jel be <u>nim</u>-ble, **Sa**-jel be <u>quick</u>…
>
> <u>Old</u> **Mar-la** **Cole** was a <u>mer</u>-ry old <u>soul</u>…

Follow-Up

Repeat this small-group activity until you have worked through the level one nursery rhymes listed below, along with any other nursery rhymes, poems, or children's stories with rhyming words close together.

Level One Nursery Rhymes

To find the page of a nursery rhyme in the *Mother Goose* book you are using, turn to the book's index.

As Tommy Snooks	Little Miss Muffet
Bow, Wow, Wow	Little Nancy Etticoat
Charley Barley	Little Poll Parrot
Charlie Warlie	Little Tee-Wee
Cross-Patch	Little Tommy Tittlemouse
Daffy-Down-Dilly	Lucy Locket
A Diller, a Dollar	The Man in the Moon… Soon
Doctor Foster	
Hark, Hark	Mary, Mary, Quite Contrary
Hector Protector	My Maid Mary
Hey Diddle, Diddle	Old King Cole
Hickety, Pickety	Old Mother Hubbard
Hickory, Dickory, Dock	Peter, Peter, Pumpkin Eater
High Diddle Doubt	The Queen of Hearts
Hoddley, Poddley	Rain, Rain, Go Away
Humpty Dumpty	Red Sky at Night
Ickle Ockle	Ring-a-Ring o' Roses
Jack and Jill	Rub-a-Dub-Dub
Jack Be Nimble	See-Saw, Margery Daw
Jack Sprat	Simple Simon
Jerry Hall	Star Light
Little Betty Blue	There Was a Little Girl
Little Blue Ben	Three Little Kittens
Little Bo-Peep	Tom, Tom, the Piper's Son
Little Jack Horner	

Related Small-Group Times

Rhyming activities 1 and 3

Copyright © 2010 HighScope® Educational Research Foundation

PA10

Copyright © 2012 HighScope® Educational Research Foundation. The owner of this book has permission to copy this page for its use in the classroom.

Level One — CONTENT AREA: **Phonological Awareness** — TOPIC: **Rhyming** — SMALL-GROUP ACTIVITY 3

SMALL-GROUP ACTIVITY

3 Learn Nursery Rhymes: Recall "Humpty Dumpty" and Other Level One Nursery Rhymes

Literacy Learning Focus

Children build a repertoire of level one nursery rhymes by recalling them from the book illustrations and from the actions and object words in the nursery rhymes. They also do this by saying as much of each nursery rhyme as they can remember.

Quick Plan
- Children guess nursery rhymes from pictures.
- Children guess nursery rhymes from actions.
- Children guess nursery rhymes from object words.

Hint: Level One Nursery Rhymes are nursery rhymes with rhyming words close together, that is, nursery rhymes with two words that rhyme within a single line or a group of four beats of the nursery rhyme—for example, "Jack and *Jill* went up the *hill*."

Materials
- ☆ A book (or books) of *Mother Goose* nursery rhymes
- ☆ Bookmarks or sticky notes marking your chosen level one nursery rhymes; for example, "Hickory, Dickory, Dock," "Humpty Dumpty," "Jack and Jill," and "Three Little Kittens" (see **Follow-Up** for a list of other level one nursery rhymes)
- ☆ Props related to nursery rhymes; for example, a large block (for a wall)—for "Humpty Dumpty"; a clock—for "Hickory, Dickory, Dock"; a mound of pillows (for a hill)—for "Jack and Jill"; and a bucket, mittens, and a pie tin—for "Three Little Kittens"
- ☆ *Mother Goose* Vocabulary: Level One Nursery Rhymes Card

Beginning
1. Gather in a comfortable spot on the floor where children can cluster around you.
2. Begin by saying something like "Today let's play a guessing game! When you see a picture, or you see an action, or you hear some words, try to guess the nursery rhyme they're from. For example, if I show you this picture *(turn to a "Humpty Dumpty" illustration)*, you might guess..." Listen to and support children's guesses and then say "Or if I do this *(pick up the clock and run your fingers up one side and down the other)*, you might guess..." Listen to and acknowledge children's ideas, and then continue by saying "Or if I said the words *hill, pail, water,* and *crown,* you might guess..." Again, listen to and support children's ideas.

Middle
3. Open the *Mother Goose* book to an illustration of a familiar nursery rhyme, for example, the three mittenless kittens crying to their mother. Invite the children to name, talk about, and say the nursery rhyme represented by the illustration. Quietly say the nursery rhyme and pat to it along with them.
4. Act out a familiar nursery rhyme. For example, sit on a wall (block), then fall off the wall (block). Invite the children to name, talk about, and say the nursery rhyme represented by these actions. Quietly say the nursery rhyme and pat to it along with them.
5. List the object words from a familiar nursery rhyme, for example, *mouse* and *clock*. Invite the children to name, talk about, and say the nursery rhyme that includes these words. Quietly say the nursery rhyme and pat to it along with them.

Copyright © 2010 HighScope® Educational Research Foundation

PA11

Copyright © 2012 HighScope® Educational Research Foundation. The owner of this book has permission to copy this page for its use in the classroom.

Lesson Plans for the First 30 Days

6. Repeat steps 3–5 until children have had a chance to guess each nursery rhyme from the book illustration and from actions and object words in the nursery rhymes. Once the children understand this guessing game, invite a child to take over your job and pick an illustration, show an action, or name objects from a nursery rhyme for others to identify. Use and talk about new words when feasible. (See the *Mother Goose* Vocabulary: Level One Nursery Rhymes Card.)

End

7. Invite the children to pick a final nursery rhyme. Then ask them to pat to or jump in place to the nursery rhyme as you say the nursery rhyme together.

8. Dismiss the children by having them say the nursery rhyme and jump to the next part of the classroom daily routine.

Follow-Up

Repeat this small-group activity until you have worked through the level one nursery rhymes listed below, as well as any other nursery rhymes, poems, or children's stories with rhyming words close together. Post a list of these nursery rhymes so that you can say, pat to, and jump to them with children as the occasion arises.

Level One Nursery Rhymes

To find the page of a nursery rhyme in the *Mother Goose* book you are using, turn to the book's index.

As Tommy Snooks	Little Miss Muffet
Bow, Wow, Wow	Little Nancy Etticoat
Charley Barley	Little Poll Parrot
Charlie Warlie	Little Tee-Wee
Cross-Patch	Little Tommy Tittlemouse
Daffy-Down-Dilly	Lucy Locket
A Diller, a Dollar	The Man in the Moon… Soon
Doctor Foster	
Hark, Hark	Mary, Mary, Quite Contrary
Hector Protector	My Maid Mary
Hey Diddle, Diddle	Old King Cole
Hickety, Pickety	Old Mother Hubbard
Hickory, Dickory, Dock	Peter, Peter, Pumpkin Eater
High Diddle Doubt	The Queen of Hearts
Hoddley, Poddley	Rain, Rain, Go Away
Humpty Dumpty	Red Sky at Night
Ickle Ockle	Ring-a-Ring o' Roses
Jack and Jill	Rub-a-Dub-Dub
Jack Be Nimble	See-Saw, Margery Daw
Jack Sprat	Simple Simon
Jerry Hall	Star Light
Little Betty Blue	There Was a Little Girl
Little Blue Ben	Three Little Kittens
Little Bo-Peep	Tom, Tom, the Piper's Son
Little Jack Horner	

Related Small-Group Times

Rhyming activities 1 and 2

Copyright © 2010 HighScope® Educational Research Foundation

PA12

Copyright © 2012 HighScope® Educational Research Foundation. The owner of this book has permission to copy this page for its use in the classroom.

VOCABULARY
Mother Goose: Level One Nursery Rhymes

New Words*

As you read and say with children the level one nursery rhymes in *Mother Goose,* you will come across these words and others that may be new to some children. Explain what they mean by connecting them to familiar experiences and words the children already know. (Some terms in the list below that may not be in the dictionary or that have more than one meaning are followed by explanations in parentheses.)

As Tommy Snooks
- tomorrow
- walking out

Bow, Wow, Wow
- art
- thou

Charley Barley
- lay (lay eggs)

Charlie Warlie
- brow

Cross-Patch
- cross-patch
- draw (pull or take out)
- neighbours (neighbors)
- spin

Daffy-Down-Dilly
- daffodil (implied word)
- gown
- petticoat

A Diller, a Dollar
- scholar

Doctor Foster
- Gloucester
- puddle
- shower

Hark, Hark
- beggars
- jags
- rags

Hector Protector
- Protector

Hey Diddle, Diddle
- fiddle
- sport

Hickety, Pickety
- doth
- gentlemen

Hickory, Dickory, Dock
- struck

High Diddle Doubt
- bridle
- doubt
- fetch
- maid
- saddle

Hoddlely, Poddley
- fogs
- mice
- poodle
- puddle

Ickle Ockle
- maid

Jack and Jill
- abate
- caper
- crown (head)
- disaster
- fetch
- nob
- paper plaster
- patched
- see-saw
- trot
- tumbling
- vexed
- vinegar

Jack Be Nimble
- candlestick
- nimble

Jack Sprat
- lean
- platter

Little Betty Blue
- holiday

Little Blue Ben
- glen
- score

Little Bo-Peep
- a-fleeting (as in fleeting)
- awoke
- bleating
- crook
- determined
- dreamt
- espied (as in spied)
- hard by (near)
- heaved
- hillocks
- lambkin (small lamb)
- meadow
- rambling

- shepherdess
- sigh
- stray
- tack

Little Jack Horner
- corner
- plum
- thumb

Little Miss Muffet
- curds
- frightened
- tuffet
- whey

Little Nancy Etticoat
- petticoat

Little Poll Parrot
- garret
- stole

Little Tee-Wee
- afloat
- bended

Little Tommy Tittlemouse
- ditches

Lucy Locket
- locket
- pocket
- ribbon
- round (around)

The Man in the Moon Came Down Too Soon
- burnt
- porridge
- supping

Mary, Mary, Quite Contrary
- cockle shells
- contrary
- garden
- maids
- quite
- row
- silver bells

More vocabulary words follow on the back of this card.

---

* Words appear as they do in Tomie dePaola's *Mother Goose* book.

Copyright © 2010 HighScope® Educational Research Foundation. The owner of this copy of the curriculum has permission to copy this card for its use in the classroom.   V15

My Maid Mary
  a-hoeing
  dairy
  maid
  morn
  mowing
  reel
  whilst

Old King Cole
  compare
  fiddlers
  merry
  rare
  soul

Old Mother Hubbard
  barber
  bare
  bow
  cobbler
  coffin
  cupboard
  curtsey
  fishmonger
  fruiterer (one who sells fruit)
  hatter
  hose
  hosier
  jig
  linen
  none
  seamstress
  servant
  tailor
  tavern
  tripe
  undertaker
  wig

Peter, Peter, Pumpkin Eater
  pumpkin
  shell

The Queen of Hearts
  knave
  tarts
  vowed

Red Sky at Night
  delight
  shepherd
  warning

Ring-a-Ring o'Roses
  a-tishoo (a word that sounds like a sneeze)
  meadow
  o'roses (of roses)
  posies (general term for flowers)

Rub-a-Dub-Dub
  baker
  butcher
  candlestick
  candlestick-maker
  rotten
  tub

See-Saw, Margery Daw
  master
  see-saw

Simple Simon
  adieu
  bids
  fair
  pieman
  roast
  sieve
  ware

There Was a Little Girl
  curl
  forehead
  horrid
  middle

Three Little Kittens
  naughty
  sigh
  soiled

Tom, Tom, the Piper's Son
  howling
  stole

Lesson Plans for the First 30 Days

ACTIVITY SUPPORT

2 How to Pat to a Nursery Rhyme

Getting Started
Teachers and children should sit comfortably so they can easily pat their palms or fingertips on their thighs or knees as they say nursery rhymes out loud.

Word Sound and Flow
Patting to nursery rhymes engages children in the pleasure of physically feeling the pulse of language. Later on, as they learn to read, they draw on their experiences with the sound and flow of words to sound out new words and read with fluency.

The Beat
Nursery rhymes are groups of stressed and unstressed syllables and words organized in sets or lines of four beats. In Growing Readers, the beats are represented by an underline: ____. A beat may fall on a stressed word (<u>rain</u>, <u>come</u>), on a stressed syllable (a-<u>way</u>, an-<u>oth</u>-er), or on a rest (____).

When you pat to a nursery rhyme, you pat once on each beat.

"Walking" Nursery Rhymes

<u>Rain</u>, <u>rain</u>, <u>go</u> a-<u>way</u>,
<u>Come</u> a-<u>gain</u> an-<u>oth</u>-er <u>day</u>.

<u>Bow</u>, <u>wow</u>, <u>wow</u>, ___
<u>Whose</u> <u>dog</u> art <u>thou</u>? ___
<u>Lit</u>-tle <u>Tom</u> <u>Tin</u>-ker's <u>dog</u>,
<u>Bow</u>, <u>wow</u>, <u>wow</u>, ___

Many nursery rhymes like "Rain, Rain, Go Away" and "Bow, Wow, Wow" impart the feeling of walking. This feeling occurs because a single beat may be divided in half, causing you to say two words or two syllables on one beat. For example, in "Rain, Rain, Go Away" beat 3 in the first line and beats 1, 2, and 3 in the second line are divided in half:

1	2	3		4	
<u>Rain</u>		<u>rain</u>		<u>go</u>	a	<u>way</u>	
<u>Come</u>	a	<u>gain</u>	an	<u>oth</u>	er	<u>day</u>	

In "Bow, Wow, Wow" beat 2 in the second line and beats 1 and 3 in the third line are divided in half.

1	2	3	4
<u>Bow</u>	<u>wow</u>	<u>wow</u>	___
<u>Whose</u>	<u>dog</u> art	<u>thou</u>	___
<u>Lit</u> tle	<u>Tom</u>	<u>Tin</u> ker's	<u>dog</u>
<u>Bow</u>	<u>wow</u>	<u>wow</u>	___

Here are some examples of other "Walking" nursery rhymes—that is, nursery rhymes in which some beats are divided into two:

Level One "Walking" Nursery Rhymes

Little Tommy Tittlemouse
Lucy Locket
Mary, Mary, Quite Contrary

Peter, Peter, Pumpkin Eater
Simple Simon

Level Two "Walking" Nursery Rhymes

Baa, Baa, Black Sheep
Cobbler, Cobbler
Dance, Little Baby
Diddle, Diddle, Dumpling

Mary Had a Little Lamb
Sleep, Baby, Sleep
Wee Willie Winkie

Level Three "Walking" Nursery Rhymes

One, Two, Buckle My Shoe
Monday's Child

"Galloping" Nursery Rhymes

<u>Hick</u>-o-ry, <u>dick</u>-o-ry, <u>dock</u>, ___ the
<u>mouse</u> ran <u>up</u> the <u>clock</u>. ___ The
<u>clock</u> struck <u>one</u>, the <u>mouse</u> ran <u>down</u>,
<u>Hick</u>-o-ry, <u>dick</u>-o-ry <u>dock</u>. ___

"Hickory, Dickory, Dock" and some other nursery rhymes mimic the feeling of galloping. This feeling occurs because a single beat may be subdivided into three smaller parts. This generally causes you to say three syllables on one beat. For example, in "Hickory, Dickory, Dock" beats 1 and 2 in lines one and four are subdivided into three parts. A "galloping" nursery rhyme may also cause you to say one word on the first part of a divided beat and one word on the third part of a divided beat as in beats 1 and 2 in lines two and three, and in beat 3 in line three.

Copyright © 2010 HighScope® Educational Research Foundation

More examples follow on the back of this card.

AS3

Copyright © 2012 HighScope® Educational Research Foundation. The owner of this book has permission to copy this page for its use in the classroom.

1			2			3			4		
Hick	o	ry	dick	o	ry	dock				—	the
Mouse		ran	up		the	clock				—	the
Clock		struck	one		the	mouse		ran	down		
Hick	o	ry	dick	o	ry	dock				—	

You will find that many of children's favorite nursery rhymes are the "galloping" type, probably because the division of the beats into three equal parts lends a waltz-like lilt or swing to the flow of words. Let's look at "Humpty Dumpty" as another such "galloping" nursery rhyme.

> Hump-ty Dump-ty sat on a wall,
> Hump-ty Dump-ty had a great fall;
> All the King's hor-ses and all the King's men
> Could-n't put Hump-ty to-geth-er a-gain.

1		2			3			4	
Hump	ty	Dump		ty	sat	on	a	wall	
Hump	ty	Dump		ty	had	a	great	fall	
All	the	King's	hor	ses	and	all	the	King's	men
Could	n't	put	Hump	ty	to	geth	er	a	gain

Here are some examples of other "galloping" nursery rhymes—that is, nursery rhymes in which the beats are subdivided into three.

Level One "Galloping" Nursery Rhymes

Hey Diddle, Diddle
Jack Be Nimble
Little Miss Muffet
Little Bo-Peep
Old Mother Hubbard
See-Saw, Margery Daw
Three Little Kittens

Level Two "Galloping" Nursery Rhymes

Dickery, Dickery, Dare
Hush-a-Bye, Baby
Ladybird, Ladybird
Little Boy Blue
Ride a Cock-Horse
Rock-a-Bye, Baby
There Was an Old Woman Tossed up in a Basket

Level Three "Galloping" Nursery Rhymes

Old Mother Goose

Making Up Rhymes

When you make up a rhyme modeled after nursery rhymes, organize the words into groups or lines of four beats:

1	2	3	4
I	like	big	rocks.
I	wear	woolly	socks.
I	wear	red	
When I	go to	bed.	

Listen for and pat on the four beats in each line. Note that a beat or pat may fall on a stressed word, on a stressed syllable, or on an unvoiced rest.

1	2	3	4
I	like	big	rocks.
I	wear	wool-ly	socks.
I	wear	red	—
When I	go to	bed.	—

Practice saying and patting your new rhyme ahead of time so you can introduce it to the children with ease.

Here is a made-up rhyme with four beats in each line. It is a "galloping" rhyme because the beats are subdivided into three parts.

1			2			3			4		
Sue			has		two	goats.				—	
Goats			rhymes		with	coats		and	boats.		

Here is another made-up rhyme with four beats in each line. It's a "walking" rhyme because the beats are subdivided into two parts. Note that the first line is a "warm up" line of four rests or unvoiced pats.

1		2		3		4	
—		—		—		—	
Have	you	seen		—		—	a
Pink		sink		pink		sink	
Pink		sink		pink		sink?	

Appendix A:
Reproducible Planning Sheets

Observations

Use this sheet to record what you saw individual children say and do today.

Follow-Up Ideas

➡

Use this sheet to write down your own follow-up ideas.

Lesson Plan Ideas

Use this sheet to make notes for your own lesson plans.

Greeting Time

Planning Time

Group 1

Group 2

Work Time

Lesson Plan Ideas

Use this sheet to make notes for your own lesson plans.

Cleanup Time

Recall Time

Group 1

Group 2

Small-Group Time

Group 1

Group 2

Lesson Plan Ideas

Use this sheet to make notes for your own lesson plans.

Large-Group Time

Other Ideas

Appendix B: Music CD Selections for Lesson Activities

Lesson Plans for the First 30 Days

The following chart is a guide for using selections from the music CD packaged with this book together with activities in the lesson plans. All songs are from HighScope's "Rhythmically Moving" CD series, a set of nine CDs that can also be used with the book *Teaching Movement & Dance* and the video series *Beginning Folk Dances Illustrated*. HighScope publishes numerous books and multimedia materials in movement and music. For more information, visit the HighScope Web site at *www.highscope.org*.

Music CD Selections for Lesson Activities

Lesson Plan Day/Activity	Music	Selection Could Also Be Used for...
Day 7: Scarves or Streamers and Music With No Words	Misirlou-Kritikos	**Large-group time** on Days 9, 18, 23, 28, and **cleanup time,** all days
Day 9: Musical Carpet Squares	Tipsy	**Large-group time** on Days 7, 18, 23, 28, and **cleanup time,** all days
Day 12: Fast/Slow Movements	Hora Hassidit	**Large-group time** on Days 7, 21, 23, and 28
Day 14: Statue Music	Seven Jumps	**Large-group time** on Day 9
Day 16: Popcorn!!!	Popcorn	**Large-group time** on Days 7, 9, 21, and 28
Day 18: Sliding/Skating to Music	Alley Cat	**Large-group time** on Days 7, 9, 14, 23, 28, and **cleanup time,** all days
Day 21: Pretend Dancing	Joe Clark Mixer	**Large-group time** on Days 7, 9, 16, 23, and 28
Day 23: Musical Shapes	Bele Kawe	**Large-group time** on Days 7, 9, 14, 18, 28, and **cleanup time,** all days
Day 28: Dancing with Letters	Carnavalito	**Large-group time** on Days 7, 9, 23, and **cleanup time,** all days
Cleanup time – all days	Pata Pata	**Large-group time** on Days 9, 14, 18, 23, and 28
Cleanup time – all days	Jamaican Holiday	**Large-group time** on Days 9, 14, 18, 23, and 28
Cleanup time – all days	Gaelic Waltz	**Large-group time** on Days 7, 18, 23, and 28
Cleanup time – all days	Korobushka	**Large-group time** on Days 9, 16, 21, 23, and 28
Cleanup time – all days	Sneaky Snake	**Large-group time** on Days 9, 18, 23, and 28

About the Authors

Beth Marshall is Director of Early Childhood Education at the HighScope Educational Research Foundation in Ypsilanti, Michigan, and has also served as a teacher and mentor in the HighScope Demonstration Preschool. Additionally, she was the coordinator for the HighScope National Diffusion Project through the U.S. Department of Education from 1992–1995. Beth has written and developed training materials for HighScope on a range of topics, including adult learning, art with young children, adult-child interactions, and the impact of brain research on early childhood practices. She contributed to the development of the Preschool Child Observation Record (COR) and Program Quality Assessment (PQA) assessment instruments. She also has conducted training projects throughout the United States and internationally and was a trainer and mentor for the inaugural Training of Trainers projects for HighScope Ireland and the Khululeka HighScope Teacher Training Centre in South Africa. She holds a master's degree in Early Childhood Education.

Beth's first step in early childhood education was a part-time job as a college student in a multicultural setting. On her first day, she was directed to a three-year-old girl from Swaziland who spoke no English (it was the child's second day at school and second week in the United States). Beth was told her job was to keep this child from running out the door! Remembering this experience has continued to give Beth empathy for others taking their first steps in this field.

Shannon D. Lockhart, a senior early childhood specialist and research associate with the HighScope Educational Research Foundation since 1988, has served as a national and international researcher, teacher, curriculum developer, trainer, and educational consultant in the United States and abroad. Her areas of expertise include child development (infant-toddler and preschool) and instrument development (observations, program evaluation, and child assessment). She also conducts HighScope infant and toddler and preschool training around the country and abroad. She has written numerous articles for the HighScope publications *Extensions* and *ReSource*, authored several chapters in the HighScope book *A World of Preschool Experience: Observations in 15 Countries* and coproduced the HighScope IEA videotape series, "Sights and Sounds of Preschool Children." Shannon holds a master's degree in early childhood education and teaches early childhood courses for Rochester College and Oakland University, both located in Rochester, Michigan.

Shannon's first step in early childhood education came through helping raise her own brothers and, particularly, her sister. As her sister grew from an infant to a preschooler and then to a kindergartner, Shannon was active in her development. When Shannon told her high school advisor that after she graduated, she wanted to work with young children, his reply was that no one knows at such a young age what they want to do for life, and he discouraged her from going into early childhood work. However, Shannon had always known that she wanted to work with children, and she has accomplished this in various ways throughout her career.

Moya Fewson was born in Belfast, Northern Ireland, but grew up in Canada. She has held a variety of jobs, including those as a reporter and columnist for a small newspaper. **Moya's first step in early childhood education** followed the birth of her children, when she moved to a country community that had a small cooperative preschool. While attending a couple of parent days per month, it became obvious to her how important play was — for instance, how much her son learned through playing with blocks, through painting a picture, or through hearing a story read. Moya had a degree in education but decided to go back to school to learn about early childhood — and was hooked. Eventually she took the helm at the co-op preschool and turned it into a full-time day care center that has more than 100 children enrolled. It was this experience that led her to become interested in HighScope.

Moya began working for Sheridan College in Brampton, Ontario, 30 years ago as a professor of early childhood and wanted to infuse HighScope principles into the college courses. She helped create the Sheridan HighScope Teacher Education Centre. When Sheridan moved in a different direction, Moya continued serving the community by opening the HighScope Teacher Education Centre for Eastern Canada.

Moya trains directly for the HighScope Foundation in the United States and for the new Teacher Education Centre in Canada. One of Moya's proudest moments was when her daughter Sarah became a HighScope trainer, and mother and daughter were able to work side by side. Moya has a passion for HighScope and a passion for her family, which includes her husband of more than 40 years, a son (also an an educator) and five of the most adorable grandchildren.